ARISTOPHANES

Plays I

ARISTOPHANES

Plays I

NEWLY TRANSLATED INTO ENGLISH VERSE
BY PATRIC DICKINSON

OXFORD UNIVERSITY PRESS

LONDON OXFORD NEW YORK

1970

Oxford University Press

OXFORD LONDON NEW YORK
GLASGOW TORONTO MELBOURNE WELLINGTON
CAPE TOWN SALISBURY IBADAN NAIROBI DAR ES SALAAM LUSAKA ADDIS ABABA
BOMBAY CALCUTTA MADRAS KARACHI LAHORE DACCA
KUALA LUMPUR SINGAPORE HONG KONG TOKYO

SBN 19 281054 5

© Oxford University Press 1957, 1970

Acharnians and *Peace* first published, in *Aristophanes Against War*, by
Oxford University Press, London, 1957

This edition first published as an Oxford University Press
paperback by Oxford University Press, London, 1970

*Printed in Great Britain
by Richard Clay (The Chaucer Press), Ltd.,
Bungay, Suffolk*

CONTENTS

To

Maurice Platnauer

TRANSLATOR'S PREFACE

P.D.	Aristophanes, tell me, as your translator—
ECHO	Later, later . . .
P.D.	Do you believe me?
ECHO	Live me, love me, leave me . . .

My vision of Aristophanes is that of a translator and a poet. I daresay I have more Greek than Shakespeare, which according to Ben Jonson wouldn't be difficult, but I give way to nobody in my admiration for this writer nor in my wish that others may find even more than I have, since first I read (acted) with that splendid scholar Dr. W. H. D. Rouse at Cambridge in 1933, when I was eighteen.

It is of no use to be categorical about translation. Samuel Johnson's words, 'Poetry, indeed, cannot be translated; and therefore it is the poets that preserve languages', have their point, but it is no *use* 'preserving' in this mean and pragmatical way. It is true that 'And be among her cloudy trophies hung' is untranslatable. Sometimes, it seems to me, such poetry is untranslatable even into spoken English. I emphasize the word *spoken*. No one, since printing began, *need* speak a poem aloud. No one yet has devised a method of acting in silence a drama, which depends on words to enforce and employ its action. Yet to many, foreign to English, our drama must be mime; to many, even though augmented with the appropriate tongues, opera *is* mime, whether in Babylon, Carthage, or New York.

Let me emphasize that Aristophanes wrote plays which were acted. They were acted in very different circumstances from those our Western world theatre has come to know. The thing is that Athenian drama, tragedy or comedy, can be acted *at all*. Their theatre is not so far away. In translating plays I think the translator has to be theatre- not study-minded. He has to think in terms of an actor performing bodily in front of an audience and of the words each actor has naturally to say in accord with who he is.

My principles in translating Aristophanes are threefold. One is to render the words, a Johnsonian impossible. At most, I do not feel that I have done his language much harm. Take on trust that he was a marvellous poet. Secondly, he was a dramatic poet, whose characters one has to explore and, as it were, expound. (I would not like to think I have got Trygaios or Anaxagora wrong.) Thirdly and most difficult, I am alive over 2,000 years later, but I have to offer my audiences and readers some sort of language, ephemeral it may be, which does not do injustice to the playwright but which does not get in the way of actors' speaking or audiences' accepting what he said; that is my aim and my claim.

What he *said*: how he said, what he said. I have not skimped nor scamped the sexual stuff; often I prefer a sort of circumlocution. (I'd prefer anything, say, to the revolting vulgarities of Aubrey Beardsley's illustrations of *Lysistrata*.) What I have written down is nothing but what is in the text; save that I think it funnier, sometimes, not to wave a real, or property, penis about when (as it does) it takes away attention from the dialogue. Very seldom (and I hope not noticeably) I have done what Aristophanes did: quote from contemporaries; my contemporaries. Rhythmically I have tried various things. I have used, for dialogue usually, a line of four stresses, not only to escape from blank verse but to move speech on in the way we speak in English now; and not far, I hope, from the way Athenians spoke Attic then.

I have used dialect—Aristophanes did—not so much by language as by characters, as I see them; and I cannot escape from Greece to England entirely. My slang is out of date; as all slang is. My justification is that it is there in his work, and not unspeakable in mine, and I have to offer recognizable people to an English- or American-speaking audience—by which I must mean at least that I have not translated these plays into diplomatic French. Now for the set pieces: the rhythms of Greek and English are wholly different. Sometimes I have offered fairly near alternatives; sometimes I have luxuriated in the cunning of offering choruses in exact line-by-line number, with quite exacting (and exacted) English stanzas; sometimes I have made poems in English which I hope are like the originals, if Aristophanes could translate them back.

This is not Aristophanes up-to-date, for that would soon be Aristophanes out-of-date. But such a master needs must be re-introduced to each generation.

What I can tell no one is how, in the turmoil of his lifetime,

Aristophanes wrote poetry; wrote great poetic comedies. It is no use if I quote a line or so of the Greek. I have the luck to hear it—maybe wrong—and you may not. All I can hope is that anyone acting in any of these plays may somehow get a Greek echo to his English speech; and maybe, if he forgets his words, and is prompted by Aristophanes, might go on in the sort of words I have given. Though I had rather he went on in the original words . . . .

P.D.

1970

Line numbers in the running headlines refer to the Greek text. Stage directions and some indications of characters and their mode of speaking have been supplied by the translator. The headnotes to the plays are by Richard Brain of Oxford University Press, who also compiled the Glossary and Index.

ACHARNIANS

The Acharnians *was first produced early in 425* B.C. *in Athens at the Lenaia, the winter Dionysiac festival at which plays, especially comedies, were performed and the audience would be practically all of Athenians, with few foreigners present. It won the first prize. Aristophanes had had two or three plays produced before, but this is his earliest to have survived (and thus the oldest complete Greek comedy extant).*

Acharnai is a village in the Attic countryside which had suffered almost annual incursions by the Spartans and their allies for the six years the Peloponnesian War between Athens and Sparta had lasted when this play was first performed. Its menfolk provide a Chorus of typical peasant Athenian citizens straightforwardly hostile to the Spartans and vehement for a brisk and successful prosecution of the war.

But Aristophanes, though only in his mid-twenties, boldly presented this comedy mocking bluff militarism, satirizing the economic and social effects of the war, and openly commending peace and the benefits (to all but wartime officials and racketeers) that would return with it. The play's hero, Dikaiopolis, not only makes the case for ending the war, he even exposes the meanness of the origins of it and puts in a word in favour of the enemy, the Spartans themselves. That he makes his plea with his head on the block symbolizes the risk Aristophanes knew he was taking; the very year before the playwright had been brought to court for attacking Athenian policy as conducted by Cleon, the principal political leader in the war against Sparta.

The navy was the Athenians' greatest strength, and the expense of providing ships (frequently mentioned in Aristophanes' plays) was chiefly borne by the wealthy citizens. But the worst burdens of the war, like most wars, fell on the old, the poor, and the simple, and on women. The farmers of Acharnai and elsewhere in Attica had their crops and stock ravaged, and old men had to man the defences of Athens; but clever young men might get sent on lengthy delegations, with lavish expenses paid, to seek aid or support from non-Greek states—as, in this play, Thrace or Persia under its Great King. Others again profited from the war as minor officials enforcing regulations against trading with enemy allies— e.g., here, the neighbouring Megarians and Boeotians, who for their part suffered economic hardship from the loss of the rich Athenian market. Almost as official were the authorities' informers and those who brought legal action against their fellow citizens for wartime offences.

Dikaiopolis attacks such self-seeking beneficiaries of the war more sharply than the direct military men like Lamachos, the real-life general represented in the play—as the mask the actor wore would make clear to the audience. It is to be free of them all, however, and to regain the easy ways—and the better food—of peacetime that Dikaiopolis makes his one-man treaty (here reified as the vintage wine which traditionally celebrated and ratified treaties) with Sparta; and both by argument (apart from the symbolic threat to the charcoal-burning industry which was the Acharnians' chief economic resource) and by tempting them with the pleasures resulting from his jealously preserved treaty, he wins the Chorus—and, Aristophanes hoped, his audience—in favour of making peace.

The Feast at the end is almost part of the ritual of the Old Attic Comedy, which was the form of most of Aristophanes' plays. Aristophanes is already in the *Acharnians* (though he didn't publicly announce it as his play) professionally fascinated by the art of playwriting. Frequently in his plays Euripides is laughed at as by a friendly critic—here for his use of tattered clothing and props for his more unfortunate characters. And in the Parabasis (pp. 26-8), a central section of most Old Comedies, Aristophanes in this play sets out his ideals in comedy-writing such as 'showing the world how a *real* democracy works'.

CHARACTERS

DIKAIOPOLIS, *a good citizen*

DEPUTIES

CRIER

AMPHITHEOS

Athenian AMBASSADORS *to the King of Sparta*

PSEUDO-ARTABAS

THEOROS

SOLDIERS

Dikaiopolis' WIFE

His DAUGHTER

SLAVES

KEPHISOPHON, *servant of Euripides*

EURIPIDES

LAMACHOS

A MEGARIAN

Twin GIRLS, *his daughters*

INFORMER

A BOEOTIAN

NIKARCHOS

SERVANT

A FARMER

A BEST MAN

A BRIDESMAID

MESSENGERS

CHORUS *of Acharnian veterans*

In the background are three houses: the centre one is Dikaiopolis'.
The other two belong to Euripides *and* Lamachos. *In the fore-*
ground is a rough representation of the Pnyx where Dikaiopolis *is*
awaiting the opening of the Assembly.

DIKAIOPOLIS. I simply can't tell you how many things there've been
  Getting me down. Am I pleased about anything? Well,
  Practically nothing—p'r'aps I could think up four things:
  But as for the others—the sand of a sand-dune's a mere
  Nothing compared . . . Oh, yes! But there was one thing
  I *was* delighted with (you'll agree, rightly I think):
  That fine of five talents Cleon had to cough up:
  That was the stuff! *that* did my heart good, I loved
  The Knights for that bit of work. That was worth something to
    Greece.
  But then what a blow! I was sitting there in the theatre
  Eagerly waiting an Aeschylus—and what did the Crier do?
  He called: 'Bring on your play, Theognis.' *Theognis*! Believe me,
  My heart nearly *froze* at the thought! Wouldn't yours?
  Then I was glad when the piper Moschos went out
  And it was Dexitheos to play the Boeotian March.
  But when *Chairis* oiled in this year . . .
  But still . . . *this* is the last straw—never since I was able
  To wash have I known such an absolute washout!
  Look:
  The Assembly opens today. This morning. Here, now. And who's
    here?
  Nobody. Where are the Deputies? Prattling in the market,
  Up and down, up and down, dodging the whips, not coming;
  Or else they'll scuttle in late, chattering, jostling, bustling
  Onto the Front Benches, in a glib conglomeration.
  But as for peace—they don't care a fig for peace.
  O City, City,
                I am always the first to come here
  And I sit alone, alone in the wide Assembly,
  Alone I sit and wait; I groan and yawn and stretch,
  I fiddle, I doodle, I tweeze out bristles,
  I add up my savings, but always I gaze

Out over the fields, craving for peace,
Hating this city, aching for my village
Where the cry isn't always '*Buy*, *haggle*, and *fleece*,'
But where there is give-and-take and a living for all . . .
So here I am ready to tackle these city speakers,
Shout 'em down, curse 'em, heckle 'em, if they debate
About anything else but peace . . .

> [*A buzz of noise.*

Ph! Here they come—our midday Deputies—
What did I tell you?—just exactly that!
And every man jack of them elbowing to the front.

> *The* Deputies *enter, herded by the* Crier.

CRIER [*stentorian guide's voice*]. Move up there! Move up! with-*h*in
the 'allowed ground!

> *A sound of running and panting. Enter* Amphitheos.

AMPHITHEOS [*to* Dikaiopolis]. Anyone spoken yet?

CRIER. Who will address the meeting?

AMPHITHEOS. I will!

CRIER. Who? Name please?

AMPHITHEOS. Amphitheos.

CRIER. Not a man?

AMPHITHEOS.   No, an immortal.
For the first Amphitheos was
The son of the goddess Demeter
(Triptolemos was his father),
And his son was Keleos, Keleos
Was married to Phainareté
And she bore my father Lykinos
—Then I'm an immortal, aren't I?
And the gods have made me, and nobody
Else, entirely responsible
For making peace with Sparta;
But, gentlemen, though I'm immortal,
I've got no money and the Deputies
Refuse to vote me any
For my mission—

CRIER.   Hey, there, Sergeant-at-arms,
Have him put out.

AMPHITHEOS [*bustled away*]. Triptolemos!
Keleos! help me! help me!

DIKAIOPOLIS [*jumping up*]. Gentlemen! Deputies! I put it to you,
It is entirely out of order in this Assembly
To have that man suppressed—he only wanted
To make peace for us—

CRIER.   Silence there!

DIKAIOPOLIS. I'm hanged if I will, by Apollo,
Unless you debate about peace and
Nothing else but—

CRIER.   Silence! Pray silence
For the ambassadors
Returned from the King!

DIKAIOPOLIS.   What sort of
A king? I'm sick of these embassies,
With their hot airs and disgraces—

CRIER. *Silence!*

               Enter the Ambassadors *with* Pseudo-Artabas.

AMBASSADOR [*a fop*]. Gentlemen, when Euthymenes was Archon—

DIKAIOPOLIS. Eleven years ago!

CRIER. Silence!

AMBASSADOR.   —you despatched us
As ambassadors to the court of the Great King
With an honorarium of two drachmas a day, each—

DIKAIOPOLIS. Eleven years of our money down the drain!

AMBASSADOR. Oh, a *hard* time we had of it,
For a journey and such a long journey,
Sauntering over the *drab* Kaÿstrian plain,
Lolling out in our soft litters—
It was really *killing*—

DIKAIOPOLIS.   I had all the luck—
Lolling out on the cosy ramparts in the muck,
That was killing too—

AMBASSADOR.   And the parties, so *exhausting*,
The silken girls bringing sherbet, you know,
And the wine, unmixed and sweet
Out of the gold and the crystal,
We *had* to drink it—

DIKAIOPOLIS.   O rugged City!
Do you hear your ambassador's insolent words?

AMBASSADOR.—But a man's manhood is measured *there* by his
Capacity to—eat and drink:

DIKAIOPOLIS [*with meaning*]. —It's different
Here: whether it's boys or whores.

AMBASSADOR. In the fourth year we came to the King's palace
But he'd just gone to—er—to relieve himself,
And there for eight months he sat on the Golden Hills
With all his men.

DIKAIOPOLIS.   —And when did the Royal Top
Recollect his Royal Bottom?

AMBASSADOR.   At the full moon.
Then he returned and there was *such* a dinner,
An ox baked whole in a pot—

DIKAIOPOLIS.   An ox in a pot?
Stop lying—

AMBASSADOR. And a bird three times the size
Of fatty Cleonymos. It was called a Quack.

DIKAIOPOLIS. And fed on drachmas I suppose? You crook!

AMBASSADOR. And now let us present to you Pseudo-Artabas,
The Great King's Eye!

DIKAIOPOLIS.   I wouldn't object to a crow
Picking out yours, my friend—

CRIER.   Silence! Silence!
For the great King's Eye!

DIKAIOPOLIS.   O Heracles, O heaven,
He looks like a man of war with that eye on his prow—
Are you coming to spy on the docks?
Is that a rowlock under your eye?

AMBASSADOR [*pompously*]. Now tell the Athenians what the Great
King himself
Instructed you to say:

PSEUDO-ARTABAS. Edditeddihenwypawlipansy.

AMBASSADOR. Do you understand?

DIKAIOPOLIS. By Apollo, no! I do NOT!

AMBASSADOR. He says the King is going to send us gold.

[*To* Pseudo-Artabas.] Here, you; tell him more plainly about
the gold.

PSEUDO-ARTABAS [*very distinctly*]. No getting gold. NOT. Greeks
all bumsuckers.

DIKAIOPOLIS. That's clear enough, good god.

AMBASSADOR. What does he say?

DIKAIOPOLIS. What does he say? He says the Greeks are suckers
If they expect to get any gold from Persia.

AMBASSADOR. No, no, he spoke of gold in *buckets*-full.

DIKAIOPOLIS. Buckets my foot. You rotten liar—get out.
I'll try him myself. Now do you see my fist?
[*A grunt from* Pseudo-Artabas.
And answer me clearly, or I'll tap your claret. Understand?
[*Another grunt.*

DIKAIOPOLIS. Does the Great King intend to send us gold?

PSEUDO-ARTABAS [*clearly*]. Oh, *no* . . .

DIKAIOPOLIS. Are our ambassadors double-crossing us?

PSEUDO-ARTABAS [*same tone*]. Oh, *yes.*

DIKAIOPOLIS [*quizzically*]. Your attendants seem to nod and beck
like Greeks
(Or pseudo-Greeks). It wouldn't surprise me if
They came from this neighbourhood. . . . Why surely
One of your eunuchs—yes of course it must be!
[*He puts on a sissy voice for this in deliberate mockery.*
Cleisthenes—Sibyrtios' son—and you come
Dressed up as a *eunuch*? But, then, you can only shave
The cheeks you sit on, can't you? (—You mincing ape!)
And, heaven! Who's the other? Not *Straton* surely?

CRIER. Sit down there! Silence! The Council invites the Great
King's Eye—to the Council chamber for a banquet.

DIKAIOPOLIS. It's enough to choke you, isn't it? Look at me
Slogging away as a soldier, on the outside;
But the door's wide open for any ruddy foreigner.
Right! Now you see, what *I* am going to do!
Amphitheos! You still here?

AMPHITHEOS. Yes, here I am.

DIKAIOPOLIS [*slowly*]. Take these eight drachmas and make a
private treaty,

Just for me and my family, with the Spartans,
For *me* and *nobody else*. See?   [*Exit* Amphitheos.
[*Raising voice.*]—As for you and your embassies,
You know what to do with them—

CRIER.   Silence!
Silence for Theoros who's come from King Sitalkes.

                         Enter Theoros.

DIKAIOPOLIS [*aside*]. O heavens, another imposter!

THEOROS [*upper class*]. We wouldn't have been so long in Thrace—

DIKAIOPOLIS.   You wouldn't
But for the pay you were getting.

THEOROS.   —but for the storms
That covered all Thrace with snow. All the rivers froze—
It was the time Theognis' play was on, *and*—

DIKAIOPOLIS.   (Yes, it was colder here.)

THEOROS.—You see, Sitalkes was such a philathenian,
So kind and nice to us all, *and*, do you know,
He used to write on the walls of his—on every wall—
'The Athenians are beautiful', *and*
Then his son (whom we'd made a citizen) *was* so longing
To celebrate his naturalization *and*
So *begged* his father to help his adopted country
(The son's I mean) that he (the father I mean)
With the deepest vows so swore to help us,
With such a huge army, everybody'd say
What a cloud of locusts is coming—

DIKAIOPOLIS.   *And*
That's the one word of truth . . .

THEOROS [*triumphantly*].   —*and* so he's sent you
The most warlike tribe in Thrace.

DIKAIOPOLIS.   —And that's more like it!
If it's only true. . . .

CRIER. Forward you Thracians, there!

                     Enter a troop of Soldiers.

DIKAIOPOLIS. Good god, what's that?

THEOROS [*proudly*]. The Odomantian Guards!

DIKAIOPOLIS. Are *those* things Odomantians? Are they *men*? Tell me,
Can they stand to attention? Or has someone cut off their—

THEOROS. Give them two drachmas a day and they'll flatten the whole of Boeotia!

DIKAIOPOLIS. *Two* drachmas a day? For these 'pitiful rascals'?
What will our sailors say, the poor devils,
Our first line of defence, our lifeguards, and
'All for a drachma a day.'
                                        Damn and blast it!
One of 'em's swiped my garlic. I'm done for!
Put down my garlic, you, or I'll—

THEOROS.   No, you don't!
My men fight better on garlic!
Don't you dare lay a finger
On my Odomantian heroes.

DIKAIOPOLIS [*appealing to the* Deputies]. Gentlemen! How can you sit there
And let these foreigners treat me
Like this, in my own country?
[*Solemnly.*] But now I must give you warning
Don't continue to hold this Assembly
To discuss the Thracians' pay. I've
Just had a portent from heaven—   [*Pause.*
A raindrop . . .
                              [*General alarm, &c.: any excuse . . .*

CRIER. Let the Thracians retire!
And return in two days. The Assembly
Is DISSOLVED!

DIKAIOPOLIS [*aside*]. —And my salad's ruined . . .
                              Enter Amphitheos.
But look who's here—it's Amphitheos
Back from Sparta. Amphitheos!
Hello there, wait! I—

AMPHITHEOS.   Can't stop! I'm sorry.
They're after me—the miners from Acharnai—
I've got to get right away.

DIKAIOPOLIS. What's the matter?

AMPHITHEOS. I was hurrying back with the treaties
   Quick as I could, but somehow
   They nosed them out, these Acharnians,
   You know, survivors of Marathon,
   Crusty old veterans tough as the ilex and maple,
   And then they all hollered 'You b——'
   (I couldn't repeat what they called me)
   'How dare you be bringing treaties
   When all our vines are cut down.'
   Then they filled up their pockets with stones and I fled,
   And they followed me bawling. . . .

DIKAIOPOLIS. Let 'em bawl. Have you got me the treaties?

AMPHITHEOS. Oh yes. Three different samples.
   These are the five-year: taste one?

DIKAIOPOLIS [*spluttering*]. Ugh!

AMPHITHEOS. What's the matter?

DIKAIOPOLIS.   Don't like 'em.
   They smell of tar and caulking
   And the fitting out of warships.

AMPHITHEOS. Then try a ten-year one.

DIKAIOPOLIS. No . . . there's a whiff of embassies
   Very urgent, to all our allies,
   And all our allies stalling. . . .

AMPHITHEOS. Then here are the thirty-year treaties
   Both for land and sea. . . .

DIKAIOPOLIS. O day of Dionysus! A sweet scent
   Of nectar and ambrosia,
   And never think of rationing any more,
   And in my mouth it says 'Go where you like'.
   Yes! This is the treaty for me, the real stuff!
   Let the Acharnians go and chase themselves!
   I'm going to hold a celebration!   [*Exit.*

AMPHITHEOS [*sadly*]. And *I'm* going to run for it! *Here they come. . .*
   Shouts of angry old men. The Chorus *of Acharnians enters.*

CHORUS. After him, hunt him, inquire for him everywhere,
   For the sake of the State it's our duty to get him,
   Has anyone seen this wanted man
   With treaties under his coat?

Gone, clean gone. We're hipped by old age.
When I was young I could pace Phaÿllos
With a sack of coal on my head—
I'd have been close on his heels, then,
He'd never have slipped off so easily.

All my joints are full of rheumatics:
The load on your legs, Lacrateides,
Is too heavy, and that's the truth. But after him, boys,
Don't let him boast he escaped us Acharnians
However long in the tooth.

Father Zeus, you listen, and all you gods:
This traitor's made a treaty
With our bitterest enemies,
On whom relentlessly we shall wage war.
We shall never relax
Till we've made it so hot for them
They'll never trample our vineyards again:
That's why we're after him,
Why we must hunt him,
By sea, by land, on the beaches, in the streets,
Till we corner him and pulp him to mummy
With volleys of stones.

Re-enter Dikaiopolis *with his* Daughter, *his* Wife, *and* Slaves.

DIKAIOPOLIS [*within*]. Silence, holy silence please!
That's right, you go a little ahead with the basket.

DAUGHTER. Yes, father.

DIKAIOPOLIS. You Xanthias, you hold up the phallic emblem.

WIFE. Now dear, we'll begin. Put down the basket.

DAUGHTER. Quick, mother, pass me the soup ladle,
So I can pour it out over the soppet.

DIKAIOPOLIS. Excellent. [*Mutters* 'Let us pray'.
O Lord Dionysus look with favour upon me
As I and my family make our sacrifice,
May you take pleasure in our festival!
(For I've finished with soldiering for ever—and, O,
Let my thirty-year treaty work out well!)

WIFE. Now, darling, carry the basket nicely;
  Put on your party smile. He's a lucky dog
  Who marries you and begets little pussies
  As sweetly scented and prettily behaved.
  Now, take particular care, in the crowd,
  Nobody nips your ear-rings. Go on, now.

DIKAIOPOLIS [*to a* Slave]. Come on, you, hold up the pole with
    Xanthias,
  A little behind my daughter with the basket,
  I shall follow and sing my phallic anthem—
  [*To his* Wife.] You, dear, you watch me from the roof-top—
  Now off we go!

[*Sings.*]   O Phales,
              Friend of Bacchus, fellow boozer,
              Night-stroller whose delight is
              All the women and the pretty boys,
                  I'm home!
              After six war-weary years
              I've made a private treaty,
              I've said my good-byes
                  To all that—
              Leaving Lamachos to fight!
              Leaving Lamachos to fight.

                  O Phales, oh!
              How immeasurably sweeter
              To stroll through my coverts
              And find a lovely girl there
                  Trespassing—
              Strymodoros' daughter Thratta—
              To detain, to tumble over,
              And trespass you know where,
                  O Phales, Phales,
              And trespass you know where;
              Leaving Lamachos to fight.

                  O Phales, come!
              Come home with us and souse yourself,
              And on the morning after,

> For your hangover we'll drink
>   A draft of Peace,
> And stuff my rotten shield up the chimney,
>   O Phales,
> And stuff my rotten shield up the chimney!
> LEAVING LAMACHOS TO FIGHT!

CHORUS. That's the fellow! Up guards and at him!
  Stone him, stone the filthy blackguard!
  Why don't you? Why don't *you*?

DIKAIOPOLIS. Heaven, what's this? Look out, or you'll smash my
    pot.

CHORUS. It's you we'll smash, you rotten swine—

DIKAIOPOLIS. What have *I* done?

CHORUS. *You* ask that? You, you disgrace, you disgusting traitor
  To your country, making treaties for yourself,
  How dare you look us in the face?

DIKAIOPOLIS. But you don't know why I did it. Listen, won't you?

CHORUS. Listen be damned! Kill you; flatten you; crush you with
    stones!

DIKAIOPOLIS. Not before you listen—do *please* be patient—

CHORUS. My patience is exhausted. Don't dare say another syllable.
  I loathe and detest you, even more than Cleon—
  And I'm going to cut *him* into boot-soles for the Knights—
  You—no long speeches from you! D'you think I'd listen?
  Making treaties with Sparta! Tcha! Punished, that's all, punished.

DIKAIOPOLIS. My good men, put the Spartans out of your minds
  And listen to me. Simply, as regards my treaty,
  Was I right to make it?

CHORUS.   How can you possibly ask that?
  A treaty with—with men for whom altar and faith and oath
  Have no significance whatever?

DIKAIOPOLIS.   I know you hate them,
  But *I* know the Spartans are not entirely to blame
  For everything.

CHORUS. Not entirely to blame? God's thunder! How dare you
  Say things like this to us openly?—And expect us to spare you?

DIKAIOPOLIS. No, I stick to it! *Not entirely*. I say so deliberately,
   And I can give many examples of *our* injustice to *them*.

CHORUS. That's a terrible thing to say, sir, makes my heart go cold—
   Do you really mean you intend to plead for our enemies?

DIKAIOPOLIS. If I don't speak the truth and cannot convince the
      people,
   I'm willing to put my head on the block as I speak.

CHORUS. Look here, why don't we finish the feller now, why not
   Batter him to bloody bits?

DIKAIOPOLIS.   A sinister ember
   Flared up in you then. Acharnians, WON'T you listen?

CHORUS. No. Never.

DIKAIOPOLIS.   That's hard—

CHORUS. May I drop dead if *I* do.

DIKAIOPOLIS. Don't say that—

CHORUS. But it's *you* who're going to die, here and now.

DIKAIOPOLIS. I'll make you suffer—I'm going to kill
   Your dearest friend—yes, I've got a hostage of yours
   And I'm going to get it and cut its throat!   [*Exit.*

CHORUS. What can he mean, Acharnians?
   Has he kidnapped one of our children?
   What's made him so suddenly cocky?
      Dikaiopolis *re-enters with a sword in one hand, a coal scuttle
                        in the other.*

DIKAIOPOLIS. See what I've got, you Acharnian miners!
   A scuttle of coal! I'll soon see
   Which of you loves his coal!
   This is what I'm going to murder:
   Go on, throw your stones, go on—
   What are you waiting for?

CHORUS. That's done it. My dearest friend,
   My love, my life, my living—
   Oh *please* don't do what you say,
   Never, never!   [*Breaks down.*

DIKAIOPOLIS. Go on, yowl. But I'll do it—
   I shan't listen to *you* now.

CHORUS [*passionate*]. I've—I've loved coal all my life—
　And I'm old now—you'd *kill me* too.

DIKAIOPOLIS. You wouldn't listen to *me*, just now.

CHORUS. But it's different now. Say what you like,
　Say you *adore* the Spartans,
　I'll never betray my scuttle.

DIKAIOPOLIS. Put all those stones down first.

CHORUS. Out they go! You—*you* put away your sword.

DIKAIOPOLIS. There may be more in your pockets—

CHORUS. All gone, I swear, all the lot;
　Don't go back on *your* word now.
　Put *your* weapon away. Look,
　I've shaken myself nearly inside out!

DIKAIOPOLIS. Oh yes, you could all shake out some tears
　When your precious coal was threatened
　—*And* by its friends' folly.
　Why even the scuttle was so afraid,
　It's squirted me black like a squid!
　Oh heaven! How can men's hearts be so bitter
　They always prefer to bluster and hit out
　Than hear a dispassionate argument?
　—Even though I'm prepared to go to the block,
　Loving my life as I do, to put the case for Sparta.

CHORUS. Then why don't you—bring out the block,
　And say this tremendous whatever-it-is
　You've got to say?—I'm really longing to hear it;
　After all, it *was* your suggestion—
　Put the block here, and get on with it.

DIKAIOPOLIS [*rhetorically*]. Here is the block! Here is the man!
　I am going to speak to you now.
　Oh, don't be afraid, I come totally unarmed,
　To say what I have to say on behalf of Sparta.
　But *I* am afraid. First, I know very well
　The ways of our country cousins—how they mop it up
　If anyone *praises* them or the City; any
　Corner tub-thumper, whether he's lying or not—
　—They don't know they're being led up the garden path.
　Then, I know the minds of the mordant old men who look

For nothing but hurting by voting-against: then, I know
What I suffered from Cleon in last year's comedy,
How he dragged me before the Council and fulminated,
Perjured, and swore like a sewer in spate, till I
Nearly died from his smears—
So before I begin, please let me dress myself
In the oldest rags I can find.

CHORUS. Why keep up this barrage of excuses and postponements?
Let the poet Hieronymos lend you the mop of hair
That makes him invisible; borrow his whole bag of tricks
From Sisyphus—we don't care—*but get on with it.*

DIKAIOPOLIS. I must be strong, now—I think I'd better
Go and find Euripides. Boy! Boy!
        [*He knocks on* Euripides' *door.*

KEPHISOPHON [*within*]. Who's there?

DIKAIOPOLIS.   Is Euripides in?

KEPHISOPHON. In and not in. If you understand me.

DIKAIOPOLIS. In and not in?

KEPHISOPHON.   That is a way of putting it.
His mind is outside, collecting snippets of poetry,
Not in, in a manner of speaking, but *he*
Is upstairs writing a play.

DIKAIOPOLIS.   Lucky Euripides!
When even his servant speaks such clever dialogue.
Call him please.

KEPHISOPHON.   Impossible.

DIKAIOPOLIS.   Oh, *really*!
No. I'll not go. I'll hammer at the doors!   [*Does so.*
Euripides, dear Euripides, if ever you listened
To anyone, listen now. It's me. Dikaiopolis.
         Euripides *appears at the window.*

EURIPIDES. I've no time.

DIKAIOPOLIS.   Come down.

EURIPIDES. There is never time to come down.

DIKAIOPOLIS.   Oh, *please.*

EURIPIDES. I shall come, and not come. I can see you;
And you, doubtless, are aware of me.

DIKAIOPOLIS.   Euripides!
  Why do you write up there and not down here?
  Is that why your characters limp? Have they fallen out?
  And why do you sit dressed up (or should I say down)
  In such sad rags? Such a pitiable object?
  I'm not surprised it's beggars you create.
  But now *I* beg *you*, Euripides,
  Give me some rags from that old play of yours,
  For I've got to make a long speech to the Chorus
  And *if* I fail, I'm to die. . . .
EURIPIDES. It depends what you mean by rags.
  Would it be the garb the poor dotard Oineus
  Wore when he entered?
DIKAIOPOLIS.   No. Not Oineus.
  Worse than that!
EURIPIDES. That which eyeless Phoenix assumed?
DIKAIOPOLIS. Not Phoenix. Someone far worse off than Phoenix.
EURIPIDES. What rags of time? What tattered outfit?
  Philoctetes?
DIKAIOPOLIS. No, *much much worse than that*!
EURIPIDES. The squalid habit lame Bellerophon wore?
DIKAIOPOLIS. Bellerophon? No. But mine *was* lame and talked,
  (Like most of your characters) talked, talked, talked . . .
EURIPIDES. Ah, you mean Telephos.
DIKAIOPOLIS.   I mean Telephos.
  Lend me his baby clothes—
EURIPIDES.   The rags of Telephos,
  Boy! Between the rags of Thyestes and Ino—
              Kephisophon *appears at the door with rags.*
KEPHISOPHON [*with distaste*]. Take 'em. Here they are.
              [Dikaiopolis *holds the rags up and looks through the
                          threadbare and holey parts.*
DIKAIOPOLIS. O Zeus, whose eye can pierce
  Through anything anywhere!
  Let me be prepared in the most
  Repulsive possible way. . . .
  [*To* Euripides.] Euripides, since you have given me these, so
    kindly,

Give me a cap to match,
For I have to act the beggar today,
[*Mocks.*] 'To be myself and not myself'
Whilst the audience know who I am
And the Chorus gape round like morons,
And I bait them with wise saws and cunning instances.

EURIPIDES. I'll give it you. You seem to me not uningenious.

[*The cap is produced.*

DIKAIOPOLIS. Good luck to you! And to Telephos—well . . .

[*He puts on the rags, &c.*

Now I've put *these* on, I'm itching with wit already!
But I must have a beggar's staff—

[*The staff is handed out.*

EURIPIDES. Take it, and leave my house.

DIKAIOPOLIS [*rhetorically*]. O soul! Cast out from the doors,
Lacking so many requisites! (Now,   [*Aside.*
Oil up to him, close and quick.) *Euripides*!
The little basket, with a hole burned in it,
That Telephos carried—please?

EURIPIDES.   What possible use
Could it be to you?

DIKAIOPOLIS.   I haven't an idea,
But I'd *love* to have it.

EURIPIDES.   Do not be importunate,
Please go away from my house!

DIKAIOPOLIS. What a shame. But bless you, and your mother.

EURIPIDES. Please, *go away*!

DIKAIOPOLIS.   Give me one thing more—
The little cup with the broken rim.

[*The basket and cup appear.*

EURIPIDES. Take it and go. You're a doom on the house.

DIKAIOPOLIS. Dear Euripides, one thing more—
The little pitcher bunged up with a sponge.

EURIPIDES. You are taking my whole play! Take it and *go*!

[*Hands him the pitcher.*

DIKAIOPOLIS. I'm going. But what shall I do?
There's one thing more, and if I don't have it I'm ruined.
Euripides, listen!

If I have this, I'll go and never come back:
Put me some withered leaves in my basket.

EURIPIDES. You're ruining me. My plays are disappearing.

[*Gives him the leaves.*

DIKAIOPOLIS. All right, I'm going. I see I'm too much of a nuisance.
—Human kind cannot bear very much reality.
Oh lord, I'm ruined! I've forgotten the *one thing*
On which everything else depends. . . . Euripides—
I swear I won't ask for anything else—
Give me some chervil from your mother's barrow?

EURIPIDES. You insult me. Bar the doors!

[*He goes in from window.*

DIKAIOPOLIS. Well, soul, we must go without our chervil.
Do you realize what a perilous performance
It's going to be? To speak for the Spartans?
On, my soul, on. Toe the line! Why are you waiting?
Swallowed Euripides neat? Feeling better?
Good! Come on, then, heart, bring head to the block;
And speak without fear what you know to be true.
Off we go! Steady. We're there. Well done! Ph!

CHORUS.   —What'll you do? What'll you say?
          Man, are you made of iron?
          Have you no conscience at all?
          —Offer your neck to the city
          Opposing us all, every one!
          —He's afraid of nothing. Well,
          Since you *will* have your way:
          SPEAK!

DIKAIOPOLIS. I trust that none of you here will think ill of me
If, dressed as a beggar, I'm bold enough to speak
To the Athenian people about the State
—And in a comedy. Even a comedy
Can tell the truth—nor can Cleon accuse me
Of inveighing against the State with strangers present.
There are no strangers present. We are alone here.
There are no emissaries from the allies. Not one.
We are here; the people, the winnowed grain of us.
Our resident aliens are not in this. We are alone.

So—just let me tell you that I loathe the Spartans,
And if Poseidon wrecked, in a bumper earthquake,
Every single one of their homes—I shouldn't worry.
But are we, I say—and we're all friends here—
(I, like you, have had my vines cut down)
Are *we* to blame the Spartans for everything?
There are those among us—I do not say the State,
Remember that, please, I do not say the State—
There are those among us, men of a sort I suppose,
Crooked, dishonest, degenerate, double-dealers,
And what have they done?
They kept on objecting and informing against
The Megarian trade in tunics—their staple trade—
And if they saw a cucumber, or a hare,
Or a sucking pig, a garlic-corm, a block of salt,
And they came from Megara, what did they do?
Had them confiscated!—And then knocked down for a song.
I suppose these were mere nothings—just our Athenian way—
The Megarians shouldn't have minded?

But when some young drunks, after a cottabos session,
Corkscrewed to Megara and abducted a whore
(Simaitha her name was), *then* the Megarians
Were really roused and proceeded, tit for tit,
To abduct a couple of Aspasia's—establishment.
My friends, the war which has spread through *all Greece*
Began for the sake of these three whores! Yes!
For in his wrath Olympian Pericles
Enacted a law (which sounded like a Calypso):
'The Megarians must not remain, nowhere, nowhere,
Not on the land, oh no!
Not on the sea, oh no, oh no!
Not in the market oh NO NO NO!
Not any place anywhere, nowhere at all.'
Then the Megarians slowly starving to death
Appealed to their friends the Spartans to see if they could
Get the Act of the Three Whores somehow rescinded.
They asked, we refused; they asked, we refused; *refused*,
REFUSED.

Then came the clash.
It shouldn't have done, you say? What else could they do?
I put it to you: If some Spartan had sailed out
To the island of Seriphos and done with the minniest mongrel
What *we* did in the market with the Megarians
Would you have sat down under it? You know you wouldn't!
Immediately, you'd have launched three hundred warships,
The whole city'd been full of soldiers' commands,
And milling round the ships' captains, wage-paying, gilding
Of figure-heads, uproar in the streets, allotment of rations,
Filling of wineskins, fixing of rowlocks, bidding for water casks,
Garlic, olives, nets of onions, garlands, pilchards, flute-girls,
And—black eyes!
In the dockyards oar-handles planed, bolts hammered,
Everything fitted out shipshape; flutes, pipes, and boatswains'
    whistles.

Well? You'd have done all this? Of course you would!
Don't you think Telephos will?—If you can think at all!
Well—?

                        The Chorus *splits.*

ANTI CHORUS. You revolting tramp, is it true?—Do you dare
    Address us like this? You! A common beggar!
    Why blame *us*, if we've got informers among us?

PRO CHORUS. He's absolutely right! Every single word is true!

ANTI CHORUS. But even if it is—was it right for him to say it?
    You can't let a man like that get away
    With saying such monstrous things—   [*Going off.*

PRO CHORUS. Where are you going? Why aren't you staying?
    If you molest this man I'll give you a double
    Dose of your own medicine—   [*Attacking.*
                                                       [*A scuffle.*

ANTI CHORUS.   Lamachos! Help, help! Hurry—
                 With your lightning-looks,
                 Your gorgon plume, come! Quickly!
                 Will nobody rush to my rescue?
                 No brigadier? Ow!
                 No general? Ow!

No commando? Ow!
He's got me pinned by the middle!
Lamachos . . . !

Enter Lamachos, *with a Gorgon's head on his shield.*

LAMACHOS [*a regular-army type*]. What's all this din? Where shall
   I help?   [*Parting them.*
And add to the row? Who woke my gorgon?
Come on, there, get up—

ANTI CHORUS [*pointing to* Dikaiopolis]. This hot-head's been ranting
   against the State.

LAMACHOS. Oh, has he? You, you beggar, you repulsive object,
   How did you dare—

DIKAIOPOLIS [*mock humble, acting the beggar*]. Oh, *Hero* Lamachos,
   I *do* beg your pardon, if I said anything wrong . . .

LAMACHOS. What did you say, then?

DIKAIOPOLIS.   Oh, I don't *know* now:
   I come over all queer when I see these weapons,
   Please put your shield down.

LAMACHOS. All right, sissy.

DIKAIOPOLIS. Upside down, so I can't see the Gorgon.

LAMACHOS. Tcha!

DIKAIOPOLIS. And give me that ostrich plume from your helmet!

LAMACHOS [*offhand*].—Mere chicken's tail—

DIKAIOPOLIS [*himself*].   Now hold my head.
   I want to be sick. I *hate* the things so.

LAMACHOS [*furious*]. Dammit! Using my feather to make you vomit?

DIKAIOPOLIS. Is it *really* a *feather*? What bird is it from?
   The Greater Bragfisher?

LAMACHOS.   Death and destruction!

DIKAIOPOLIS. Oh, Lamachos, *no*—not for *you*. You're too strong.
   You're *so* very strong, and so *very* well armed
   You could cut off my—foreskin.

LAMACHOS [*beside himself*].   You . . . you, a *beggar*,
   Insult me, a *general*!

DIKAIOPOLIS.   Am I a beggar?

LAMACHOS. What the hell else?

DIKAIOPOLIS.   I'm an honest citizen,
  Not a careerist. And since the war started
  I've been on active service. *You've* simply been
  At the base, in a sinecure, and after more pay—

LAMACHOS. I was specially appointed—

DIKAIOPOLIS.   By three stooges, I know.
  's why I made my treaty. I hate these rackets—
  Seeing grey-headed men slave in the ranks
  And young good-for-nothings like you malingering—
  Some off to Thrace at three drachmas a day
  (All indispensable experts: at doing nothing),
  Some off with Chares, some to Chaonia,
  Some to Kamarina, some to—

LAMACHOS [*breaks in*]. They were specially appointed by—

DIKAIOPOLIS [*equally breaks in*]. Isn't it strange?
  Somehow or other, *you* always get pay—
  These fellows NEVER. Marilades, tell me,
  You're grey, were *you* ever an envoy? NEVER.
  But he's able-minded, and active in body—
  Euphorides, tell me, and Drakyllos, and Prinides,
  Have *you* seen Ecbatana? Have *you* been to Chaonia?
  None of you. NEVER. But *Lamachos*,
  And all the young nobles, oh yes, *they've* been.
  And just before the war they were so deep in debt
  That even their friends (if they saw them in time)
  Shouted 'Look out! Keep away!' as if they were slops
  Chucked out in the evening from bedroom windows.

LAMACHOS. O Democracy! Can I stand it?

DIKAIOPOLIS. You can't—if you get no pay.

LAMACHOS [*marching out*]. But I, and all good Athenians,
  Shall fight on for ever and harry
  The Spartans by land and by sea
  To the utmost. Upon my life!   [*Exit.*

DIKAIOPOLIS. And I, to all good Megarians,
  And all good Boeotians, announce
  They may trade and do business with me—
  But Lamachos? NOT ON YOUR LIFE!   [*Exit.*

CHORUS. He's certainly won the debate and convinced
    The people we need a treaty.
    But just for the moment let's take off our make-up
    And speak for ourselves.

From the time Aristophanes first began to write,
He's never come into the open as frankly as this.
And you Athenians, renowned for your quicksilver wit
—You've seen him attacked by unprincipled enemies
Who say he slanders the State (and so, you) in his plays.
He's ready to answer; he knows you, quicksilver, too,
For the truth if it's offered you. Hear what he says. He says
He deserves your approval: hasn't he held before you
The mirror in which you see yourselves flattered and tricked
By any slick foreign envoy?—right from the time
Some smarmy called Athens 'violet-crowned' and you stuck
Yourselves up, and sat on your bottoms and beamed?
And if anyone sucked up and simpered 'Athens so glistening'
You'd do *anything* for them (though the epithet better applies
To a sardine). But now, as you listen
To the truth from your poet, won't you reward him for
    this?
—And for showing the world how a *real* democracy works? If
I told you they'll come simply *pressing* tribute upon you
—Just for a glimpse of the poet who risked his life
To tell the Athenians the truth—it'd *be* the truth.
Why, the report of his courage has spread so widely already
The King of Persia asked the envoys from Sparta,
First, what nation was the greatest power at sea,
And then, *whose* poet was the hardest hitter,
The most fearless satirist. Then the King added this:
'The people that have *his* advice will fight better, they'll win
The war for a cert!'—Aren't the Spartans suing for peace,
At the moment, because of this? Demanding the cession of
    Aegina,
Yes (though they don't give a damn for the place),
But hoping to whittle the poet away with it. YOU
Must never allow that! For he tells the truth in his plays
And he's still got a packet to say, and *all for your good.*

And you know him: he doesn't toady, suck up, blather, or lie;
He has only the best to offer you. He offers it fearlessly!

> Let Cleon direct against me
> As much smear and smut as he likes—
> I've got Right on my side. I don't mind!
> My conscience is clean, as regards the State.
> *Him*! Well, you know what a coward *he* is,
> And what sort of jobs for the boys *he* finds . . .
> You know I am not like that!

Come O fiery Muse, hot-tempered, Acharnian, eager,
Springing up like a spark; fanned into flame, from the charcoal,
When the *fritto misto* is cleaned and lying there ready for frying,
And someone is mixing the Phasian sauce for the fish to be dipped
    in,
Come oh as proud, oh as strong, rustic song as a folk song,
Come O fiery Muse—

We ancients, we old men, censure the City.
Is it fair that we who fought your battles,
And *should* be cosseted, so should suffer?
They take us to court, us old fellows,
To be mocked at by clever young counsel;
We are dull old dodderers, we dither,
Our sticks our only support;
And there in the courtroom we mutter;
Lost in the legal darkness,
In the hopeless mazes of our cases.
Then some young pig of a prosecutor
Who wangled the job, who knows how,
Turns us inside out with a quick-fire
Volley of villainous epigrams,
Sets traps in his cross-examination,
And so tears, twists, and troubles old Tithonus
That the old buffer bumbles and stumbles and goes off, Guilty!
Then weeping and keening, he complains to his cronies,
'The very cash I'd saved up for my coffin's
Filched from me to pay the fine. . . .'

Can it be right to ruin us greybeards

Just on account of the passing of the years?
We who have worked so, have wiped so much sweat from
Our manly young brows on behalf of the State?
Didn't we fine lads all rally to Marathon,
At Marathon conquer and kill and pursue?
Now, old, *we* are sued and pursued by these bloodsuckers!
Can anyone give us an answer? Can YOU?

Look at that bent old chap there—Thucydides—
Lost, like a babe, in the Scythian forests
Of Kephisodemos' clever-clever eloquence.
I can't tell you how much it upset me to see the
Old veteran pricked by the shafts of that creature.
Why, were he 'the great Thucydides whom we knew'
He wouldn't have stood it a minute, a second!
He'd have floored ten wrestlers as tough as Euathlos,
Roared down with his word-of-command a whole company
Of archers three thousand strong, and shot his accuser's
Whole family—going to Scythia to do it!

But if you won't let us sleep in peace,
Sort out the writs again;
Let one toothless old gaffer prosecute another
—And as for a young man:
Let some smart pansy, like the son of Cleinias,
Knock the bottom out of his case!
Now, in the future, as to fines and banishments:
It will be a scandalous disgrace
If we don't reform the courts and arrange things
Where they belong:
Leave the old men to deal with the old men,
The young with the young.

                    Re-enter Dikaiopolis.

DIKAIOPOLIS. Look! Here are my market boundaries,
    And any Boeotian and any Megarian
    Can trade with me here. But Lamachos? No!
    And these three good thongs—I'll make them clerks of my market,
    And if any informer or creature of that kidney . . .

                              [*Crack of whip.*

Now, I'll fetch my treaty pillar, and put it up,
Here, where they all can see it.   [*He goes out again.*

Enter Megarian *with two little* Girls *of about eight. The*
Megarian *has a North Country accent.*

MEGARIAN. Good morning Athenian market! And love from
  Megara!
By gum, I've missed you like mother.
Now you, you two wretched brats of a feeble father—
If you're after a bit o' duff,
Listen with all your guts:
Now: Would you rather be sold or hungry?

GIRLS. Sold! Sold!

MEGARIAN. Right enough. But who's such a damned idiot
As to give owt for you, y' couple o' dead losses?
. . . But I know a little Megarian trick:
I'll say I've a couple o' piglets.
Put up your hands. Now, tie on these trotters—
Behave like you come from a good pig-family—
For if I can't sell you, if I have to take you home again,
You'll be as hungry as never.
Now, put on these dear little snouts and get into the sack.
Now, grunt and squeal like pigs at a sacrifice, see?
I'm going to call Dikaiopolis. . . . *Dikaiopolis*! ! !
D'ye want any pigs today?

Re-enter Dikaiopolis.

DIKAIOPOLIS.   What is it, Megarian?

MEGARIAN. I've come to t'market.

DIKAIOPOLIS.   How are you doing?

MEGARIAN. Shrinking to death, by the fire . . .

DIKAIOPOLIS. Drinking to death? How delightful—with music, I
  hope?
What else are you doing in Megara?

MEGARIAN. Well, I came up this morning
From t'town, and I left the elders debating
How we could die most quickly . . .

DIKAIOPOLIS.   —I suppose it's a way
Out of your troubles. . . .

MEGARIAN. You're right there; an' no mistake about it.

DIKAIOPOLIS. What else now? Tell me; the price of grain for example?

MEGARIAN. Terrible! The gods are high. But *it's* higher. Much higher.

DIKAIOPOLIS. Any salt?

MEGARIAN. You control our salt.

DIKAIOPOLIS. Any garlic?

MEGARIAN. Garlic?
—And you raid us like field-mice and root it all up? Garlic?

DIKAIOPOLIS. Then what *have* you got?

MEGARIAN. Mystery pigs.

DIKAIOPOLIS. Let's see them.

MEGARIAN. Champion, they are. Pick 'er up if you like,
She's lovely and plump—

DIKAIOPOLIS. God in heaven, what's this?

MEGARIAN. A pig, like enough.

DIKAIOPOLIS. What do you mean?
Whatever sort of a pig?

MEGARIAN. A Megarian pig . . .

DIKAIOPOLIS. Doesn't seem like a pig.

MEGARIAN. Eh! Doesn't believe me!
Not a pig? *This* not a pig? I bet you a pinch
O' salt, she's a pig in our Greek
Sense of the word, fair enough. Would you like
To hear them grunt?

DIKAIOPOLIS. Yes, I would.

MEGARIAN. Come on, my porkers, quick now, your grunts—
[*Silence.*

You won't?—Not a grunt, you gormless young wretches?
D'you want me to take you home?

1 GIRL. Wee! wee! wee!

MEGARIAN. Is *that* a *pig*, or isn't it?

DIKAIOPOLIS. Yes, more like a pig
—But in five years, what'll she be?

MEGARIAN. Just like her mother.

DIKAIOPOLIS. But no good for sacrifice—

MEGARIAN. Why ever not?

DIKAIOPOLIS.   Got no tail.

MEGARIAN [*producing the other*]. She's young yet. When she's grown
    up—
  If you'd rear them, this one's a beauty!

DIKAIOPOLIS. It's as much a pig as the other. . . .

MEGARIAN. From the same father and mother!
  Just fatten her up, and wait till she grows her bristles,
  She'll be a beautiful sacrifice—
  To the goddess of Love!

DIKAIOPOLIS. To Aphrodite? A pig? You couldn't do that!

MEGARIAN. To her alone of the gods—the flesh of these piglets,
  Hot on a spit, is any man's dish—it's delicious—

DIKAIOPOLIS. Can they feed themselves yet? Without their mother,
  I mean?

MEGARIAN [*sardonically*]. Yes, and without their father.

DIKAIOPOLIS. What'll they eat?

MEGARIAN. Whatever you give them. Ask 'em.

DIKAIOPOLIS. Piggy, piggy, piggy . . .

GIRLS. Wee wee wee.

DIKAIOPOLIS. D'you like peas?

GIRLS. Oh wee oh wee—

DIKAIOPOLIS. And Phibalean figs?

GIRLS. WEE WEE WEE.

DIKAIOPOLIS. Both of you?

GIRLS. *Wee wee wee*.

DIKAIOPOLIS. They squeal superbly for figs! Hey! Someone in there
  Bring figs for these two little grunts—little *pigs*, please!
  Glory be! Look at them eating! *What* sort of pigs did you say?
  Eatallian pigs?

MEGARIAN [*munching hungrily*]. They haven't ate *all* the figs . . .
  Eh? I've picked up *one* for myself.

DIKAIOPOLIS. They're fat little creatures. What d'you want for
  them?

MEGARIAN. Λ corm of garlic for one; for t'other
  A measure of salt, if you like.

DIKAIOPOLIS. I'll take 'em! Wait here.

> *[Going off to get them.*

MEGARIAN.   —I'll wait! Eh! By Hermes!
  I'd sell wife and mother for terms good as these.

> *Enter an* Informer.

INFORMER [*icy*]. Excuse me, but who are you?

MEGARIAN. A pig merchant from Megara.

INFORMER. Then I'll denounce you! You're enemies, enemies!

MEGARIAN. Here it comes again. The whole bloody nonsense.
  This is where we left off.

INFORMER.   I'll make you suffer
  For being Megarian. *Put down that sack!*

MEGARIAN. Dikaiopolis! Dikaiopolis! I'm being informed on!

> Dikaiopolis *rushes in.*

DIKAIOPOLIS. Who by? Where is he? [*Cracks whip.*] Clerks!
  Why don't you keep these informers out?

INFORMER [*retreating*]. They're our enemies! [*Crack.*] It is our
  duty! [*Crack.*]
  To show them up! [*Crack.*]

DIKAIOPOLIS [*driving him off*]. Get out! Get *out*! Show somebody
  else up—   [*Exit* Informer.

MEGARIAN. Eh! Proper curse they are, to all you Athenians—

DIKAIOPOLIS. Never mind. Here's the garlic and salt,
  The price of your—pigs . . . and good luck to you.

MEGARIAN. We need it in Megara.

DIKAIOPOLIS.   You'll get it
  Or I'll know the reason why—

MEGARIAN [*gently as he goes*]. Well, my piggies,
  Good-bye. You must do without your father
  And learn to eat salt with your duff—if anyone gives you some . . . .

> [*Exit.*

DIKAIOPOLIS [*calls after him*]. Good luck, Megarian!

> [*He goes inside with* Girls.

CHORUS. Lucky man. How well your plan is going;
  Sitting there, prospering, in your private market!
  Let Ctesias come or any damned informer
  —You'll send him packing!

No under-counter cheat shall get ahead of you;
No pansy provoke; no blustering Cleonymos;
But cleanly you'll go; no Hyperbolos shall profit from
   Bringing an action.

Nor shall Cratinos, self-evident adulterer,
Walk in your market, nor Artemon the stinker,
Too clever by half (you can smell him a mile off,
   Like that old goat his father).

Nor shall Pauson, the master crook, mock at you,
Nor Lysistratos the curse of the Cholargians,
The double-double-crosser, perpetually hungry—
   None shall molest you!

               Enter Boeotian *and his slaves.*

BOEOTIAN [*Welsh accent*]. Ph! By Heracles! My shoulder's rubbed
   raw, indeed!
Now, *very* carefully, put down the bundle
Of pennyroyal and blow on your pipes, my son.
                              [*Tuning up of bagpipes.*
         Dikaiopolis *dashes out of his house.*

DIKAIOPOLIS. Stop that row! Get away from my doors, you drones!
   God, where've *you* come from, you bumble bagpiper?
   —You're worse than Chairis—you'll murder me.

BOEOTIAN. To goodness, stranger, you are right; the wasps was
   terrible
All the way from Thebes they followed us—
And battered the blossom off all my herbs . . .
[*He gets going.*] But look you, buy—I've got chickens, and
   marvellous
Birds with *four* wings—

DIKAIOPOLIS [*interrupting*]. My dear Boeotian doughnut, what *have*
   you got?

BOEOTIAN [*off again*]. Every good thing that's coming from my
   country.
Origanum, pennyroyal, rush mats, wicks,
Ducks, daws, snipe, coots, dotterel, dabchicks—

DIKAIOPOLIS.—Foul weather for my market!—

BOEOTIAN [*flowing on*].—And geese, look you, hares, fox furs, moles,
  Hedgehogs, weasels, beavers, ferrets, otters, and—   [*Pause.*
  Eels from Lake Copaïs.

DIKAIOPOLIS. Not *eels*? Oh bringer of the most delicious succulent
  Pleasure of the palate, NOT EELS?
  Let me greet these eels—if you've really got EELS?

BOEOTIAN. 'Fairest of Copaïs' fifty daughters'—come out there!
  Say 'how-do-you-do?' to the stranger.

DIKAIOPOLIS [*in ecstasy*]. O dear most desirable darling,
  The Chorus's craving, and mine!
  Bring out the bellows and brazier, my boys,
  Regard this most beautiful eel!
  Longed-for for six war years, and at last
  She is coming, my own, my sweet!
  Children salute her, let me make up the fire
  And all for her darling sake!
  Out with her! Never, oh never again,
  Not even in death, may I ever be severed
  From a *heavenly* stewed eel!

BOEOTIAN. But what are you giving me for it?

DIKAIOPOLIS. *You* shall *give* it to *me*, as a market-toll.
  But these other things—are *they* all for sale?

BOEOTIAN [*eagerly*]. For *sale*, indeed yes.

DIKAIOPOLIS.   How much?
  Or would you consider swapping?

BOEOTIAN. For something you have, and we haven't, I would.

DIKAIOPOLIS. Sprats? Or pottery?

BOEOTIAN.   We've got them. No.
  Something we've nothing of, look you,
  And you have too much of—

DIKAIOPOLIS.   I KNOW.
  An INFORMER! I'll pack one up
  Like pottery for export.

BOEOTIAN [*delighted*].   An informer!
  Splendid! I'll make a great fortune, indeed,
  From his cunning deceits, the monkey—

DIKAIOPOLIS. And here is Nikarchos coming
  To inform on you—

BOEOTIAN [*doubtfully*]. He's *very* small in stature—

DIKAIOPOLIS. But every inch guaranteed bad!

Enter Nikarchos.

NIKARCHOS. Whose are these goods?

BOEOTIAN. Mine; I am from Thebes.

NIKARCHOS. I hereby denounce it as enemy—

BOEOTIAN.   Stuff and nonsense!
Do you make war on the little birds, is it?

NIKARCHOS. Yes, and you too.

BOEOTIAN. What have *I* done?

NIKARCHOS.   For the sake
Of all you bystanders—I'll tell you. Listen,
You've brought lantern-wicks from enemy—

DIKAIOPOLIS [*breaking in*].   *Lantern-wicks?*
You'd denounce him for lantern-wicks?

NIKARCHOS. Certainly!

DIKAIOPOLIS. What could a lantern-wick do?

NIKARCHOS. Set the docks on fire!

DIKAIOPOLIS. In heaven's name, how?

NIKARCHOS.   If a Boeotian
Stuck a wick on a water beetle
And sent if off to the docks, down a gutter,
Waiting for a strong north wind, then IF
The ships caught fire—they'd be burned in a flash!

DIKAIOPOLIS. Go, burn yourself!   [*Crack of market whip.*
What, burnt by a beetle   [*Crack.*
With a wick on its back?   [*Crack.*

NIKARCHOS. Witness! Witness! I'm being assaulted!

DIKAIOPOLIS [*holding him*]. Gag him, and bring me chips and straw,
And I'll pack him as safe as a pot,
So he shan't break on the way!

> [*Throughout the following scene* Nikarchos *makes
> inarticulate cries at intervals as he is packed.*

CHORUS. Now do the package up
So carefully for this stranger,
That nobody bearing it
Could break it.

DIKAIOPOLIS. I'll certainly do that,
    For it makes inarticulate noises.
    And it's cracked, and anyhow   [Nikarchos *groans*.
    The gods hate it.

CHORUS. What will he use it for?

DIKAIOPOLIS. You can use it for anything—
    A mug for evil, a jug
    For writs, or a stand for audits,
    Or simply a bitter cup
        Of unkindness.

CHORUS. But how could anyone
    Use this disgusting vessel
    About the house? It groans   [Nikarchos *groans*.
    Without ceasing—

DIKAIOPOLIS. It's very tough, my friends:
    Even if you hang it head downwards,   [*He does so.*
    Or swing it by the heels,
        You can't break it!

CHORUS [*to* Boeotian]. He's doing a beautiful job—

BOEOTIAN. And I'll reap a beautiful harvest, indeed.

CHORUS [*to* Boeotian]. Reap if you can, my friend—
    You've certainly got the best
    Informer going—so *go*, now!

DIKAIOPOLIS [*out of breath*]. Just managed it! He nearly finished me!
    Take up your pot, Boeotian!

BOEOTIAN. Come on, Ismenos, heave him up!

DIKAIOPOLIS. Carry him carefully home! Hold him tight.
    You've got a bit of no goods *there*, all right.
    And if you can make a profit out of him
    You've got a wonderful way with informers.
    Good luck to you—   [*Exit* Boeotian.

        Enter a Servant.

SERVANT [*shouting*]. Dikaiopolis!

DIKAIOPOLIS. What is it? Why are you shouting?

SERVANT. It's Lamachos. It's the Feast of Pitchers. He says—

DIKAIOPOLIS. Well?

SERVANT. Give him some thrushes for this drachma,
  And, for these three, an eel . . .

DIKAIOPOLIS [*offhand*]. Who is this Lamachos wanting an eel?

SERVANT. The tough one, the one with the Gorgon
  On his shield, and three shadowing plumes—

DIKAIOPOLIS. Him? Not likely? Not even if he *gave* me his shield!
  Let him twiddle his plumes at his iron rations,
  If he doesn't like it—I'll send for my clerks!   [*Cracks his whip*.
  As for me I'm going indoors with my goods—
  Under the wings of my blackbirds and thrushes.   [*Exit*.

CHORUS. Look, everyone, look
    At this superintelligent brilliant chap
    Who's made his treaty; he's goods to sell
      Imported from everywhere:
    Household goods, high quality foods,
    —The wealth of the world falls into his lap
      Without his raising a finger
          At all!

  I'll never invite War back to my house
  With his bawdy soldiers' choruses, never
      Shall he sit at the same table;
  For he's always tipsy or fighting drunk,
  He assaults his hosts, and breaks the place up
  And when you soothe him and say 'Sit down
  For a loving-cup'—all the louder he raves
  And smashes the vines, and burns the vine poles
  Spilling the wine in the very grape—
      He can't help it.

    Oh, Dikaiopolis! Look!—
  He's preparing his dinner; he's so at peace
  With the world he has chucked these plumes
      Out of his door to rot!
  O Peace, you who dwell with the beautiful
  Goddess and all the Graces, O how
      Have I missed your entrancing
          Sweet face?

Yes, Love, unite me with *you*, sweet Peace
(Love, just as he's drawn with a crown of flowers),
   Do you think me so altogether
Too old? If you'll have me, I'll show you what.
Three things: for first, I'll plant you a grand
New wineyard; and second a green young fig;
And third, though I'm old, my darling, I can. . . .
And there in a ring of olives we'll live
And love when the light of the new moon shines.
   Will you have me?

Enter the Crier.

CRIER. ATTENTION! ATTENTION PLEASE!
  When the Trumpet sounds empty your pitchers
  In the good old-fashioned way—and *whoever wins*,
  He shall have a skinful of wine
  As large as the skin of—old Ctesiphon!

Re-enter Dikaiopolis.

DIKAIOPOLIS. Boys! Girls! Didn't you hear?
  What are you doing? Didn't you hear the announcement?
  Boil up the stew! Bake! Turn the roast!
  Take off that hare! Get the garlands made!
  Bring out the spits! I'll do the thrushes myself—

CHORUS. How I envy your whole scheme; and even more
  Your present well-being—

DIKAIOPOLIS.   You mean, when you see me
  Grilling these thrushes?

CHORUS.   —The very words are food
  To my ears!

DIKAIOPOLIS. Poke up that fire, there!

CHORUS.   D'you hear how expertly,
  How like a chef, how elegantly, deftly he does it all?

Enter a Farmer.

FARMER [*wailing*]. God help me . . . God help me . . . ruined,
  ruined . . .

DIKAIOPOLIS. Great heavens; who's this?

FARMER. An unlucky farmer—

DIKAIOPOLIS [*sharply*]. Then keep your bad luck to yourself!

FARMER. But only *you* have a treaty. Be a good fellow,
  Measure me just five years, five years of peace. . . .

DIKAIOPOLIS. What's the trouble?

FARMER. I've lost my two oxen. . . .

DIKAIOPOLIS. Where from?

FARMER. The Boeotians rustled them. Phylé. That's where from.

DIKAIOPOLIS. Bad luck. But why are you wearing *white*?

FARMER [*sadly*].   I can now . . .
  Now they're gone. . . . They *kept* me. Up to the neck in muck. . . .

DIKAIOPOLIS. Well, what d'you want?

FARMER.   I've *ruined* my eyesight now,
  Weeping. For *them*. Derketes from Phylé, that's me.
  Be a good fellow. Peace-ointment; that's what I want—
  To rub on my eyes—

DIKAIOPOLIS.   You fool! *I'm* not a doctor.

FARMER. Oh, I implore you. Then I might find my oxen. . . .

DIKAIOPOLIS. *No*! Pittalos, he's the doctor. Go and weep at *his* door.

FARMER. Just *one drop*. Just one. Enough to put on this pinhead.

DIKAIOPOLIS. Not the teeniweeniest! Go and moan somewhere else.

FARMER [*as he goes*]. I'm ruined, ruined, oh my two oxen . . . oh
  What a life. . . . Who'd be a farmer? . . . Ruined . . . Ruined . . . .   [*Exit.*

CHORUS. This man has found how sweet
  The taste of his treaty is;
  He isn't going to share it
  With any Tom Dick or Harry . . .

DIKAIOPOLIS. Pour the honey over the rissoles!
  Give the cuttlefish a stir!

CHORUS. Did you hear him, what ringing words!

DIKAIOPOLIS. See those eels are properly done!

CHORUS. Oh Dikaiopolis, *don't*!
  You're whetting our appetites,
  You're killing us—we can't bear it.
  We're so famished.

DIKAIOPOLIS.   Now roast all these!
  —See they're well browned, please.

Enter a Best Man *and a* Bridesmaid.

BEST MAN. Dikaiopolis!—

DIKAIOPOLIS. Who is it, now?

BEST MAN [*nervously*]. My friend—just married—I was the best
man—
He's sent you this meat from the wedding breakfast—

DIKAIOPOLIS.   Splendid!
Whoever he is—

BEST MAN.   —And he's asked, in exchange for the meat . . .
Well, er, you see . . . he's just married, he wants to—
To—er—*be* with his wife, and not to be called up.
. . . Could he have just one drop of Peace-ointment, in this pot?

DIKAIOPOLIS [*mock anger*]. 'Take the nasty stuff away, I won't
have any meat today.'
I wouldn't give him a drop, not for ten thousand drachmas.
[*Whistles.*] But, who's this . . . ?

BEST MAN. She's a bridesmaid. And I think she's got a message
From the bride—for you, alone. . . .

DIKAIOPOLIS [*fondly*]. Well, my dear, what do *you* want?
                                                  [*A whispering session.*
[*Roars with laughter.*] What a thing to ask!
So *that*'s what she wants! Quick, bring me my treaty,
I'll give her some. *Only her.* She's a woman:
She wasn't built to bear war.
Now, hold the box underneath. That's right!
Do you know how to use it?
You—tell—her—when there's a call-up,
Rub this on EVERY NIGHT.
No, my dear, *not* on his face!
She's married. She'll know.
Now take the treaty away, and bring me the wine-jar;
I'll fill all the cups for the feast.
                    A Messenger *enters. He knocks at* Lamachos' *door.*

MESSENGER. O Battles! O Fatigues! O LAMACHOS!

LAMACHOS [*within*]. Who the—who's banging at my door?

MESSENGER [*sing-song voice*]. An order from the generals. H-arm
yourself;
Fall in your men, and pro-ceed himmediate,

To keep tabs on the Passes.
[*Ordinary voice: delighted.*] And it's snowing!
Hintelligence 'as come through,
A gang of Boeotians 'as it in mind
To make things 'ot at this feast-time.
Got it?   [*Exit.*

                    Lamachos *opens the door.*

LAMACHOS. Confound the generals! There are so many, you'd think
   They could muster *one* brain between them.
   Can't they even leave me alone
   To enjoy a feast in peace?

DIKAIOPOLIS [*overhearing*]. In peace? Oooh Lamachos! The great
   fire-eater?

LAMACHOS [*shudders*]. *You* again. Must you insult me so?

DIKAIOPOLIS [*still mocking*]. Don't you *want* to fight, not even
   With a four-winged monster—like me?

LAMACHOS. Oh god! What a hell of a message he's brought me.

A VOICE. Dikaiopolis!

DIKAIOPOLIS. Oh hell, what a god of a message—

                    Enter Messenger.

   Have you got for *me*?

MESSENGER. Dikaiopolis?

DIKAIOPOLIS.   That's me.

MESSENGER [*out of breath*]. Come to dinner *at once*!
   Bring all your provisions and wine—
   The priest of Dionysus—he sent me—
   And *hurry*—you're keeping the dinner;
   Everything else is ready and waiting:
   The couches, the tables, the cushions,
   The rugs, the garlands, the myrrh,
   The sweets and the *girls* . . .   [*He draws breath.*
   The shortbread, the cheese cake, the sesame,
   The honey cake, and the *honeys*—
   What *girls*, what *lovelies*, what—
                              [*Words fail him, he merely thinks.*
[*Coming out of daze.*] Well, come as quick as you can!   [*Exit.*
                              [*Lamachos groans in despair.*

DIKAIOPOLIS. All right, you *chose* the great Gorgon, didn't you?
You can have her! Pack up the supper!
We must be off!

LAMACHOS. Come on, boy, bring out my knapsack.

DIKAIOPOLIS. Come on, boy, bring out my hamper.

LAMACHOS. Fetch me some salt and onions.

DIKAIOPOLIS. Smoked roe for *me*. I hate onions.

LAMACHOS. Bring me an old salt fish in a vine leaf.

DIKAIOPOLIS. Bring me some new fresh meat in a vine leaf. I'll
cook it now.

LAMACHOS. The plumes for my helmet!

DIKAIOPOLIS. My pigeons and thrushes!

LAMACHOS. This ostrich feather is nice and white!

DIKAIOPOLIS. This pigeon's breast is nice and brown!

LAMACHOS [*furious*]. Don't keep mocking at my equipment!

DIKAIOPOLIS. Don't keep looking at my thrushes.

LAMACHOS. Get my crest case, with my three crests in it.

DIKAIOPOLIS. Get my hamper with my cooked hare in it.

LAMACHOS. I think the clothes moths have been at these—

DIKAIOPOLIS. I think *I'll* snatch a little snack before dinner—

LAMACHOS [*can stand no more*]. Look here, will you kindly *not*
speak to me!

DIKAIOPOLIS. But, look here, my boy and I can't agree.
[*To boy.*] Let's have a bet, boy—Lamachos will decide.
Which is the better; raw locust or roast thrush?

                          [Lamachos *makes inarticulate noises of anger.*
Locusts, he says. Fancy that!—

LAMACHOS [*tries to go on*]. Boy, get my spear off its hook.

DIKAIOPOLIS. Boy, take my sausages off—

LAMACHOS. Hold hard, while I pull it from its case.

DIKAIOPOLIS. Hold hard, while I pull 'em off the spit.

LAMACHOS. Bring the prop for my shield.

DIKAIOPOLIS. Bring my food for a prop.

LAMACHOS. Now I'll fix on the Gorgon—

DIKAIOPOLIS. And I'll have a biscuit.

LAMACHOS. This is mockery—for everyone to see!

DIKAIOPOLIS. This is pastry—for everyone to eat!

LAMACHOS [*gritting his teeth*]. Pour on the oil. . . . In my shield
   I see an old man reflected—
   Charged with cowardice. *Get on!*

DIKAIOPOLIS. Pour on the honey! I spy
   With my little eye an old man
   Still laughing at Lamachos.

LAMACHOS. My breastplate to protect my exterior—

DIKAIOPOLIS. My wine to preserve my interior—

LAMACHOS. I must arm against the foe!

DIKAIOPOLIS. I must fortify myself
   For the rigours of the feast!

LAMACHOS. Boy, tie up my blankets to my shield.

DIKAIOPOLIS. Boy, tie up my food in my hamper.

LAMACHOS. Nothing for it. I must put on my pack. . . .

DIKAIOPOLIS. Nothing for it. I must put on my best. . . .

LAMACHOS. Boy, shoulder the shield! . . . *Snowing* . . .
   O god, what a ghastly prospect!

DIKAIOPOLIS. Boy, hoist the hamper! Supper!
   What a prospect! What a *prospect*. . . .

                                      [*Exeunt.*

CHORUS.   Then go your ways my heroes—
                They're certainly rather different.
                Lamachos out in the *cold*,
                    Watching, worn to exhaustion;
                Dikaiopolis drinking there
                In the lap of—luxury—and if
                He's worn out—it's the *heat*
                    Of his own exertions!

Now let Zeus destroy Antimachos, the stuttering pest,
The lousy poet who had me shut out of the feast
Of Lenaia—and if he craves for a cuttlefish
   Let it come sizzling hot from the sea
   To run aground at his table and *just*
As he's going to eat it, may a mongrel harpy
   Snatch it and bolt.

That's for the day. Now let this happen at night.
As he's homing from riding, let Orestes roaring tight
Cosh him hard on his head, and in dizzy darkness
  Let him scrabble about for a stone and pick up
As filthy a dollop of muck as he is himself
And aim at Orestes and missing him hit Cratinos
  Plumb in the eye!

Enter a Messenger

MESSENGER [*shouting*]. Help, you servants of Lamachos; put on a
  pot
Of water to boil! Get bandages! Ointment! Lint!—
Your master is wounded, stuck by a stake
As he jumped a ditch, and then as he turned
To wrench out his ankle, he fell and he struck his head
So hard the Gorgon leapt clean off his shield!
Then his bragfisher feathers flew off on the rocks,
And he started to wail like this—
  'Great Eye of the sun, it's the last time I look on you,
  I'm leaving the light of day—I'm done in—'
And he fell back into the ditch as he finished speaking!
But he was up again, bravely barring the way
And prodding the gang with his spear as they fled defeated.
But look, here he is! Open the doors!

Re-enter Lamachos.

LAMACHOS.　　　O hellish day!
　　　　　　What appalling sufferings!
　　　　　　I'm stuck by a spear, I'm dying—
　　　　　　But worse than this, far worse,
　　　　　　　If Dikaiopolis sees
　　　　　　Me wounded and mocks my woe.

Enter Dikaiopolis.

DIKAIOPOLIS [*overhearing—tipsy*]. O heavenly day!
　　　　　　Their breasts so plump and firm!
　　　　　　How they loved me, golden-lying,
　　　　　　How they could kiss and kiss!
　　　　　　　—I was tongue-tied with bliss,
　　　　　　But I won the drinking, too!

LAMACHOS. My miseries, my ghastly wounds!

DIKAIOPOLIS [*embracing him*]. Hey there, hullo there!
   Dear ol' Lamachos, how are you?

LAMACHOS. Terrible!

DIKAIOPOLIS [*belching*]. I'm terrible too.

LAMACHOS. Why did you kiss me then?

DIKAIOPOLIS. Why did you bite me then?

LAMACHOS. How they charged and charged—

DIKAIOPOLIS. *I* wasn't charged—it was all free
   At the feast—and easy too . . .

LAMACHOS. O Paian, god of doctors!

DIKAIOPOLIS. It isn't *his* feast today.

LAMACHOS. Hold me up, my friends, hold me up,
   I can hardly stand.

DIKAIOPOLIS. Hold me down, darlings, hold me down!
   I *can*.

LAMACHOS. My head's in a whirl from that blow
   On the stone; I feel dizzy—

DIKAIOPOLIS. I'm dizzy too, but I can stand up
   And I *want* to lie down. . . .   [*Giggles.*

LAMACHOS. Take me, friends, with gentle hands
   To Doctor Pittalos. . . .

DIKAIOPOLIS. —Take me to the judges! Where's the Master of
   Ceremonies?
   GIVE ME MY PRIZE!

LAMACHOS. I'm pierced to the bone. . . .   [*Exit.*

DIKAIOPOLIS. I'm dry as a bone—
   Look here, this is empty—
   Hurrah for the winner!
   But WHERE'S MY PRIZE?

CHORUS. Hurrah for the winner!

DIKAIOPOLIS. I filled it with neat wine,
   And I drank it at a go!

CHORUS. Hurrah for the winner, here
    Take your prize and go!
    Take your wine-skin and go!

DIKAIOPOLIS. Come on, everyone, follow me!

CHORUS [*cheering*]. We'll follow you! We'll follow you!
    We'll follow you, Dikaiopolis,
    And sing your praises—
    [*Single voice.*] So long as you've got that wine-skin.
    [*All.*] We'll follow you, follow you!

KNIGHTS

Aristophanes presented the Knights, *like his preceding play, at the Lenaia, a year later, in early* 424 B.C. *Again it won the first prize, and again the veteran comic playwright Cratinos, who is mentioned in the central Parabasis (pp. 71-4), came second. It was the first play of Aristophanes produced under his own name, his earlier ones having been put on through others.*

None the less the *Knights* is a consistent and vicious attack on Cleon, the most popular man in Athens and the most powerful in the Athenian alliance waging war against Sparta and her allies. Cleon could—and did—claim to be the servant of the state and working for the people's good; by his success as a mass orator, he certainly held the acclaim of the citizens who attended the Assembly (Ecclesia). Aristophanes in this play presents him as the new and favourite slave of Demos ('the people'), a rather bad-tempered, gullible, materialistic, and ungenerous old man. Two other slaves of Demos, Demosthenes and Nikias, are actual political and military leaders, but, unlike Cleon, from old-established, upper-class families. Aristophanes said no mask-makers dared do one for Cleon; so the latter is brought on the stage, still easily identifiable, as Paphlagon. (Paphlagonia was indeed a country where slaves were got from, but the name suggested also the Greek for, as it were, 'yap yap, blah blah blah'.)

Cleon-Paphlagon is under attack chiefly by the device of introducing someone even worse than himself and thereby better at winning the favour of Demos. This is the Sausage-seller; Cleon's connection with trade, through his father, a successful leather-tanner, is not *quite* so bad. The Sausage-seller can cap any dishonest or disreputable line that Cleon may have played. Winning the votes of the people, like all electioneering, is a matter of competing in exaggerated promises, often not kept, and contriving material advantages for the masses. Under Cleon certainly the fee for anyone attending courts as a juror was raised to three obols a day. In the *Knights* it is implied that he also got large sums of money or property confiscated from wealthy citizens convicted on trumped-up charges; organized special religious festivals with state banquets to appeal through their stomachs to the urban poor; exacted excessive sums as tribute from the islanders in the Athenian alliance; imposed unfair duties on the rich in fitting out ships for the navy; encouraged informers and wrongly challenged officials on their use of public money at the audit of their accounts; continued the war even when the Spartans offered a treaty; brought armed gangs into Athens to intimidate possible opponents; made himself rich all the while; and in particular cashed in on the credit for the Pylos-Sphacteria victory the year before. In that campaign,

Cleon, having accused the two generals, Nikias and Demosthenes, in open Assembly in Athens, of cowardice for not forcing the surrender of a body of blockaded Spartan troops, accepted the challenge to take command himself in place of Nikias. He promised to bring the Spartans in prisoners within twenty days, and then carried out plans already prepared by Demosthenes—but kept his promise, and the glory for the victory.

The Knights (the cavalry) in Athens were drawn from fairly well-to-do citizens, and are therefore, as the Chorus, very ready to join in the charges on Paphlagon-Cleon from the start. Their own inclinations are more to horse-riding and wrestling than, say, the craze for enigmatic oracles and prophecies, which Aristophanes ridicules in general.

In the Parabasis, the author explains further his views on the art of writing comedy, to which he has committed himself in this first play expressly his own. And after a kind of transformation scene near the end of the play, when the Sausage-seller declares his name as Agoracritos and Demos turns into a figure of grandeur, some serious political reforms are suggested.

Was Cleon really as bad as Aristophanes makes out? It mustn't be forgotten that the *Knights* is a comedy, and the comic playwright's 'truth' is in a relationship between his play and the audience who *knew* the facts that historians and posterity can only suppose.

CHARACTERS

NIKIAS
DEMOSTHENES } *slaves wearing masks in the likeness of the Athenian generals Nikias and Demosthenes*

SAUSAGE-SELLER, *later named as Agoracritos*

PAPHLAGON, *a slave (actually the demagogue Cleon, though not in his likeness)*

DEMOS, *an old man representing the 'people' of Athens*

Girls representing TREATIES

CHORUS *of Knights*

In the background the house of Demos; *three doors out of which*
Nikias, Demosthenes, Paphlagon, *and finally* Demos *enter. In
the foreground a rough representation of the Pnyx.*

Enter Demosthenes *and* Nikias.

DEMOSTHENES. This bloody swine of a new slave!
  It's nothing but floggings for the rest of us
  Since he was bought—all fixed by him:
  No peace in the house at all. May the gods
  Blast him to the bottom of hell!

NIKIAS. I wish they would. This Paphlagon's
  The dirtiest, vilest liar ever.

DEMOSTHENES. How do you feel?

NIKIAS.   Awful. Like you.

DEMOSTHENES. Let's get it out of our systems. What
  About one of Olympus's laments?

DEMOSTHENES. ⎫
NIKIAS.   ⎬Wow wow wow wow wow!
             ⎭

DEMOSTHENES. We can't go moaning for ever—
  See if we can find some means
  Of getting away.

NIKIAS.   How? You tell me.

DEMOSTHENES. No, you tell *me*, or we might fall out.

NIKIAS. No! I'll fall in with anything. After *you*.
  I'll say what . . . I'll say.

DEMOSTHENES. 'If only you'd tell me what I ought to say!'

NIKIAS. I haven't the guts, and I can't quote
  A neat bit of Euripides to the point. . . .

DEMOSTHENES. Please don't. Don't stuff me up
  With sage sprigs of *his* wit!
  We simply want some common-or-garden way
  Of slinking off from master.

NIKIAS. Well, say the syllable 'sert'.
  Clip it short.

DEMOSTHENES. Right. Sert.

NIKIAS. Now 'de'.

DEMOSTHENES.   *De.*

NIKIAS.   Perfect.
Now relax and start off slowly
Saying 'sert', then 'de', and quicken
And crisp it up.

DEMOSTHENES.   Sert-de-
Sert-de—Sert-de-sert desert—
Desert!

NIKIAS.   Exactly. Splendid, isn't it?

DEMOSTHENES. I'm not so sure. The word's
Ominous—it gives me gooseflesh.

NIKIAS. Why?

DEMOSTHENES. They flog deserters.

NIKIAS. Then we'd better go and kneel
At the s-s-s-statues of the gods.

DEMOSTHENES. S-s-statues? What's the matter?
You don't really think there *are*
Gods still?

NIKIAS.   I know there are.

DEMOSTHENES. What proof have you?

NIKIAS.   Because
They hate me so. There must be.

DEMOSTHENES. Yes, that's convincing. We must find
Some other way. Would you like me
To put our case to the audience?

NIKIAS. Not a bad idea. But ask them
To give us a clear lead first
If they approve of our behaviour.

DEMOSTHENES. I'll tell them now. [*To audience.*] Our master's rather
A boor, a fanatical voter, a gloomy
Old bear, and more than a bit deaf.
His name is Demos or Pnyx Place.
Now, at the beginning of last month
He bought a new slave, a tanner,
Called Cle—, I mean Paphlagon—
The filthiest, most blatant, lowest-down
Liar of all time. And he soon
Rumbled his master's weaknesses

And sucked-up, arse-licked, and soft-soaped
Until he had him where he wanted. . . .
Went oiling-up with little snippets, scraps
Of greasy cunning: fawning, whining,
'Demos, don't *tire* yourself; judge one,
Just *one* case—all of three obols' worth—
Then relax in your bath and build
Yourself up with a real blow-out,
Bloat yourself—let yourself go. You
Need it! Shall I lay supper now?'
Then he nips out and snaps up
What one of us has just got ready,
And sets it before master, as if
He'd cooked it himself.

              This happened to me:
I'd baked Demos a Spartan cake
At Pylos—then *he* barged in,
In the most monstrous barefaced manner,
Swiped it, served it, and took the credit
Belonging to me. And he kicks us out,
And no one but him must wait on master.
Then, standing at table he flicks off
All opposition speakers like flies
With his leathery garland. He intones
Oracles till the poor man is
Befogged with sibyls! Then when he sees
The old fogey mooning, he gets to work
And smears us all with his hints and slanders.
Then we're flogged, and Paphlagon sidles
Scurrying round from slave to slave;
Begs and blackmails, takes bribes, hissing
'See Hylas getting his? *I* fixed that.
Want to be done today? You don't?
Keep in with *me* then.'—So we pay up.
If we don't, we get it from Demos
Four times as bad. . . .

              Look, we *must* think
Where to go and who to go to.

NIKIAS. I still like that 'sert' affair best.

DEMOSTHENES. But Paphlagon misses nothing. He has
   An eye for everything—he straddles
   One foot in Pylos, the other in
   The Assembly, and his arse is right
   Bang above open-mouthed Chaonia,
   His fist in Beggarland, and his wits
   In the Borough of Theft.

NIKIAS.   There's nothing
   Left but to die. What do you think
   The most manly death?

DEMOSTHENES.   Most manly death?
   What do *you* think?

NIKIAS.   Should we drink
   Bull's blood? That's what Themistocles
   Chose—

DEMOSTHENES. Blood! Not on your *life*! No.
   Neat wine's the stuff; and drink to our own
   Spirit of Luck. Some really brilliant
   Idea might . . . come out with the stopper.

NIKIAS. Neat wine? I don't see it at all.
   How can you think straight if you're drunk?

DEMOSTHENES. Nonsense, you piddling pussyfoot!
   Do you dare knock the powers of wine?
   Can you think of anything more effective?
   When a man drinks, he's rich, he gets
   A magic touch, he wins his lawsuits,
   He helps his friends. . . . Quick now,
   Get me a jar to whet my wit
   And I'll say something to the point.

NIKIAS. What good'll drinking do? I still
   Don't see it.

DEMOSTHENES. I don't see it—yet.
   Go get it quickly!   [*Exit* Nikias.
   I'll just lie down
   And when I'm drunk I'll throw up gobbets
   Of ideas and schemes and opinions.

Re-enter Nikias.

NIKIAS. What a bit of luck! Nobody
Saw me stealing the wine in there.

DEMOSTHENES. What was Paphlagon doing then?

NIKIAS.—Bolting cakes, as fast as he whips
Confiscations up. The soak's passed out
And snoring slumped on his stinking hides.

DEMOSTHENES. Pour me out a double, then—
For the libation—don't be mean.

NIKIAS. There. To our own good Luck! Here's
To real vintage Pramnian Fortune!

DEMOSTHENES. Here's to it! Now, *this* is *your* idea,
Not mine.

NIKIAS.   *What's my* idea? Tell me.

DEMOSTHENES. Go and steal Paphlagon's oracles
While he's asleep and bring 'em along.

NIKIAS. Well . . . I hope my luck will hold
And not turn bad. . . .   [*Exit.*

DEMOSTHENES.   And I'll just pull
The jar into my reach—my mind
Needs flagons in a steady downpour
To revive the springs of my flagging
Wit.

Re-enter Nikias.

NIKIAS. Paphlagon's farts and snores
Are so loud he never heard me,
And I've got away with the oracle
He never lets out of his sight.

DEMOSTHENES.   Splendid!
Give it to me to read—and pour me
A refill. Yes . . . I think I know
What's here. Oh, prophecies! *Come on*!
Give me that drink!

NIKIAS.   All right, all right.
What does it say?

DEMOSTHENES.   Another drink.

NIKIAS. 'Another drink'. Are these words really
In the oracle?

DEMOSTHENES. O Bakis!

NIKIAS.   What?

DEMOSTHENES. Quick, another cupful!

NIKIAS.   Bakis
   Seems very partial to the cup. . . .

DEMOSTHENES. Repulsive Paphlagon! I'm not surprised
   He's hung on to this so carefully.
   No wonder he's afraid—this is all
   About himself.

NIKIAS.   But what does it *say*?

DEMOSTHENES. How he'll be done for. It's all here.

NIKIAS. How?

DEMOSTHENES. It's as clear as day.
   First comes an oakum-seller
   To manage affairs of state.

NIKIAS. Right. One seller, and after him?

DEMOSTHENES. A sheep-seller.

NIKIAS.   Two sellers.
   And what's *his* fate?

DEMOSTHENES.   He'll be
   In power till a more disgusting
   Blackguard appears than he is,
   And that puts paid to him.
   The new one's a leather-seller,
   That's Cle— Paphlagon, a crook,
   A leather-lunged line-shooter
   With a voice like a river in spate.

NIKIAS. Then—it's there in the oracle?
   The sheep-seller's thrown out
   By the leather-seller?

DEMOSTHENES.   It's there.

NIKIAS. Oh heavens. Is there no other
   Seller of anything left?

DEMOSTHENES. Yes. It's a curious calling.

NIKIAS. What does he do? Please tell me.

DEMOSTHENES. Shall I? . . .

NIKIAS.   Go on. . . .

DEMOSTHENES.   *Sausages!*
   He outs the leather-seller.

NIKIAS. A sausage-seller! Poseidon!
   What a trade. Where'll we find one?

DEMOSTHENES. We must look for one.

NIKIAS.   Hey!
   There's one coming—maybe
   He's bound for the market-place.

DEMOSTHENES. Oh! Blessed sausage-seller,
   Come here, dear fellow. '*Enter*
   The Saviour of the State'
   —And incidentally us.

                  Enter Sausage-seller.

SAUSAGE-SELLER. Here, what's up? What're you bawling
   At *me* for?

DEMOSTHENES. Come here. I *must* tell you
   Your amazing fabulous luck!

NIKIAS. Have him put down his meat-board
   And give him the facts—tell him
   What the oracle says will happen.

DEMOSTHENES. O blessed, O rich as Croesus!
   Today—a nobody,
   Tomorrow—omnipotent!
   O happy Athens, happy
   In such a ruler.

SAUSAGE-SELLER. Come off it!
   Let me get on with trimming
   My tripes and selling my sausages, stop
   Taking the mickey out of me!

DEMOSTHENES. You fool, I'm not. Talk about tripe,
   D'you see those rows and rows and rows
   Of citizens in the Assembly?

SAUSAGE-SELLER. I got eyes, haven't I?

DEMOSTHENES.   You
   Shall be the supreme ruler
   Of the whole blasted lot—
   In market and harbour and Pnyx.
   You shall trample the Council under foot,

You shall cut the generals down to size,
Chain 'em up, clap 'em in gaol,
And use the Assembly Hall
—To have your women in.

SAUSAGE-SELLER. The Assembly Hall—for that?

DEMOSTHENES. Why certainly, if you like.
But that's not all. Get up
On your board and have a look
Round the horizon. See
All the islands?

SAUSAGE-SELLER. Clear as day.

DEMOSTHENES. And the markets and merchant ships?

SAUSAGE-SELLER. I see them.

DEMOSTHENES.   Aren't you the lucky one!
Swivel your eyes right round
From Caria in the north
To Carthage in the south—

SAUSAGE-SELLER. Aren't I in luck—to crick my neck!

DEMOSTHENES. All this is yours to deal in,
For you shall become what the oracle foretells—
The Greatest of Men, the Governor of the People!

SAUSAGE-SELLER. What *me* a sausage-seller? Me like that?

DEMOSTHENES. But that's exactly *why*.
You've got every quality:
Market morality, a natural bent
For lying and sharp practice—

SAUSAGE-SELLER. I'm not worthy of having power. . . .

DEMOSTHENES. Great heavens! 'Not worthy'—you?
Don't say you've a pang of conscience?
You weren't born a gentleman, surely?

SAUSAGE-SELLER. Anything but. Me, I'm scum from the slums.

DEMOSTHENES. That's more like it. What
A wonderul start for public life you've got!

SAUSAGE-SELLER. But, mate, I don't know nothing
But the old alpha-beta,
And I'm not so hot on that.

DEMOSTHENES. —Pity you know that much;
  It might be held against you.
  It's no use thinking decent
  Or educated men
  Can be leaders of the people—
  That's left to the illiterate
  And dishonest nowadays.
  But you mustn't lose the chance
  The oracle gives you!

SAUSAGE-SELLER. How does it go?

DEMOSTHENES.   The gods
  Have wrapped it enigmatically
  In a cunning riddle. Listen:

      When the leather eagle, the hook-beak,
      Shall seize in its jaws the snake,
      That dim-witted drinker of blood—
      Then shall the bitter brine
      Of the house of Paphlagon
      Evaporate to naught! And god
      Shall grant to the gut-retailers
      Great glories beyond the telling,
      Unless in their choice they falter
      And continue sausage-selling.

                            [A long pause.

SAUSAGE-SELLER. Sorry, I don't get it.
  What's it to do with me?
  Give me a line on it.

DEMOSTHENES. The leather eagle is Paphlagon.

SAUSAGE-SELLER. And the hook-beak—what's that?

DEMOSTHENES. Speaks for itself. He hooks
  His crooked fingers on to
  Whatever he wants to grab.

SAUSAGE-SELLER. O.K. What about the snake?

DEMOSTHENES. Obvious, isn't it?
  A snake's long and squirmy,
  A sausage's long and squirmy;
  A snake drinks blood, a sausage
  Drinks blood—got the hang of it?

So it says the snake shall do for
The leather eagle, unless
It's somehow talked out of it.

SAUSAGE-SELLER. Does me proud, that oracle does.
But how could I ever govern
The people—*me*, what *I* am?

DEMOSTHENES. No trouble at all!
Do just what you're doing now.
Mince everything up together
And keep the people sweet
And on your side with neat
Little savoury phrases to whet
Their appetites. You've got
The lot for a demagogue:
A voice like a saw, low birth, and market morals
—All you need for politics today.
So put your garland on, and drink to—
Crass stupidity!
Now, brace yourself for the fight
With Paphlagon.

SAUSAGE-SELLER.   Who's to help me?
The rich are . . . in his pocket;
And the poor simply cringe.

DEMOSTHENES. A thousand good men and true
Who hate his guts—the Knights
Are with you, and every honest
Citizen in the audience.
I am, myself; and god
Will support you, don't be afraid.

                              [*He turns to the audience.*

He's not represented as he is.
None of the mask-makers
Dared, for fear, to portray him.
But everyone here in this quick-
Witted audience will recognize
Cle— er—recognize the man.

NIKIAS.   My heaven!
Here's Paphlagon coming now.

Enter Paphlagon.

PAPHLAGON. By the twelve gods you'll pay for this—
  You're always plotting against the people.
  What's *this* doing here? A *Chalkidian*
  Wine-cup? Obvious. You're inciting
  The Chalkidians to revolt. I'll have you
  Liquidated, blotted out,
  You treacherous bastards.

DEMOSTHENES [*to* Sausage-seller]. Here, where are *you* off to?
  Don't walk out on us now—
  Don't let us down, brave noble sausage-seller!

Enter the Chorus *of Knights.*

  [*To the* Chorus.] Come to the rescue, Knights; now's the critical
    moment.
  Simon, Panaitios, set the right wing in motion.
  They're coming! Brace yourself, turn, and back to the onset!
  [*To the audience.*] Look at the whirling dust cloud as they gallop
    in close order—
  That's it! Repel and attack him—hurl him headlong.

                          [*The* Chorus *assault* Paphlagon.

CHORUS. Hit him! Hit him! The persecuting pest incessantly need-
    ling
  Us Knights—the tax-extorter, the bottomless pit, the Charybdis
  Of rapacity! Crook! crook! crook—if I shouted it daily
  As often as he's engaged in crooked business I'd never
  Say anything else. So hit him, hurt him, hate him, as we do!
  Bustle the brute, hustle him—see that he doesn't evade you;
  He's slippery as an eel and he knows how Eucrates managed
  His vanishing trick and fled and hid himself in his bran store.

PAPHLAGON. Heliasts, old men, members of the three-obol society,
  Don't I yell out my guts for *your* sake, don't I provide for you
  By fair means or foul? Show your gratitude—come to my rescue!
  I'm being beaten up by a gang of rebellious traitors!

CHORUS. Serve you right: since you help yourself to the public
    money,
  And squeeze informers like figs, and prod our administrators
  To test which is ripe or not—which is ready for extortion.
  And if you find a simple and easygoing booby

You screw him back from the Chersonese and, locking him
In a brutal hold, twisting his shoulder, you throw him
And fall full-weight on his beaten body and flatten him.

PAPHLAGON. *You* rounding on *me*? When it's all for your sake, masters,
I'm being pilloried now—just when I had it in mind
To propose the setting up of a monument to your manly
Prowess.

CHORUS.   What a two-faced twister! See what he'll stoop to,
To wheedle himself into our good graces—as if we
Were utterly gaga. If he comes *this* way, he'll take it
Straight; if he dodges *that* way, he'll stun himself on our shin-
bones.

[*A mêlée.*

PAPHLAGON. O City! O my people! What kind of bestial monsters
Are kicking me in the guts?

CHORUS.   The usual ranting and roaring!
The usual routine for upsetting the city's business.

SAUSAGE-SELLER. I'll be the first to upset him, by shouting him
down.

CHORUS. If you can beat him at bawling, you're worth our raising a
paean;
Or cap his sheer effrontery—you win us the first prize.

PAPHLAGON. I lay a formal complaint against this man. I accuse him
Of smuggling gear to the Spartans their triremes are hungry for.

SAUSAGE-SELLER. And I denounce him for crashing into the dining-
hall
With an empty stomach, and staggering out stuffed to the eyebrows.

CHORUS. And he pouches bread and meat and salt fish; which is
strictly forbidden—
A right that was never allowed even to Pericles.

PAPHLAGON. You're for instant execution,
Both of you!

SAUSAGE-SELLER. I can shout
Three times as loud.

PAPHLAGON.   I can
Outshout your shouts.

SAUSAGE-SELLER.   I can
    Outbellow your loudest bellow.

PAPHLAGON. Be general—I'll backbite you.

SAUSAGE-SELLER. My dog-whip'll bite your back.

PAPHLAGON. My lies'll make rings round you.

SAUSAGE-SELLER. I'll chop your fingers off.

PAPHLAGON. Look me straight in the eye.

SAUSAGE-SELLER. Where d'you think I come from?
    The market same as you.

PAPHLAGON. One growl out of you,
    And I'll slice you to bits.

SAUSAGE-SELLER. One snarl out of you,
    And I'll cart you off like shit.

PAPHLAGON. I admit I steal. You don't.

SAUSAGE-SELLER. Hermes, god of the market,
    Hear that? *Me* steal? I'll say!
    And if I'm copped, I swear
    Black's white I never done it.

PAPHLAGON. You're using my technique
    And pretending it's yours—you cheat!
    I'll accuse you before the Prytanies,
    As the owner of sacred pig's guts
    You haven't declared for tax.

CHORUS. Revolting, repellent brass-mouth!
    The whole land, the Assembly,
    The Treasury, the Tribunals,
    The law courts brim with your brashness,
    Muck-raking, trouble-making
    The length and breadth of the city—
    Whose raucous harangues have deafened
    Our Athens, as from a rock-ledge,
    Like a fisherman sighting tunny,
    You halloo the shoals of—Tribute!

PAPHLAGON. *I* know where this plot was stitched together.

SAUSAGE-SELLER. If you don't know a stitch, *I* don't
    Know how to stuff a sausage—*you*!
    Cutting the hide of a rotten ox

On the slant so it looks like quality,
And foisting it on to rustics who
Hadn't worn it a day before
It stretched to over twice.

DEMOSTHENES.   By heaven!
He pulled that one on me. And my friends
And fellow councillors didn't let
Me forget it. Before I got half-way
To Pergasé my feet were skating
About inside my shoes.

CHORUS. Right from the start you've displayed
That wanton disregard
For truth which was exclusively
The orators' stock in trade.
And principally you've used
These means to foster trust,
Then fleeced the wealthy foreigners you duped,
While Archeptolemos watched and wept.
                    But now there climbs to office
                    A criminal I delight in;
                    Beside him you're a novice.
He'll block you, outwit you, outmock you, defeat you—
He knows every trick of the game plus ten.
The scale of his duplicity is so gigantic
You don't stand a chance.
[*To* Sausage-seller.] Now, my dear fellow, you come from the class
That bears our *greatest* men:
                    Show us how little use
                    A liberal education is.

SAUSAGE-SELLER. First I'll tell you what sort
Of citizen he is.

PAPHLAGON. Kindly let me speak first.

SAUSAGE-SELLER. By god, I won't. I'm a crook too.

CHORUS. If he doesn't give in to that,
Say, 'like all my ancestors'.

PAPHLAGON. Kindly let me speak first.

SAUSAGE-SELLER. By god, I won't!

PAPHLAGON.   By god,
   You shall!

SAUSAGE-SELLER. I'll argue that:
   Who's to speak first. *You* won't—

PAPHLAGON.—I'll burst!—

SAUSAGE-SELLER [*carrying on*]. —You won't, I tell you.

CHORUS. Please heaven, let him burst!

PAPHLAGON. What makes you think you can
   Compete with me? What've *you* got?

SAUSAGE-SELLER. I know how to speak all right.
   I can lay it on rich and thick.

PAPHLAGON [*sneering*]. So you know how to speak? So you think it
      comes easily
   As serving up raw gristle masked by a tasty garnish?
   I know your sort. I know them by the thousand.
   You conduct one case in a provincial court
   Against some alien half-wit—mugging it up
   All night, and mumbling it to yourself as you meander
   Through the streets; and with sips of water you show it off
   To your friends till they're dying of boredom—and you think
   You've got the gift of the gab—you poor fool!

SAUSAGE-SELLER. Hgh! And what sort of dope do *you* swallow
   To get the people to swallow you, just you,
   As they mope in tongue-tied silence like deaf-mutes?

PAPHLAGON. I'd like to know who you'd compare me with!
   Me, I can polish off a plateful of hot tunny
   And a skinful of neat wine and smear the generals
   At Pylos with stinking libel—all at a sitting.

SAUSAGE-SELLER. Me, when I've scoffed an ox paunch and some
      pig's guts,
   And swilled them down with the greasy juice from the pot,
   I won't wait to wash—I'll throttle all the orators
   And freshen up Nikias.

CHORUS.   We've approved of all
   You've said so far, but one thing we don't like.
   You speak as if you sat down by yourself
   To this delicious meal. . . .

PAPHLAGON. He can hardly eat their bass
And then do down the Milesians.

SAUSAGE-SELLER. Not like you did, I wouldn't.
When *I've* downed my breast of beef
I'll buy silver mines for the State.

PAPHLAGON. I'll burst into the Council
And kick 'em out by force.

SAUSAGE-SELLER. I'll stuff your guts up your arse.

PAPHLAGON. I'll hoick you up by the rump
And throw you inside out.

CHORUS. Poseidon! If you do, you do me as well.

PAPHLAGON. I'll lock you in the stocks.

SAUSAGE-SELLER. I'll charge you with cowardice.

PAPHLAGON. I'll tan your skin.

SAUSAGE-SELLER.   I'll make
A thief's purse out of yours.

PAPHLAGON. I'll peg your legs on the tan-house floor.

SAUSAGE-SELLER. I'll mash you to meatballs.

PAPHLAGON. I'll tweeze out your lashes.

SAUSAGE-SELLER. I'll slit your gizzard.

DEMOSTHENES. By god, prise his jaws wide open
And hold 'em with a clamp,
As cooks do with a pig
Then tug his tongue right out
And look into his guts
Down to his fundament and see
If he's got any spots
Like the diseased pig that he is.

CHORUS. There are things hotter than fire is,
There are speeches even fouler
Than the besmutted speeches
Of our gross and libellous rulers.
It's no easy job you've got there.
Snatch him, wrench him, screw him;
You've no time for half-measures
If you intend to throw him.
You've got him gripped round the middle—

Sock him, soften up the creature,
And you'll find he's a coward.
I understand his nature.

SAUSAGE-SELLER. He's been yellow from birth. Why, he has what
reputation
He's got by reaping a harvest he hadn't sown, and the ears
Of corn he brought back from Pylos he's got tied up in prison
To dry like they was in sacks—and sell them back to the Spartans!

PAPHLAGON. I'm not afraid of you while the Council survives and
the moonface
Of Demos gawps from his seat.

CHORUS.   You see how he's quite impervious?
He doesn't change colour even. By god, if I don't detest him
I'll be Cratinos' sheepskin sodden with piss; or, worse,
I'll have Morsimos coach me as Chorus for his play.

Your key to corruption, you
With your nose for ever deep
In the stinking blossoms of bribery
Snuffing the gold and sucking
It up with your slobber-lip—

May you throw up your pickings as quick as they went down!

Then I'll sing nothing but
'Drink, drink, to this happy event!'
And I know the son of Iulios
Who keeps a loving eye
On the bread and the young crusts

Will shout out 'Bacché-Bacchus!', and raise a paean of joy.

PAPHLAGON. Do you think you can go one better than me? No, by
Poseidon!
Or I'll give up my share of the feasts of Zeus-of-the-Market.

SAUSAGE-SELLER. By the tough school of knuckles I was forced to
from a child,
And the bashes of butchers' knives, I know how to do you down
Or I was fattened for nothing—on a diet of bread-pellets
The rich clean their fingers on.

PAPHLAGON.   Bread-pellets like a mongrel?
Do you suppose, you gutter-licker, you can fight me on the diet
Of a scavenging cur? Me—a great dog-headed monkey?

SAUSAGE-SELLER. By god, when I was a boy I had more tricks than
a monkey:
I diddled the cooks like this: 'Look up!' I'd shout. 'D'you see it?
Look up, my lads, it's spring! A swallow, there's a swallow!'
And up they gaped, and I swiped a steak from under their noses!

CHORUS. That was a brilliant stroke! You had an eye to the future
And got your meat in season—just as the lifters
Of winter artichokes wait till it's almost springtime.

SAUSAGE-SELLER. Nobody ever pinched me. But if I was ever
suspected
I hid the meat in my crutch, and by every god in heaven
I swore I'd never done it. And one of them orators
Was struck with the performance and he said, 'One day this
nipper
Will make his mark—he'll even govern the people, see if he don't!'

CHORUS. How right he was to perceive the essential qualifications
Of a ruler: stealing, perjuring, and hiding the swag where no one
Would think of looking. . . .

PAPHLAGON. I'll gag your insolent mouths! I'll hurtle down on you
Like a whirling hurricane flaying land and ocean piecemeal!

SAUSAGE-SELLER. I'll reef my sausages and ride you out—and go
sailing
On a nice calm flood of fortune—and you can laugh yourself sick
On the other side of your face!

DEMOSTHENES.   —And if there's a leak
We'll look after the bailing.

PAPHLAGON.   By the holy goddess Demeter!
You shan't get away with the pile of talents you've filched from
Athens.

CHORUS. Look out! Let go the sheet. He's bellowing like a nor'-
easter—
Or a roaring sycophanter.

PAPHLAGON.   I know you got ten talents
Out of Potideia.

SAUSAGE-SELLER. *You should* know.—How about taking one
And keeping your mouth shut?

CHORUS.   Why—it's second nature!
You can hoist full sail now.

SAUSAGE-SELLER.   —The wind's certainly slackened!

PAPHLAGON. I'll bring four actions against you,
   A hundred talents a suit,
   For bribery and deceit.

SAUSAGE-SELLER. I'll bring twenty for cowardice
   And a thousand-odd for theft.

PAPHLAGON. You trace your pedigree,
   I swear, from those atheistic
   Aristocratic snobs of
   Alcmaionidai.

SAUSAGE-SELLER. Your father was bodyguard to—

PAPHLAGON. Well, go on, say it—

SAUSAGE-SELLER. To Hippias' jock-strap.

PAPHLAGON. You dirty louse!

SAUSAGE-SELLER. You bloody flea!

CHORUS. Lay off and sock him!

PAPHLAGON. Ow! These plotters! Help! Help!
   I'm being bashed to pulp.

CHORUS. Give him another! Here, slash him
   With this stinking string of guts
   —Just the thing to use on *him*!

O noblest of mortals, fairest spirit in the world,
Shining saviour of our city, of our nation,
With what a masterly wit you trounced him in debate!
Would we could find the words to match our admiration.

PAPHLAGON. By Demeter! Do you suppose I wasn't
   Aware of these plots being assembled,
   This chariot of revolt being pinned
   And glued together?

CHORUS.   Can't you counter
   With some wheelwright's technical jargon?

SAUSAGE-SELLER. Do you suppose *I* wasn't aware
   What he's been up to in Argos?
   Making friends with them for *our* sake
   (So he says) and holding secret
   Conferences with the Spartans

On his own account. I know their drift:
He's welding them together on
The matter of the prisoners.

CHORUS. A good touch! Welding for gluing.

SAUSAGE-SELLER.—And there are Spartans hammering at
That particular proposition too.
But no bribe of gold or silver, nor
Sending persuasive friends to shut
My mouth will stop me speaking out
To the Athenians, spilling the beans
About your double-dealing.

PAPHLAGON.   Right!
I'm going straight to the Council, now,
To inform them of *your* plots, your nightly
Huddles in the city, your overtures
To the Medes and the Great King—and your feelers
To the Boeotians. . . .

SAUSAGE-SELLER.   I like that!
What's the price of cheese in Boeotia
To *you*?

PAPHLAGON. I'll lay you out stone-cold,
By Heracles!   [*Exit.*

CHORUS. What's in your mind now? What are you going to do?
It's the moment to show if you're really the clever sharper
That got away with the meat as you said. You haven't
A moment to lose. Get to the Council at once,
For he'll thrust his way in and bellow and bluster
In a thunderous volley of lies against us all.

SAUSAGE-SELLER. I'm going, but I must stow my tripes
And my knives first.

DEMOSTHENES.   Here, take this grease.
Rub your neck with it so you can ease
Your arguments under his guard of lies.

SAUSAGE-SELLER. Spoke like a trainer! Good!

DEMOSTHENES.   And this—
Swallow it.

SAUSAGE-SELLER. What is it?

DEMOSTHENES.   Garlic,
  To fire the fight in you. Off, quick.

SAUSAGE-SELLER. I'm off!

DEMOSTHENES.   Above all, take our advice.
  Get straight in with your teeth, savage
  His crest, tear at it, sever it,
  Worry his wattles off—and don't come back
  Till he's a total wreck.

CHORUS. Go and good luck to you, go in good spirits, accomplish
  All that is in our hearts.
  May Zeus-of-the-Market keep you
  Till you return to us, in triumph, crowned with flowers.

                                        [*Exit* Sausage-seller.
  Now, for a while, we ask you, members of the audience,
  To concentrate on us and listen to our anapaests—
  You, who yourselves have tried to master all styles and metres.
  If a poet, one of the old brigade of comedy-writers,
  Had approached us with a request to perform a chorus in public,
  He wouldn't have found us easy to get.
                                  It's a different matter
  With our poet today. We need no persuasion to act for a poet
  Who shares our hatreds, who dares to speak truth, without
      reservation,
  Who courageously tilts alone at the typhoon and the whirlwind.
  He tells us that many among you are puzzled and put him the
      question
  Why he has never before asked for his own chorus.
  Now *we* are empowered to answer. After working so hard it was
      never
  From listlessness that he lingered—nor stupidity; but solely
  Because he considered the mastery of the comedy chorus the
      hardest
  Task in the world. Many have tried but few have succeeded.
  Till now he's observed how your favours are short-lived as annual
      flowers
  And how you neglect and reject, in their old age, poets who pleased
      you.
  So he saw Magnes suffer in grey-haired decline—once winner

Of countless chorus contests. So wide was the range of his genius,
He mimicked the music of harp-string, bird-wing, Lydian patois,
Fig-fly, green-dyed frog—yet it wasn't enough; in his dotage,
The prime of his life long past, he was hissed from the stage the
    instant
His powers of mockery flagged.

                          Then our poet thought of Cratinos
Who flooded the level plains in a torrent of adulation
Sweeping all snags before him, rooting up oak and enemy,
Critic and plane-tree. Never was banquet held but they chorus'd
His 'Doro Sandalled with figs' or 'You makers of intricate verses',
He was such a popular poet. But now when you see him
Drivelling round the streets, those inlaid amber embellishments
Fallen out of the lyre of his genius, the strings broken,
The framework warped and cracking, you haven't a shred of
    pity!
Now he is old he reels and totters mopping and mowing,
Drunken as Connas, mad with thirst—for whom a fitter
Reward would have been to drink his fill in the Prytaneium
For the sake of his former fame, not to lurch about in a stupor,
But to sit well-groomed and rich in the finest seat in the theatre
By the statue of Dionysus.

                        Consider the brutal treatment
Crates had to endure from you with your gibes and hisses:
Admitted, he offered up the sparest and driest of tidbits
From his meagre larder of wit, and in or out of your favour
Merely survived—as if that were in itself an achievement!

So our poet lingered long in fear, and in meditation:
You must master the art of rowing before you can handle the
    tiller;
Then take the for'ard look-out and learn to gauge the wind,
And only then can you be your own and competent pilot.
If you approve of his wisdom in waiting till he was ready,
Now is the moment to give him a real Lenaian reception,
Recognition, acclamation—the full heart of your praise!

              And let him depart in a haze
              Of delight at your delight,
              Rejoicing in his prize,

His soul afire with pride,
And his whole being ablaze
To the top of his bald head.

Poseidon, lord of horsemen,
You who take delight in
The clash of armoured cavalry,
The whinneying and neighing:
You who take delight in
The dash of dark-prowed triremes
Manned by fearless mercenaries,
And the brilliance of young charioteers,
Flashing, crashing; O come,
Gold-tridented dolphin-master
On Sunium crowned and Geraistos,
Dearest of gods to Phormion,
Son of Cronos, O come,
Be with our Chorus!

Let us praise our gallant fathers, heroes worthy of our country,
Names to weave upon the Peplos, victors everywhere in war,
Land and sea alike, who ruled us and adorned our ancient city.
None among them ever stopped to count the number of the foe,
But on sight his ardent spirit drove him headlong into combat.
Should one sink down to his shoulder, hastily he'd wipe the stain,
Swear he'd never fallen and at once rejoin the mêlée.
Never general begged a public feast from Cleon's father *then*;
Now, if they're not fêted, seated in the place of honour,
They refuse to fight! But *we* fight, giving loyal service free
To the gods and holy Athens, as our fathers did before us,
Never asking pay—conceiving this our privilege by birth.
But when the war is over and a treaty ends our labours
Do not grudge us our long ringlets and the pleasures of the bath.

O Pallas our protectress,
Ruler over the holiest
People of all, the mighty
In war and in her poets,
The nonpareil of countries,
O come, be with us,
And bring with you our ally

In our battles, our abetter
Against every rival chorus,
Victory. Now if ever
Appear to us, great goddess,
Infuse our every sinew
With the utmost of endeavour,
Come to us, now!

Let us praise our gallant horses, heroes worthy of our country,
Bearing witness of their exploits, all the glorious fights and frays
We've survived on land together, which *we* almost take for
    granted
Since *they* took to sea—embarking in the transports undismayed,
With their drinking cups and garlic, and sat down upon the
    benches,
Taking oars like any mortal and whinnying for joy,
'Pull stronger there my hearties! Heigh, Sanbrand there! You're
    shirking!'
Till they disembarked at Corinth and the juniors with their hoofs
Started scraping holes to sleep in and went foraging for bedding.
They ate crabs instead of fodder, which they trapped along the
    shore
And even snatched them scutttling from their crannies on the
    bottom
Till, Theoros says, a crab of Corinth raised a bitter plea:
O Lord Poseidon, pity us, our fate is over-cruel
If we've nowhere to escape these Knights, neither by land nor sea!

Enter Sausage-seller.

CHORUS. Why, dearest and toughest of men,
Your absence has been agony:
Here you are safely back again!
Tell us, how did it go? Did you . . .

SAUSAGE-SELLER. What d'you think? 'Course I did!
Beat the lot of 'em all ends up.

CHORUS. Magnificent! Superb! We'll crack
Heaven open with our paean.
Friend, if your words sound good,
Your deeds sound better still.
Tell us the whole tale,

So we can follow step by step
The same heroic track.
Don't be afraid to tell us all—
You know we'll hang on every word.

SAUSAGE-SELLER. —And a damn good earful at that!
Well . . . I came in hard on his heels,
And there he was spewing out
A bellyfull of thundery muck,
A rancorous, raucous hullabaloo
Of rambling, rumbling, windy crap.
(Never heard anything like it!)
On the rampage he was, laying
For the Knights with every dirty
Twist of his black tongue, calling
Them all conspiring bastards;
And you could see his lies seeding
And sprouting in every Councillor's ear—
They put on their mustardy look
And frowned like murder.
                              When I saw
They were had for suckers and he'd got them
Eating out of his greasy hand,
'Gods,' I said to myself, 'you gods
Of lechery, treachery, butchery,
Bribery, robbery, clobbery,
Slobbery, and hobnobbery—
You market, as punched me up
—Give me an endless supply of
Bare-faced abuse, back answers, and sauce!'

As I mulled this over a bugger
Farted on my right and 'Bless you,'
I said, and sticking my arse hard
Against the bar I burst it in,
Opened my trap and yelled, 'GOOD NEWS,
COUNCILLORS!—and you're the very first
I'm bringing it to—GOOD NEWS!
Never, *never* since war broke out,
Have I seen anchovies as cheap as

They are today!' That put the sunshine
Back on their mugs, and they crowned me
For my *wonderful* news'. So I hissed,
'Keep it dark, see? An' if you want
Them fish at an obol a pound—you impound
All the tradesmen's wine-cups.' They applauded,
Goggling at me like I was a freak.
But Paphlagon—he was onto the game;
He knew at once what line to take
And proposed this resolution: 'Gentlemen',
(He says) 'it seems to me, on account of
This great news we've been brought,' (he pauses)
'It'd be proper to sacrifice
A hundred oxen to the goddess!'
—So they switches back to him again
And I—I saw I was being smothered in dung
So I raised the bid and yelled 'Two hundred',
And added a promise to sacrifice
A thousand nanny-goats to Artemis
The Huntress, the next morning, IF
Anchovies sold at an obol a stone.
So they switched back to me again,
And Paphlagon was rocked on his heels
And went vaguely muncering on until
The Prytanies and the Specials took him
In tow. And the Councillors stood up
Cheering for the anchovies,
And he kept bawling, 'Wait a bit,
Wait till you hear the Spartan herald—
He's come to discuss peace!' 'What? Peace?
With fish at the price it is?' (they said).
' 'Course *they* want peace, but what do *we* want
With a treaty now? Let the war go on!'
—Then they voted to pack it in, and started
Jumping the barriers. . . .

But I

Sneaked out, went to the market quick
And bought up the whole stock of leeks
And coriander: then handed it out

Free, gratis, as seasoning for the fish.
They couldn't make head or tail of *that*
But they took it all right, crowding round
And lushing me up proper till I left.
—So I got the Council under my thumb
For an obol's worth of coriander!

CHORUS. All a coming man should do
As he rises to fame, you've done.
You're incomparably superior
In every single one
Of his grubby ways. It looks
Like total eclipse for him.
But he's not done yet, you must plan
How best to wage the rest
Of your campaign—and you know
We're behind you to a man,
As we have always been!

SAUSAGE-SELLER. Look, here's Paphlagon now,
Rearing along like a wave
In a rough sea, all a splutter
And flurry of foam and fury.
He wants to swallow me up;
To hell with his b-lether!

Enter Paphlagon.

PAPHLAGON. If I've got a single one
Of my old tricks left in the bag,
And I don't do for you,
I'll simply disintegrate.

SAUSAGE-SELLER [*simpering*]. I just adore your threats,
You great big empty windbag!
You make me positively
Giggle and dance and waggle my bottom
And go Cuckoo! cuckoo! at you.

PAPHLAGON. By Demeter! if I don't eat you
Clean up—I can't live.

SAUSAGE-SELLER. If you don't eat me . . . I
Won't live if I don't drink you,
Swill you down whole and burst.

PAPHLAGON. By god, by the seat of honour
I won because of Pylos,
I'll do you—

SAUSAGE-SELLER. The seat of honour?
I'll show you a back seat, soon!

PAPHLAGON. It's the stocks for you, by god.

SAUSAGE-SELLER [*mocking*]. My—he's ever so fierce!
What does'ms like to eat?
Whats'ms favourite? Purses?

PAPHLAGON. I'll scratch your filthy guts out
With my own nails.

SAUSAGE-SELLER.   I'll scratch you
Off the public-dinner list.

PAPHLAGON. I'll drag you to Demos—he'll give me justice.

SAUSAGE-SELLER. I'll drag you first—and give you smear for smear.

PAPHLAGON. You fool. He won't take any notice of you.
But I can twist him round my little finger.

SAUSAGE-SELLER. You seem darn certain Demos
Is yours—

PAPHLAGON. I *know* he is.
I know what he specially fancies.

SAUSAGE-SELLER.—And feed him like a nurse does.
Chew up a great chunk
In your own mouth, and pop
A tiny morsel in his,
And *you* swallow three times as much.

PAPHLAGON. By god, I can make him expand
Or contract by my own skill—

SAUSAGE-SELLER. I can do that with my arsehole.

PAPHLAGON. My friend, you'll find insulting me
In the Council's a different matter
From coming before Demos.

SAUSAGE-SELLER. Well, I'm not stopping you—
Get on with it, why are we waiting?

[*They go to* Demos' *door.*

PAPHLAGON. Come out—dear Demos!

SAUSAGE-SELLER. Come out—dear Father!

PAPHLAGON. Demos, dearest Demos,
  Hear how I'm being brutally
  Browbeaten and ill-treated.

                    Demos *opens the central door.*

DEMOS. What's all this blasted row?
  Go away from my door, will you?
  You've smashed my harvest wreath!
  Oh, it's *you*, Paphlagon. What's the matter?

PAPHLAGON. I'm being knocked about
  By this lout and by the Knights,
  All because of you—

DEMOS.   Why?

PAPHLAGON. Because of my unswerving
  Love and devotion to you.

DEMOS [*to* Sausage-seller]. And who are *you*?

SAUSAGE-SELLER. His rival. And I've loved you
  For years and craved to serve you,
  I and a thousand other
  Good honest men, but *he*
  Won't let us. And you, sir
  (Forgive my saying so),
  Are like them fancy-boys
  And their lovers—*you* won't accept
  Good honest men, but take up with
  Lantern-sellers and stitchers
  And shoemakers and tanners.

PAPHLAGON. I do my best for Demos.

SAUSAGE-SELLER. Such as what?

PAPHLAGON.   I stole a march
  On the general, Demosthenes—
  Sailed to Pylos, took the Spartans,
  And brought them back prisoner.

SAUSAGE-SELLER. All right, I did the same—
  Slinked round and stole from the workshop
  Someone else's boiling soup-pot—

PAPHLAGON. Now, Demos, call an Assembly
  And find out which of us loves you

The better, and so decide
Which of us two you'll favour.

SAUSAGE-SELLER. By all means make your choice,
But *not* in the Pnyx.

DEMOS.   No. No.
I'll sit in the Pnyx or nowhere.

SAUSAGE-SELLER [*aside*]. Then I've had it. Blast my luck!
The old man's up to the mark
And quite quick-witted at home.
But once he's on that hard
Stone seat he gapes like a half-wit
Bobbing for figs.

CHORUS. Now you must loose all sail—must exert your utmost will
power
And inveigle him into arguments that cannot be answered,
For he's adept at getting himself out of the tightest corners.
You must thrash down upon him like a whirlwind—but be care-
ful:
Don't give him a chance to attack, but have your weights at the
ready
To crash down on his deck before you grapple and board him.

PAPHLAGON. I pray you, Mistress Athene presiding over the city,
If I be found the fittest to serve the people of Athens
(Apart from Lysicles and those whores Salabaccho and Kynna)
Let me dine at the public expense (for doing nothing, as ever),
But if I be found to hate you, and not press to the fore to protect
you,
Destroy me, saw me in half, and cut up my skin for harness.

SAUSAGE-SELLER. Demos, if I don't love you, *love* you, I'm perfectly
willing
To be sliced up into mincemeat, and if *that* doesn't convince you,
Let me, here on the spot, be grated and mashed with cheese
Or dragged by the balls with my own flesh-hook to Kerameikos.

PAPHLAGON. How could there ever exist a citizen who adored you
More than *I* do? From the moment I became your adviser
I filled your treasury. . . . It may be I had to resort to
Begging, the rack, or other means of applying pressure—
To please *you* I was indifferent to people's personal hardships.

SAUSAGE-SELLER. That's nothing to boast about; I can do that
     myself:
Steal someone else's bread and give it to you, Demos.
He doesn't really care a rap for you, let me tell you,
Except to see that he gets his nice little cosy corner
By the fire. But as for you, who fought to the death at Marathon
To save all Greece from the Medes, and left us a glorious legacy
Of inexhaustible song—he pays you no attention
As you sit on your hard stone seat; not, as *I* do, bringing
This cushion I've made you special. . . . Heave yourself up a
     moment.
Fine! You'll be comfortable now and no longer blister a bottom
That sat on the benches at Salamis.

DEMOS.   Are you a descendant
Of Harmodios? Who *are* you? This is a truly noble
And Demos-loving act.

PAPHLAGON.   With that mean little bit of flattery
You get in his good books.

SAUSAGE-SELLER.   Not so mean as the baits *you*
Hooked him with!

PAPHLAGON.   I swear there has never, in our history,
Been a man so devoted to the welfare of his people.
I'll stake my head on that!

SAUSAGE-SELLER.   And *how* you show your devotion!
You saw the poor refugees living cooped in barrels and crannies
And dovecotes, eight long years, and *you did nothing* except to
Keep them confined and bleed them white. You expelled Archep-
     tolemos
When he tried to make peace; and the embassies
As came to propose truces—you ran them out of the city,
And kicked them in the teeth.

PAPHLAGON.   But of course! I did it for Demos,
So he can rule all Greece! Doesn't it say in the oracle?
'In Arcadia he shall judge, receiving five obols a day,
If he remain steadfast.' Meanwhile it's I who feed him and
Wait on him hand and foot; and I'll get his *three* obols for certain,
However I have to do it.

SAUSAGE-SELLER.   What, Demos *rule* over Arcady?
Not likely! But so as *you* can comb your way through its cities,
Thieving, extorting, and bribing. And 'cause of the war and smoke he
Can't see what dirty work you're up to, but sits there moony,
Half starving and worried silly, dependent on you for his payroll.
You just wait till it's peace and he goes back to his farming,
Peps himself up with porridge and platefuls of pressed olives;
He'll soon discover the good living you swindled him out of
While he paid you in the forces. Then he'll be after you
Like a hunter hot on the scent of an angry vote against you.
You know this clear as day, so you try and double-cross him
And stuff him up with dreams about your wonderful virtues.

PAPHLAGON. To hear you slinging mud like this is really distressing,
After all the things I've done for Demos and the Athenians—
Far more indeed than Themistocles did in his time for the city.

SAUSAGE-SELLER. City of Argos! Do you hear what he says? What colossal
Brass! Do you dare compare your lousy self with Themistocles?
—Who finding the city like a half-empty wine-cup filled it
Right to the brim; Themistocles, who grafted the Piraeus
On to it like a titbit, adding new fish to our menu
But losing none of the old. And what's *your* contribution?
Partition walls that diminish the city and make the Athenians
Appear provincial and petty—that; and *oracles*—I ask you!
And you dare compare your lazy lousy self with Themistocles!
And *he* went into exile and *you* stay, wiping your fingers
On the best bread.

PAPHLAGON.   Demos, how long have I to listen
To this sewer of abuse—and all because I love you?

DEMOS. Oh, shut your mealy mouth. You've had your dirty fingers
On my bread for far too long—and I never noticed.

SAUSAGE-SELLER. Dearest Demos, O just get an eyeful of him—
He's the nastiest piece of pollution,
Crime, and corruption that ever poisoned the city.
And while you're gawping about,
He gets his teeth in the root
Of the juiciest audit and swallows it whole,

And, armed to the elbows, ladles out
Public funds from the treasury
With both hands—that's from his left
To his right, see?

PAPHLAGON. You won't be so pleased with yourself
When I shop you for stealing a cool
Thirty thousand drachmas. . . .

SAUSAGE-SELLER. Do you *have* to thresh about like this?
You don't *need* to tell the Athenians
What a shark you are. They know.
I'll die if I can't prove you took
A bribe from the Mytilenians
Of forty minas or more. . . .

CHORUS. Your eloquence fills us with awe. You're of paramount
     service
To all mankind—go on like this and you'll be the greatest
Of all Athenians, our sole ruler, wielding the trident
Over our allies too; by your energies amassing
Enormous wealth. Now, if he gives you an opening,
Don't let go. With lungs like yours you should easily silence him.

PAPHLAGON. Not yet, by a long chalk!
You seem to forget Pylos. Mention that to my enemies
And they don't know where to look. They're struck dumb.
They know the fame of my exploit there will last
While there's a shred left of the prisoners' shields.

SAUSAGE-SELLER. Stop at those shields! You've given me a hold.
If you love Demos why did you hang them up
With their handles ready for action? Right, I'll tell you:
If you propose to punish him he'll stop you.
See his squad of muscle-men, tough young leather-sellers
And round them the honey- and cheese-sellers, all his men?
Any hint of trouble against him, any toying with ostracism,
And they'll all gang up, swoop on the shields one night,
And take control of the food supplies!

DEMOS.   Great gods!
Their handles at the ready? [*To* Paphlagon.] You treacherous
     scoundrel,
You've cheated and double-crossed us long enough.

PAPHLAGON. My dear fellow, don't trust a word he says.
  You'll never find a better friend than I am.
  I'm your watchdog—I nose out these plots;
  Nothing brewing in this city gets by me,
  But I expose it at once—loudly and fearlessly.

SAUSAGE-SELLER. I know your technique—like them eel-fishers.
  If the lake's clear and they catch nothing
  They stir up the mud and pull them in—that's you
  Stirring up the muck and getting your rake-off.
  Now tell me this: you do a roaring trade
  In skins: have you ever given Demos as much
  As a scrap of leather to patch his shoes?

DEMOS. No, by Apollo, never!

SAUSAGE-SELLER.   Just his sort.
  Now, look what I brought—a nice strong pair o' shoes
  Special to give you. . . .

DEMOS.   Really, of all the people
  I've ever known, you're the most generous
  And considerate to the people—and their feet.

PAPHLAGON. Isn't it monstrous that one pair of shoes
  Can wipe out the memories of my manifold
  Good works? I, who stamped out buggery and had
  Gryttos struck off the roll of citizens. . . .

SAUSAGE-SELLER. Isn't it typical you should spend your time
  Spying on buggers—and the fact is you stopped them
  Not because you were against them, but because
  You were afraid they'd become orators
  And speak against you. And there's poor old Demos
  Without a cloak and you care for him so little
  You can't be bothered to give him a thick one
  With sleeves—and in winter too. *That's* left to me.

DEMOS. Oh thank you! Why, even Themistocles
  Never thought of this. I grant you the Piraeus
  Was a brilliant idea; but if I have to choose
  Between the two, I reckon I'm for the tunic.

PAPHLAGON. What shocking methods you're using to discredit
  me!

SAUSAGE-SELLER. When a chap's gone to a dinner and got soused,
And he's taken short, he grabs anyone's shoes;
So I—step into *your* methods. . . .

PAPHLAGON.   I can out-blarney you
Any day of the week. I'll wrap him up—
In *this*. [*Produces leather.*] Go on, whine about it. . . .

DEMOS.   Ugh. *I* will!
The stink of leather! Chuck it to the crows.

SAUSAGE-SELLER. He did it on purpose—he was trying to choke you
And he's tried it before. Don't you remember?
When asafoetida stalks were going so cheap—

DEMOS. I do.

SAUSAGE-SELLER. He was certainly at the back of that,
And saw that everyone bought and ate them; and then
In the courts the jurymen had such wind they nearly
Asphyxiated each other—

DEMOS.   By Poseidon, yes—
A shit of a man from Copros told me about it!

SAUSAGE-SELLER. And you all got worse and dirtied yourselves
    farting—

DEMOS. God, I remember—and a dirty trick it was.

PAPHLAGON. What revolting and vulgar smut you use to bait me.

SAUSAGE-SELLER. The goddess bid me beat you—with your own
    weapons.

PAPHLAGON. You won't. Now Demos, just relax. Do nothing
And I'll see you get a good full plate of—pay.

SAUSAGE-SELLER. Accept this charming little pot of ointment
And rub it into the sores on your shins.

PAPHLAGON. I'll pick out your grey hairs and make you young.

SAUSAGE-SELLER. Have this hare-scut to dab your darling eyes—

PAPHLAGON. Dear Demos, blow your nose
And wipe your fingers in my hair—

SAUSAGE-SELLER.   *Mine*'s cleaner!

PAPHLAGON [*losing control*]. I'll fix you in command
Of a trireme—at your expense.
I'll see she's an ancient hulk
With rotting canvas and never,

Never will you be finished
With fitting her out or *paying*
Through the nose!

CHORUS. Stop him! He's boiling over.
Here, someone, take this bailer
And draw some threats off, quick!

PAPHLAGON. I'll sting you where it hurts, I'll
Fix your name in the list
Of the super-tax class—I'll soak you
Till you've nothing! . . .

SAUSAGE-SELLER.   Me,
I won't even threaten *you*.
I'll just pray there's a pan
Of cuttlefish sizzling hot
On your stove, and, that very moment,
You remember you've *got* to speak
In the Assembly on
The Milesians (and make a talent
If you make your point), and you think
You can eat your cuttle and *still*
Get there in time, and then
A bloke rushes in to fetch you,
And you think of that lovely talent,
Gulp down the fish, and CHOKE!

CHORUS. Amen. By Demeter, Zeus, and Apollo!

DEMOS. By and large this sausage-seller seems
To be an outstanding citizen.
I don't know of a time when anyone
Did more for so many—for one obol.
But you, Paphlagon, protesting
You love me, train me on garlic.
I'm sick of your stewardship;
Take off my ring. You're sacked.

PAPHLAGON. Here it is . . . but if *I* don't do your work,
You'll only get somebody worse.

DEMOS.   This isn't
My signet ring—this isn't my device,
Or can't I see straight?

SAUSAGE-SELLER.   What's on yours?

DEMOS. A fig leaf stuffed with beef fat.

SAUSAGE-SELLER.   No,
    That's not there.

DEMOS.   What is it?

SAUSAGE-SELLER.   A gaping
    Cormorant haranguing from a rock . . .

DEMOS. Horror!

SAUSAGE-SELLER. What's up?

DEMOS.   Chuck it away!
    It belongs to fatty Cleonymos.
    Take this one, and be my steward.

PAPHLAGON. Not yet, I beg you, sir! Please wait
    Till you've heard my oracles.

SAUSAGE-SELLER.   And mine!

PAPHLAGON. If you take any notice of his,
    You'll be no more than a wine-skin.

SAUSAGE-SELLER. If you take any notice of *his*,
    He'll have the skin off your cock.

PAPHLAGON. *My* oracles foretell that you
    Shall rule over all the land—garlanded
    With roses.

SAUSAGE-SELLER. Mine, that you'll put on
    A purple robe and a crown and pursue
    Pansy Smikythé and his 'spouse'
    From a golden chariot—

PAPHLAGON.   Then go
    And get your oracles—let *him* hear them!

SAUSAGE-SELLER. By all means. And you get yours—

PAPHLAGON. Very well.

SAUSAGE-SELLER.   Then what are we waiting for?

                                    [*Exeunt.*

CHORUS.   Sweetest light of day to us
          And our children's children,
          Day of Cleon's downfall!
          But some cynical old brokers

On 'Change are putting forward
A counter-theory—
That were he not in power the State
Would lack two useful tools:
A pestle and a ladle.

For our part we're amazed at
His swinish taste in music:
His schoolmates say he'd only
Deign to attempt the Dorian
Mode on his lyre—till his wrathful
Teacher expelled him
Saying, 'He'll master nothing but
The Cashadorian mode
Of bribery and corruption!'

Re-enter Paphlagon *and* Sausage-seller, *laden.*

PAPHLAGON. Look at this lot—and I've got plenty more!

SAUSAGE-SELLER. God, what a weight—and I've got plenty more!

DEMOS. *What's* this?

PAPHLAGON.   Oracles.

DEMOS.   What! *All these?*

PAPHLAGON. Are you surprised? I've got cupboardsful
At home still.

SAUSAGE-SELLER. I've got an attic full,
And two cellars.

DEMOS.   Very well, let me see:
Whose oracles are these?

PAPHLAGON [*smugly*].   *Mine*
Are by Bakis.

DEMOS [*to* Sausage-seller]. And yours?

SAUSAGE-SELLER.   By Glanis . . . Bakis's
Big brother.

DEMOS.   What are they about?

PAPHLAGON. The Athenians, Pylos, you, me,
And everything.

DEMOS [*to* Sausage-seller]. And yours?

SAUSAGE-SELLER.   Oh—Athens,
   Porridge, Spartans, fresh mackerel,
   Short weight among the barley-sellers
   In the market, you and me.
   He can go and bite his cock off!

DEMOS. Expound them to me. The one I specially
   Like is where I soar as an eagle
   Into the clouds. . . .

PAPHLAGON.   Then follow me closely.
   'Son of Erechtheus, heed the drift of my oracle,
   Which, from his inmost sanctuary, Apollo
   Has vouchsafed to you, his sacred tripods tolling:
   Keep safe, he bids, the jaggéd-toothéd holy
   Watchdog that yawns at your feet or ferociously
   Snarling defends you, for he will furnish
   Your pay—and if he fails to, he will perish;
   For many a jackdaw hates you both, about you croaking!'

DEMOS. By Demeter, I haven't a clue
   What it says—what has Erechtheus
   To do with a dog and jackdaws?

PAPHLAGON. I'm the dog. I bark for you. Apollo
   Says you must cherish this dog—me.

SAUSAGE-SELLER. Nonsense! *That's* not what it says.
   This dog has chewed a bit off the oracle
   Like he does off a door. I'll put you
   Straight about this crooked dog.

DEMOS. Please do. But first I'll get a stone,
   In case this dog-oracle snaps at me.

SAUSAGE-SELLER. 'Son of Erechtheus, heed! This man-snatching
      Cerberus
   Of a dog that wags his tail as you dine—he's watching
   Your every move with eyes fast-fixed and if your attention
   Wanders a moment— Zip! He swipes your portion.
   And dogwise by night he sneaks into the kitchen
   And licks the plates clean—like he does the islands.'

DEMOS. By Demeter! I like Glanis better!

PAPHLAGON. Listen again before you choose:
   'A woman shall be delivered

Of a lion in holy Athens,
Which lion shall fight for Demos
With an army of mosquitoes
As fiercely as for his litter;
Build palisades to protect him,
And iron towers to defend him!'
Do you understand what it means?

DEMOS. Not a single word, by Apollo!

PAPHLAGON. The god says guard me close,
I'm your lion-of-defence.

DEMOS. Strange that I never noticed!

SAUSAGE-SELLER.—But he's purposely forgotten
To tell you one thing. He's never
Told you what the contraption
Of wood and iron you've ordered
To keep him safe in, *is*.

DEMOS. Then what does the god mean?

SAUSAGE-SELLER. The stocks-cum-pillory.

DEMOS. That certainly might come true.

PAPHLAGON. Heed not the jealous crows that croak against me,
But love your falcon; recalling
Who delivered you, bound in fetters,
Those Spartan fledgeling ravens.

SAUSAGE-SELLER. He'd never have had the guts
If he hadn't got plastered first!
'O son of Cecrops! You counsel ill (and no error)
If you think this a mighty achievement.
For a woman will bear a weight
If a man impose it upon her:
But she cannot fight—if she struggles,
She simply piddles for terror.'

PAPHLAGON. Remember the oracle: 'Pylos
Before Pylos and there is Pylos
Before Pylos still.'

DEMOS.   What *does* he mean,
All this piling up of Pyloses?

SAUSAGE-SELLER. He means that pile of bathtubs
   In the bathhouse—he's going to pinch them.

DEMOS. Then I won't get my splash today.

SAUSAGE-SELLER. Maybe. But listen to this,
   It's about the fleet—please
   Give all your mind to it.

DEMOS. I will—but expound to me first
   How we're going to pay the sailors.

SAUSAGE-SELLER. 'Son of Aegeus, beware of the tricky hound fox!
   If he can, he'll get round you, sidling
   Secretly up to nip you, swift to retreat and wily,
   Adept in deceit . . .'
                              Do you get it?

DEMOS. Philostratos the pander?
   He fills the bill.

SAUSAGE-SELLER. Not him.
   No. No. He's continually
   Demanding your speediest triremes
   To fetch more tribute. Apollo
   Says: 'Don't you give him none!'

DEMOS. How can a trireme be
   A hound fox?

SAUSAGE-SELLER. A trireme's speedy,
   So is a hound speedy.

DEMOS. Why add the fox bit though?

SAUSAGE-SELLER. 'Cause the men go scrounging
   Through the farms eating all
   The grapes off of the vineyards

DEMOS. I see . . . and the pay for these little foxes?

SAUSAGE-SELLER. *I'll* provide it within three days.
   —But listen to this:
                              'The son
   Of Leto bids you beware
   Of the ever-open hollow.'

DEMOS. The ever-open hollow?

SAUSAGE-SELLER.—Paphlagon's open palm,
   And his endless demands to fill it.

PAPHLAGON. No, no, Apollo meant
    Diopeithes' crippled hand!
    But look, here's a winged oracle:
    'Transformed into an eagle,
    You will be lord of all lands.'

SAUSAGE-SELLER. Mine's better. 'Lord of all lands
    And of the wine-dark sea,
    And in Ecbatana dispenser
    Of justice, your judgements tempered
    With the delight of sweetmeats.'

PAPHLAGON. I have dreamed a dream. Athene
    Appeared to me holding a *ladle*
    From which she poured an elixir
    Of health and wealth for the people.

SAUSAGE-SELLER. I have dreamed a dream. Athene
    Descended from the citadel,
    An owl upon her shoulder,
    And she poured out from a *bucket*
    On to Demos' head ambrosia,
    And on *his*, sharp garlic pickle.

DEMOS. Splendid! There's never been
    A prophet wiser than Glanis!
    [*To* Sausage-seller.] I put myself in *your* hands.
    You shall teach me again and put
    New sense in my old brain.

PAPHLAGON. Not yet, not yet! I'll provide you
    With barley and daily bread!

DEMOS. I'm sick of eating your promises!
    You and your secretary
    Have tricked me once too often.

PAPHLAGON. I'll give you pre-ground flour.

SAUSAGE-SELLER. I'll give you pre-cooked cakes
    And pre-baked fish—DO NOTHING
    BUT EAT.

DEMOS.   Get on with it then.
    And I'll hand the reins of office
    To whoever does me best.

PAPHLAGON. I'm bound to win.

SAUSAGE-SELLER. That's what *you* think!

             [*Exeunt* Paphlagon *and* Sausage-seller.

CHORUS.
    Consider what wonderful powers
      We delegate to you
    As if you were dictator,
    O Demos—and then how easy
      You are to lead by the nose,
    How you dote on being flattered
    And gulled to believe as gospel
    Whatever the glib and specious
      Offer your scatter-brain.

DEMOS.
    You keep your brain in your hair if
      You think I never think.
    I play the fool on purpose
    Because I delight to loiter
      And booze the day away;
    And I choose to fatten one super-
    Thief in the government stable
    Till he's completely bloated—
      Then, pht! I squash him flat!

CHORUS.
    Are you really as Machiavellian
      As you make out? If so,
    You have our fullest approval,
    So nourish up your nasty
      Politicians in the Pnyx.
    Then pick the ripe and juicy
    When you feel you want to tickle
    Your palate with something tasty
      And serve him piping hot.

DEMOS.
    Observe how circumspectly
      I keep an eye on them
    As they practise their dirty dodges,
    And never one instant notice
      I'm on their trail until
    I seize them and thrust my surgical
    Probe down their throats and compel them
    To disgorge the swag they've stolen
      —They discover too late—for ME!

Re-enter Paphlagon *and* Sausage-seller.

PAPHLAGON. You, you . . . go to heaven!

SAUSAGE-SELLER. You too . . . you hell's best bet.

PAPHLAGON. Demos, *I've* been ready waiting
　　To serve you for three ages.

SAUSAGE-SELLER. And I for ten, twelve, a thousand,
　　A thousand thousand—

DEMOS. And *I've* been waiting thirty
　　Thousand thousand thousand
　　Till I hate you both.

SAUSAGE-SELLER. Do you know what?

DEMOS. 　　　　　　　　　　　　　No,
　　But you'll tell me if I don't.

SAUSAGE-SELLER. Start us from the gate.
　　Dead equal, no favouritism.

DEMOS. Indeed I will. Get set . . .

PAPHLAGON *and* SAUSAGE-SELLER. We are.

DEMOS. Go!

SAUSAGE-SELLER [*to* Paphlagon].—And don't cut in!

DEMOS [*aside*]. My heaven, I'd be too good to be true
　　If I didn't enjoy myself today
　　At the expense of this loving pair.

PAPHLAGON. See! I'm first to bring you a chair.

SAUSAGE-SELLER. But not a table—I'm firster there.

PAPHLAGON. I've got you this tasty pasty cooked
　　From the grain I got at Pylos.

SAUSAGE-SELLER. I've got these dollops of dough scooped
　　By the goddess's very own ivory hand.

DEMOS. What enormous fingers she must have got!

PAPHLAGON. Here's some pea soup. It's lovely and fresh and hot,
　　Pallas, victrix of Pylos, stirred the pot.

SAUSAGE-SELLER. See how she spoils you, holding up
　　This *whole tureenful* of soup.

DEMOS. Do you think if she hadn't the city would have survived?

PAPHLAGON. Look at this fillet of fish
　　The Petrifier of Foes
　　Has fried for you . . .

SAUSAGE-SELLER.   —This delicious
   Beef broth the Nobly-Begotten
   Has boiled and a prime portion
   Of innards and tripe . . .

DEMOS.   (A kindly
   Return for the Peplos, bless her.)

PAPHLAGON. The Gorgon-Crested craves
   You taste this *feathery* shortcake
   And row with a *longer* stroke.

SAUSAGE-SELLER. *Please* have *these*!

DEMOS. What on earth shall I do with pig's guts?

SAUSAGE-SELLER. —For the bellies of our ships.
   Clearly the goddess favours our fleet.
   Now drink this excellent wine,
   Two parts neat to three of water.

DEMOS. Zeus, but it's strong; it can take
   The dilution all right.

SAUSAGE-SELLER.   Athene
   The Triton-born mixed it herself.

PAPHLAGON. Have a cut of this succulent cake . . .

SAUSAGE-SELLER. Have a *whole* cake!

PAPHLAGON.   But you can't
   Give him a hare, because *I* can.

SAUSAGE-SELLER [*aside*]. Where can I get a hare?
   I must think up something quick!

PAPHLAGON [*crowing*]. D'you see this, you bastard?

SAUSAGE-SELLER. D'you think *I* care?
   . . . Why, there they are at last—
   Hull*o* there!—coming to me at last. . . .

PAPHLAGON. Who are?

SAUSAGE-SELLER.   Nothing much . . . .
   Some envoys with sacks of silver. . . .

PAPHLAGON. Where are they? Where? Where?
                   [Sausage-seller *snatches the hare.*

SAUSAGE-SELLER. What does it matter? Let
   The poor strangers alone! Demos,

Dear Demos, look at this
Beautiful hare I've brought!

PAPHLAGON. Great god, he's grabbed my hare!
Here, it wasn't yours to give him.

SAUSAGE-SELLER. Oh yes it was! You did the same at Pylos.

DEMOS. Tell me, who put the idea in your head?

SAUSAGE-SELLER. Athene. It was *her* idea. I *had* to do it.

PAPHLAGON.—It was I had to risk it! It was I had to cook it!

DEMOS. But *he* served it up! He gets the credit.
You've missed it. He took it.

PAPHLAGON. Gods! I've been out-twisted!

SAUSAGE-SELLER. Now Demos, why not decide it?
Which of us is the better
To you and your stomach?

DEMOS. What do you think the audience
Would accept as evidence
Of a just and sensible judgement?

SAUSAGE-SELLER. I'll tell you. Don't say a word,
Creep up to my basket first
And see what's in it. Then Paphlagon's.
You can't go wrong like that.

DEMOS. What's in yours?

SAUSAGE-SELLER.   Don't you see?
'S empty. Nothing. Everything
I had, I've given *you* . . . father.

DEMOS. Why, certainly this basket
Has Demos' stomach at heart.

SAUSAGE-SELLER. Quick now, see what's in *his*.

DEMOS. Why it's *crammed*! Look what a prize
Of a cheese cake he's put aside.
And look at the wretched sliver
He gave me . . . it's hardly visible!

SAUSAGE-SELLER. Just what he did before—
Gave you a sliver and kept
A great hunk for himself.

DEMOS. You greedy deceiving swine!
And 'I stuffed you wi' duff'. . . .

PAPHLAGON [*self-righteous*]. *If* I stole, *I* stole for the city.

DEMOS. Enough of that! Off with your crown!
  At once! I want to crown him.

SAUSAGE-SELLER. Jump to it! You . . .

PAPHLAGON.   Not likely;
  I've a Delphic oracle
  Describing the only man
  That can defeat me.

SAUSAGE-SELLER.   —Describing
  Me and perfectly clearly.

PAPHLAGON. Right, then I'll test you out and see
  How closely you match up
  With the god's predictions. First,
  Let me ask you this: who taught you
  When you were a boy?

SAUSAGE-SELLER.   Hard knuckles
  Knocked me to shape in the kitchens.

PAPHLAGON. What's that? (It's close to the oracle—
  Far too close for my liking.) What
  Did you learn from your school instructor?

SAUSAGE-SELLER. What d'you think? If I was caught
  Stealing, deny it flat—and not
  Bat an eye but stare 'em down.

PAPHLAGON.   O Phoebus!
  What trade did you follow—when you grew up?

SAUSAGE-SELLER. Sausage-selling and—

PAPHLAGON.   Well?

SAUSAGE-SELLER [*simpering*].   Can't you guess?
  I was ever so nice. But I had my price.

PAPHLAGON. This is the end—I've had the lot.
  I've only a flicker of hope left.
  Tell me, where was your pitch?
  In the market or by the gates?

SAUSAGE-SELLER. By the gates where they sell salt fish.

PAPHLAGON. I'm done for! It's all come true,
  Every black word of it! Roll me down
  And out in my misery!

Dear crown, good-bye, good-bye.
It's agony letting you go—
To a *luckier* man, perhaps,
But *not* a bigger crook. . . .

SAUSAGE-SELLER. Zeus of all Hellas, yours is the victory!

CHORUS. Great conqueror, all hail!
(And bear in mind our loyal support
In your climb to fame. But for us . . .
And perhaps I might venture a small request
If the job's going? Your signer of writs?
Yes? . . .) —But tell us your name.

SAUSAGE-SELLER.   Agoracritos.
For I've lived on my wits in the market,
And I'd die if I couldn't haggle—

DEMOS. Very well, Agoracritos,
I commit myself to you—
And Paphlagon to your mercy.

SAUSAGE-SELLER. And I'll give you the best of my service, too,
So everyone shall agree
No one has ever been better than me
To this noble city of—nitwits.

                                        [*Exeunt.*

CHORUS.   Could we select a theme more apt
                        For beginning and ending
                  Than to sing of the headlong speed
                        Of the charioteer and his horses?

            Why with deliberate malice
                  Impugn Lysistratos?
            Or with a mean indifference mock
                  Poor Thumantis,

            Who starving clutches your quiver
                  In a waterfall of weeping,
                  O Apollo, and begs relief from
                        His abject poverty.
It is never invidious to mock at the mockworthy.
To every honest man it's a matter for approbation.
Now if the man whose filthy behaviour merits

Public exposure were notable himself
I would not mention the name of one I admire.
Everyone knows Arignotos. Anyone who can tell
White from black can distinguish his music from other players.
But his brother Ariphrades—you wouldn't believe him a brother
He's so utterly unlike in every possible way—
If he were just an ordinary pervert
I wouldn't waste time on him. But he's invented
A new, an unspeakably revolting vice
So inconceivably bestial even the whores shudder
When he erects his lecherous tongue in the brothel.
Never shall lips so defiled, depraved, disgusting
Sully a cup of mine.

        'Oft in the stilly night'
        This puzzle keeps me wakeful,
        And I wonder where Cleonymos got
          His fabulous appetite.

        They say there's nothing harder,
        Though he guzzles at the lavish
        Boards of the generous and rich,
          Than to tear him from the larder.

        People fall on their knees
        And beg, beseech, implore him,
        'Mercy, dear fellow, go, do *go*;
          Spare our table, please.'
Our triremes met together once, so the story goes,
For a debate, and one of them, a senior ship, began:
'Sisters, what d'you make of this? They say they mean to hand us
Over to that Hyperbolos, the sour and worthless lout
For a sally against Carthage—a hundred of our line!'
This monstrous proposition met with rage and dismay;
Then a virgin, not yet out of port, protested to her elders,
'He'll never take *my* helm! I'd rather moulder, here at anchor,
Gnawed to bits by woodworms. Not with a single plank
Of all my fir and timber shall *Nauphante* nor her builder
Submit to him! And if the people let him have his way
I propose we sail for sanctuary, making for the shrine
Of Theseus or the Holy Gods. Never shall he exploit

The city in this shameless way. Never shall he command us.
If he likes to launch the trays he sold lamps on—let him man one,
And take a little voyage, single-handed, to the crows!'

Re-enter Sausage-seller.

SAUSAGE-SELLER [*pompously*]. Keep holy silence, everyone!
Call no more witnesses!
Close the law-courts, though we love them,
Let the theatre ring with paeans
At the good news I bring!

CHORUS. Light of ancient Athens, warden of our islands,
What good news shall kindle
The altars in our streets?

SAUSAGE-SELLER [*reverting*]. I've boiled old Demos up a bit
(Or rendered him down), but anyway
I've renewed his youth.

CHORUS. You're a genius for extraordinary
Inventions! Where is he now?

SAUSAGE-SELLER. In this here violet-crowned, ancient,
Famous Athens—as usual.

CHORUS. How can we see him? What's he wearing?
What's he looking like?

SAUSAGE-SELLER.   Like he was
In the old days when he was mates with
Miltiades and Aristides.
You'll see him for yourselves—the doors
Of the Propyleia are opening.
So raise a cheer for the grand old days
Of Athens come back again, the renowned
And celebrated in song—where
Noble Demos has his abode.

CHORUS. O shining bright, O violet-crowned,
O justly envied City, show us
The lord of Hellas and our land.

Enter Demos.

SAUSAGE-SELLER. Look at him in his glorious old-
Style clothes and the gold cicala

In his hair—not stinking of votes,
But sweet with the scent of treaties,
Perfumed with myrrh!

CHORUS.   Lord of the Greeks,
All hail! We duly rejoice with you
In your new noble guise, the very
Spirit of Marathon flashing in your eyes.

DEMOS. Agoracritos, my friend, come here!
What marvellous good your boiling did me!

SAUSAGE-SELLER. Really? If you remembered what
You were like before, and all you did,
You'd think I was a god!

DEMOS.   Tell me,
What did I do? What was I like?

SAUSAGE-SELLER. Well . . . if anyone in the Assembly said
'Demos, I love and adore you. *No one*
But me has got your interests
Really at heart' . . . if anyone shot
Soft smarmy lines like that, you flapped
Your cock's wings and crew, and tossed
Your bull's horns, and lapped it up!

DEMOS. I did?

SAUSAGE-SELLER. Then he'd cheat you all he could
And leave you flat!

DEMOS.   Truly? They did
This to me and I never knew?

SAUSAGE-SELLER. They did! Because, by god, your ears
Opened and shut like a sunshade.

DEMOS. Was I so brainless and doddering?

SAUSAGE-SELLER. And if two speakers proposed, one
To build ships, the other to step up
Civil servants' pay, the pay-man
Always beat the ship-man hollow.
Why are you hanging your head? Why
Are you shifting about?

DEMOS.   I'm ashamed
Of my former faults.

SAUSAGE-SELLER.   The blame's not *yours*;
    You mustn't think that. The blame's on all
    Who cheated you. Now answer me:
    If any blustering crook of a pleader
    Should say to the jurors, 'No barley
    If the prisoner gets off,' what
    Would you do to the scum?

DEMOS.   I'd tie
    Hyperbolos round his neck and chuck him
    Into the pit.

SAUSAGE-SELLER. Sensible chap; that's good.
    What's your policy in general?

DEMOS.   First,
    As soon as the fleet puts in, I'll pay
    The sailors' arrears in full.

SAUSAGE-SELLER.   Many
    A callused bottom'll bless you for that!

DEMOS. Then when a soldier has been posted
    He must stay on his list. He shall *not*
    Get a transfer by graft, but stick
    To his original posting.

SAUSAGE-SELLER.   That's
    Given Cleonymos' shield-strap
    A nasty nip!

DEMOS.   And no pretty boys
    Shall use the market as a rendezvous.

SAUSAGE-SELLER. That's tough on Cleisthenes
    And Straton.

DEMOS.   No, no, no! I mean
    Those know-all creatures lolling about
    The scent-shops drawling 'Phaiax—the fella's
    Brilliant. *Mar*vellous resource
    Or he'd be dead. I mean to say,
    He's such a stickler for fact,
    So accurate and exact, but with what tact,
    How per*sua*sively he sparkles and *ab*solutely crackles
    With epigrams—and the way he tackles hecklers,
    My *dear* . . .'

SAUSAGE-SELLER. You're not in favour of
   These quacking little duckies?

DEMOS. By heaven, no! I'd make them all
   Chuck politics and go hunting!

SAUSAGE-SELLER.   Then
   Accept this folding stool, and a well-
   Developed boy to bear it for you
   (And he's got other uses too)!

DEMOS. I shall be like I was of old!

SAUSAGE-SELLER. You'll say that when I offer you
   These treaties-for-thirty-years!—Now
   Step forward, my dears . . .

          Enter the Treaties, *lovely girls.*

DEMOS.   Zeus, they're sweet!
   I'd like to g-ratify them all!
   Wherever did you get them?

SAUSAGE-SELLER.   Paphlagon
   Kept them hidden so as you
   Should never have them. Now they're yours
   To take back to your farms.

DEMOS.   And how
   Will you punish Paphlagon—the root
   Of all our troubles?

SAUSAGE-SELLER.   I won't do much.
   He can take on from me . . . sole rights
   Of sausage-selling at the gates.
   Let him mince dog- and donkey-meat,
   Get drunk and bicker with whores
   And quench his thirst on bathwater.

DEMOS. Excellent! Just what he's fit for,
   To brawl with bath attendants
   And trollops in the gutter.
               —But as for you,
   I invite *you* to a banquet
   In the Prytaneium, where Paphlagon once
   Got rich by his dirty dealing.

Put on this emerald mantle,
And follow me to the table.

                    And as for *him*—
Let them cart him off to his squalid pitch
Where citizen and stranger,
Every single one of his victims,
Shall see him—sausage-selling!

CLOUDS

The Clouds *was first produced in the spring of 423* B.C. *at the Great Dionysia, the main dramatic competition and festival in Athens, which foreigners and official visitors frequently attended. Because it only won third prize* (Cratinos *having won the first), Aristophanes wrote a revised version (which may never have been performed in ancient Athens), part of which is incorporated in the text which has survived.*

The war was still on, and the economic hardship resulting from it may be reflected in the indebtedness from which this play's leading character, Strepsiades, is suffering, and in the avidity with which public feasts are mentioned and welcomed. But the *Clouds* is not directly concerned with politics at all; it draws its fun rather from two styles of life—the rustic, practical, and traditional contrasted with the urban, intellectual, and modern. (One consequence of the war must have been to set off these two by juxtaposition, with large numbers of country people obliged unwontedly to stay in the city of Athens for protection from enemy attacks.)

Strepsiades is a farmer and, by city lights, a fool. He is bewildered by the fashions in behaviour, dress, and speech of the young generation; he dislikes contemporary music, songs, and verse; he blames his debts on his wife's extravagant purchases of new things and his son Pheidippides' passion for the latest vogue, horse-racing. Most of all he cannot understand recent educational ideas and methods—those of the Sophists.

Socrates is presented as the typical Sophist—a cross between an academic and a guru. Old Strepsiades can neither make anything of, nor get anything from, the Sophists' interest in science, their scepticism about religion, their analytical discussion of meaning and morals, let alone their asceticism and meditations. The Clouds who appear as the Chorus are just what Strepsiades might expect the gods or goddesses of the Sophists to be, in place of the conventional gods of Athens; and dialectical argument and logical ingenuity are presented, as Strepsiades would see them, in the debate between True and False Logic. (In this translation True Logic is made to speak, in the main argument, in traditional blank verse, and False Logic in modern syllabics, in the hope of underlining their differences.) Young Pheidippides learns a thing or two, but Strepsiades' final reaction is simply one of violence against the new-fangled intellectuals.

Aristophanes much resented the failure of the *Clouds*, as is clear in the Parabasis, which is from the revision he made a few years later; he attacks other playwrights for following fashions in characters and subjects, and cannot see why his clever and original play wasn't acclaimed. It was evidently too subtle for his audience, and the revised version we now have probably attacks Socrates and the Sophists much more crudely; had Aristophanes earlier underestimated the number of Strepsiades in his audience?

CHARACTERS

STREPSIADES
PHEIDIPPIDES, *his son*
SLAVE *of Strepsiades*
STUDENTS *of Socrates*
SOCRATES
TRUE LOGIC
FALSE LOGIC
PASIAS, *a money lender*
WITNESS
AMYNIAS, *a money lender*
CHAIREPHON, *a famous student of Socrates*
HERMES, *a god*
CHORUS *of Clouds*

At the back of the stage are Strepsiades' *house and* Socrates' *Logic factory. It is night.* Strepsiades *and* Pheidippides *are asleep.*

STREPSIADES [*groaning*]. Oh . . . oh . . . oh . . . oh Zeus!
How endless, oh great god, how endless
The nights are: will day never come?
It was hours ago I heard a cock crow,
But the servants are still snoring—nothing's
What it used to be. There are heaven knows
How many reasons for avoiding
War—and one's enough: I'm afraid even
To beat the brutes. And here's my son,
My splendid boy, he's not wakeful, oh no,
He's deep in fine blankets snoring and farting.
I'll try myself, wrap up and join the band. . . .

[*He tries to sleep.*

No good at all. I can't get off.
I'm bitten to the bone by the debts
His horses and his extravagances
Have run me into. Look at him,
With his smart long hair, his curricles—
He loves horses, so I'm ruined, I'm also-ran;
But the days are running out horribly,
It's nearer the end of the month
And I'll have to pay up.
                          Boy! Light a lamp—
Bring my account book!

            Enter Slave *with lamp and book.*
                          I must check up
Who I owe and how much. *Twelve minae*
To Pasias! Twelve minae
To *Pasias*! Why on earth . . .? What did
I spend that on? Oh yes, I got
That confounded Corinthian hack from him.
I wish I'd walled my eye with a stone first. . . .

PHEIDIPPIDES [*muttering in his sleep*]. Philon, you're cutting in!
   Keep
   To your own lane! Keep straight, damn you.

STREPSIADES. Horse-mad. That's what has finished me.
   Even in his dreams he's obsessed with horses.

PHEIDIPPIDES. How many laps do the war-
   Chariots have to drive . . .?

STREPSIADES.   You've driven
   Your father round the bend often enough!
   Now who's competing with Pasias? Amynias.
   Three minae for a sports chariot
   And spare wheels. . . .

PHEIDIPPIDES.   See my horse has a proper
   Roll, and then take him to the stables!

STREPSIADES. You've rolled me properly—clean out of everything,
   What with summonses and threats
   To distrain all my possessions . . . oh . . . oh . . . *oh*!

PHEIDIPPIDES [*waking*]. Whatever's the matter, father—bumping
   And boring all night like this?

STREPSIADES. There's a big bug-ger of a dun biting me
   In the bedclothes.

PHEIDIPPIDES.   Pipe down, old boy,
   Give me some peace.

STREPSIADES.   Peace—all very well.
   Sleep now if you can, in the end
   It's you that'll have to pay—not me!
                              [Pheidippides *goes back to sleep*.
   Oh curse the confounded matchmaker
   Who jockeyed me into marrying
   Your mother! There was I, leading
   A blissful country life, shabby
   And dirty and happy-go-lucky with piles
   Of olives, flocks in my folds,
   Bees in my hives—and then I had
   To marry this blue-blooded bit.
   Me a farmer, she the niece
   Of nobility, a town-bred,

Stuck-up, finicky, classy lady
And *I* married her! Me, stinking of wine
And fig-boards and oily with raw wool,
And she all cloyed with expensive
Scents and saffrons, and tricksy kisses,
And parties, and stuffing herself, and sex.
I don't say she did nothing, no!
She went the pace and I told her so,
Showing her my more-than-worn-out cloak:
'You're burning it up too fast,' I said.

SLAVE. Sir, there's no oil left in the lamp!

STREPSIADES. Why did you have to light that one?
It *drinks* oil. Come here and I'll beat you!

SLAVE. Ooh sir, whatever have *I* done?

STREPSIADES. Put in a thick wick, you fool!
. . . Well when at last our son was born
She opted for a high-class name—
Xanthippos, Charippos, Callipides.
Pheidonides was what I wanted
After his grandad. So we quarrelled.
In the end we compromised in favour
Of Pheidippides—and she used to take
The boy and cuddle him and whisper:
'When you're big, darling, you'll drive
Your chariot to the city dressed
Like Megacles in purple.' Then
I'd say, 'When you drive the goats
Down from the rocks and screes togged up
Like your father in working leather . . .'
But he took no notice of what *I* said.
So he's driving me to rack and ruin
With his mania for horses.. . . .
                              But now
After cogitating the whole night
I've hit on a way, an immutable
Divine and curious way to save myself—
That is, if he'll agree: I wonder
What's the least painful way to wake him?

—Phei—Phei . . . dippides . . . easy . . .
Come up my little colt . . . easy . . .

[*He wakes his son.*

PHEIDIPPIDES. What is it now?

STREPSIADES.   Give me a kiss
And your right hand.

PHEIDIPPIDES.   What's the trouble?

STREPSIADES. Do you love me?

PHEIDIPPIDES.   By Poseidon,
God of horses, of course I do!

STREPSIADES. No, no, no! Not *that* god, please!
He's at the bottom of all my troubles.
But if you love me with all your heart
Will you do what I ask?

PHEIDIPPIDES.   Ask away.

STREPSIADES. Give up your present ways completely,
At once, now, and begin learning
What I'll tell you to.

PHEIDIPPIDES.   Learning what?

STREPSIADES. You'll truly do what I say?

PHEIDIPPIDES.   By Pos— Dionysus!

STREPSIADES. See that little door and that little house?

PHEIDIPPIDES. I do. What is it?

STREPSIADES.   A Logic factory
For the extra-clever. There are men there
Who can convince you heaven's a sort
Of fire-extinguisher all around us
And we're like cinders—yes, and they teach you
(If you pay enough) to win your arguments,
Whether you're right or wrong.

PHEIDIPPIDES.   Who're 'they'?

STREPSIADES. I don't quite know, but they're deep
Analytical thinkers and of course
Real gentlemen—

PHEIDIPPIDES.   Ph! Stinkers.
I know that lot: barefaced, wheyfaced,

Barefoot, big-mouths—that lousy Socrates
And Chairephon . . .

STREPSIADES.   Really now,
Don't speak like that, but if you care
Twopence for my crops go to them now
And chuck this craze for horses.

PHEIDIPPIDES.   No!
By Dionysus, no! Not even if
You gave me the pick of Leogoras' stud!

STREPSIADES. Dear, dear boy, *please* go and learn.

PHEIDIPPIDES.   Learn what?

STREPSIADES. They say they've two systems
Of Logic: you can argue from a basis
Of True, and False. They can teach you
To win with the False and *if* you can learn
To do this for me I won't have to pay
An obol, not a single obol
Of all the debts that *you've* run up.

PHEIDIPPIDES. I'm damned if I'll go. I couldn't bear
The Knights to see me like an indoor sissy.

STREPSIADES. Then, by Demeter, you don't eat
Another mouthful in this house!
Nor your carriage-horses and race-horses!
Out you go, my lad! You can go to hell.

PHEIDIPPIDES.—I'll go to my Uncle Megacles,
He wouldn't like me to be without
A horse! I won't give you another thought!

                                           [*Exit.*

STREPSIADES. I've tripped up, but I won't stay down.
I'll pray to the gods and I'll—I'll go myself
To this Logic factory, and be taught myself.
How shall I learn to split hairs? Me—
I'm bald, old, forgetful, and slow,
But it's needs must, so why am I hanging about?
Why not knock on the door? Boy! Boy!

                        [*He knocks at the factory door.*
                A Student *appears.*

1 STUDENT. Blast you with your knocking! Who are you?

STREPSIADES. Strepsiades, Pheidon's son,
Strepsiades of Kykinna.

1 STUDENT. Zeus!
You're a fool whoever you are,
Banging and clattering at the door
Without thinking; but *I* was thinking
And you've given me a miscarriage.

STREPSIADES. I'm so sorry. I come from the country.
What have I made miscarry? Tell me.

1 STUDENT. Oh, I couldn't. It wouldn't be right
Except to a fellow-student—see what I mean?

STREPSIADES. You can tell me. You see I've come
To enroll at this Logic factory.

1 STUDENT. All right, I'll tell you, but you've got
To remember these things are sacred mysteries.
[*In awed tones.*] Socrates asked Chairephon
A few minutes ago how many lengths
Of its own foot could a flea jump.
(After biting Chairephon it hopped
Out of his eyebrow on to the smooth
Curve of the Master's head.)

STREPSIADES. And how did Chairephon cope
With this weighty problem?

1 STUDENT [*seriously*]. Ever
So cleverly! He warmed some wax,
Then grabbed the flea and plunged its feet
Into the wax and, you see, when the wax
Cooled off the flea had on a pair
Of Persian slippers which Chairephon then
Took off and used them to measure
The space between.

STREPSIADES. Almighty Zeus,
What amazing subtlety of mind!

1 STUDENT. What would you say to this device
Of Socrates then?

STREPSIADES. Please tell me.

1 STUDENT. Chairephon
Put up two theories: do gnats buzz

Through their mouths or their backsides;
Which did he think?

STREPSIADES.   And which did he?

1 STUDENT. He said their guts are narrow and
That along this narrow pipe the air
Is forced at pressure towards the
Hollow of the rump, and being forced
To escape through the arsehole, at
This pressure, it makes it whistle.

STREPSIADES. So a gnat's arse is a trumpet.
How incredibly lucky a man must be
With such an exquisite entrail-insight.
It would be child's play to escape justice
If one were an expert in gnats' guts!

1 STUDENT. He lost a sublime thought last night
Because of a lizard. . . .

STREPSIADES.   How was that?

1 STUDENT. He was rapt. He was gazing up
Open-mouthed at the winding paths
Of the moving moon, and meditating
Upon them, when a lizard pissed
Down onto him.

STREPSIADES.   Pissed on Socrates!
That's rich. I like that!

1 STUDENT.   Yesterday
We'd got no dinner.

STREPSIADES.   How did he manage
To conjure your barley up?

1 STUDENT.   —Sprinkled
A layer of dust on a table, bent
A rod into compass-shape, and hooked up
The wherewithal from the wrestling school.

STREPSIADES. And we still marvel at Thales! Open
This Logic factory up at once;
I must see Socrates, I must
Enroll this minute! Open the door!   [*They go in.*

The scene changes to the inside of the Logic factory. Several
Students *are at work;* Socrates *is above, in a basket. Enter*
Strepsiades *with* First Student.

STREPSIADES. Great Heracles! What weird, wild freaks!

1 STUDENT. What's wrong? What d'you think they're like?

STREPSIADES. The Spartan prisoners from Pylos.
Why are they glowering at the ground?

1 STUDENT. They're probing under the surface.

STREPSIADES.   For truffles?
Tell them not to bother, I know
Where the biggest and best grow. Why are
These ones bent double?

1 STUDENT.   They're sounding
The darkest depths of Tartarus.

STREPSIADES. And why are their bottoms pointing to heaven?

1 STUDENT. Their bottoms are separately taking
A course in Astronomy.
[*To other* Students.] But let's go in, we mustn't be caught
Loitering by him.

STREPSIADES.   Wait!
Wait just a moment, I want to tell them
My own case.

1 STUDENT.   No. Staying outside
In the open air is too much waste
Of time.

STREPSIADES. By Zeus, whatever's this
Contraption?   [*Pointing.*

1 STUDENT.   Astronomy.

STREPSIADES. And this?

1 STUDENT.   Geometry.

STREPSIADES. What's it used for?

1 STUDENT. Measuring the land.

STREPSIADES. Do you mean lots for allotment?

1 STUDENT. No, no—*the whole earth*, I mean.

STREPSIADES.   That's true
Democracy, if anything is!

What a useful idea: to be
Simply allotted the whole earth!

1 STUDENT. See, here's a map of the world. That's Athens—

STREPSIADES. Athens? Nonsense? I can't see any
Law courts in session.

1 STUDENT.   Truly this
  Is Attic territory.

STREPSIADES.   Where are
  My neighbours in Kykinna?

1 STUDENT.   Here.
  And that's Euboia, that narrow strip
  Stretched out along there.

STREPSIADES.   Stretched is right!
  By us and Pericles. Where's Sparta?

1 STUDENT. Sparta? Sparta? . . .Er . . . oh yes! Here it is.

STREPSIADES. How *horribly* close! Now apply your mind
  To moving it farther away—much farther!

1 STUDENT. We can't do *that*.

STREPSIADES.   You can't do that?
  The more fools you. Who's the old bastard
  Up in the basket?

1 STUDENT [*with horrified awe*]. It's . . . Himself.

STREPSIADES. Himself who?

1 STUDENT.   Socrates.

STREPSIADES.   Socrates?
  Give him a shout!

1 STUDENT [*coldly*].   Give him a shout
  Yourself. I haven't time. . . .   [*Exit.*

STREPSIADES.   Socrates!
  Dear Socratesicles . . .

SOCRATES.   Why are you
  Addressing me, my fellow mortal?

STREPSIADES. Well, for a start, what are you doing up there?

SOCRATES [*grandly*]. Pacing the Air, conning the Sun.

STREPSIADES. Oh, I *see*. You're being truly high-minded!
  You look down on the gods—from your basket.
  That is, if you believe in . . .

SOCRATES. How could I come to any proper
    Conclusions about celestial problems
    Had I not so suspended my
    Perceptions and so intermingled my
    Delicate thought in a like element?
    How could I do this on the earth,
    For the earth compels the mind's
    Essence to itself, like watercress.

STREPSIADES. Really? The essence of one's mind
    Is drawn into watercress? Socrates!
    Come down at once and teach me all
    I need to be taught, please!

SOCRATES. What have you come for?

STREPSIADES.   To learn
    To equivocate like a lawyer.
    I'm up to the ears in pressing debts.
    The bailiffs are in, but I'm cleaned out.

SOCRATES. How did it happen? Didn't you see
    What was coming?

STREPSIADES.   It was horse-fever.
    It nearly killed me. Please teach me
    Your alternative system of argument—
    How not to pay debts. I'll pay *you*
    Anything—I swear by the gods.

SOCRATES. Which gods? I warn you, we don't regard
    The gods as viable currency.

STREPSIADES. What d'you use then? Byzantine iron?

SOCRATES. Would you really like to know the truth
    About heaven?

STREPSIADES.   By heaven, if there *is* any.

SOCRATES. And embrace the Clouds, our virgin
    Goddesses—in colloquy?

STREPSIADES.   I would.

SOCRATES. Then sit on that holy bed.

STREPSIADES.   I'm on it.

SOCRATES. And take this chaplet.

STREPSIADES.   Socrates—
Oh my lord, you're not going to offer me up
Like Athamas?

SOCRATES.   No, no, we perform
These rights by way of initiation.

STREPSIADES. But what shall I get out of it all?

SOCRATES. You'll become an assured, glib
Confidence-man, with a shifty tongue;
You'll sift words fine as flour; but please
Be quiet now.

STREPSIADES.   By Zeus, as it is
You're grinding and sprinkling me like flour!

SOCRATES. Keep holy silence now, old man, and attend to our
        prayer!
O Master, Lord, O Measureless Air that cradles the earth
In space, O shining Aether, O holy Cloud-goddesses,
Authors of thunder and lightning, rise! Manifest your presences,
Poised in the mid-heaven. Appear to your votary!

STREPSIADES.—Please wait a moment till I fold
My cloak over my head; like a fool
I've left my rainproof hat behind!

SOCRATES. Come then, all-hallowed Clouds, appear to this mortal
        man—
Whether you rest on the holy height of snow-crowned Olympus
Or in the watery bowers of Father Ocean, you dance
The choric measures to entrance the Nymphs, or it may be
Scoop up the waters of Nile-mouth in golden ewers,
Or parade the Maiotic lake or the high white crag of Mimas—
Hear our prayer and receive our sacrificial offerings!

                    Enter the Chorus *of Clouds.*

CHORUS.   O everflowing Clouds
               Come rise, appear,
               Our spirits dewy-bright
               From the deeps of Father Ocean!

               Come soon to the tree-crowned heights
               Of the peaks and let the full
               Far-stretching view of the distant
               Ranges be our horizon!

Let us view the earth and her crops
Ripe on her breast of water!
The divine flowing of rivers,
And the belling of the deep,

For the unwearying eye
Of Aether fires the Cosmos
With its light-kindling gaze.

Let us shake off the dark
Cloaks of cold-shrouding mist
From our immortal frames and sweep
The whole world with a look!

SOCRATES. Superbly, O Holy Goddesses, have you given
  A clear reply to my call. Did you not hear
  Their voices' ringing echo in the bellowing of the thunder?

STREPSIADES. Oh, I did, I worship you Holy Ones,
  But I can't help but compete
  Against your thunder with a fart.
  I'm so dithering with terror,
  Whether you like it or not,
  I can't help it, I'm taken short!

SOCRATES. Don't play the fool or behave like those dolts of comic
  poets.
  Keep a respectful silence—a great swarm
  Of goddesses comes humming with their song.

CHORUS.   Rain-bearing maidens come
               To the rich land of Pallas,
               The dear, dear land of Cecrops,
               The nurse of heroes,

               Where secret rites are celebrated
               In the numinous halls of Eleusis,
               Mystic initiations
               And sacrifice to the gods:

               The holy-of-holies disclosed,
               The votive gifts, and the blessed
               In solemn rapt processions
               And garlands everywhere.

Here festivals abound,
Hours of feasting and joy,
For seasons, for fecund spring.

The thrilling inspiring tones
Of the choric hymns,
The deep, enchanting notes
Of the clear flutes!

STREPSIADES. By the gods, Socrates, tell me
Who are these noble singers
—Daughters of antique heroes?

SOCRATES. No, no, they're heavenly clouds—great
Goddesses of the empty-headed.
They fill us with skill in Logic
And brain-waves and *savoir-faire*,
And the art of duping fools,
Garbling the truth, talking
Beside the point, spell-binding,
Meaningless oratory, and browbeating.

STREPSIADES. I shuddered to hear them, to the depths
Of my soul. And already I'm craving to babble
And argue about sweet nothings,
Put two and two together and make five
And then minus five. . . . If it's possible,
I'd like to see them clearly.

SOCRATES. Look there, towards Mount Parnes,
I can see them there already
Settling down softly.

STREPSIADES.   Where? Show me!

SOCRATES.   In a body,
Gliding slantwise over
The hollows and thickets . . .

STREPSIADES.   What's come over me?
I can't see them.

SOCRATES.   By the entrance . . .

STREPSIADES. I just caught a tiny glimpse.

SOCRATES. Now surely you can see them,
   Unless your eyes are stuck up
   With pumpkin-size lumps of gum.

STREPSIADES. I see them, the all-hallowed,
   By Zeus, they're everywhere.

SOCRATES. Didn't you know they were goddesses?

STREPSIADES. Good heavens, no! I'd been led
   To believe they were foggy dew.

SOCRATES. Then you don't know that they keep
   Most of the sophists fed,
   And the proselytizing prophets,
   Quack doctors, and long-haired poseurs
   Whose fingers you can't see
   For their rings, and the fake weather-
   Forecasters, and the poets,
   The metre-weavers and the chorus-coilers,
   And every layabout
   Who writes them a praising poem.

STREPSIADES. Ah! So that's why they write:
   'The swirling-vapourous-whirling-bright-
   And-violent-rushing' and
   'The locks of a hundred-pated Typho'
   And 'whirlwindy hairblowings' and 'air-floating birds'
   'Crook-talon'd solitary gliddering eagles'
   And 'dewy effluence moist with watery gushings'
   And for that crap, they gulp
   Great slices of eel and choice
   Thrush pies!

SOCRATES.   Isn't that right and proper?

STREPSIADES. If they're really and truly clouds,
   Please will you tell me why
   They're shaped like mortal women?

SOCRATES. What do you think they're like, then?

STREPSIADES. Can't say, exactly. Up there they seem
   Like spread-out fleeces, not at all
   Like women—and anyway, those have noses.

SOCRATES. Now answer my question.

STREPSIADES.   Get on
   And ask it then.

SOCRATES.   Have you never
   Looked up and seen a cloud
   Shaped like a centaur, or
   A leopard, or a wolf, or a bull?

STREPSIADES. Well, yes, I have. But why . . .?

SOCRATES. They assume what shapes they like.
   If they meet some matted shaggy
   Drunken boor—say like the son
   Of Xenophantes—they mock his
   Behaviour and turn into centaurs.

STREPSIADES. What do they do if they see
   That cash-grabbing harpy Simon?

SOCRATES. Embody his spirit and turn into wolves.

STREPSIADES. *I* see. And if they were quick enough
   To see the back of Cleonymos,
   After he'd chucked his shield away
   In a paroxysm of terror,
   I suppose they'd turn into deer?

SOCRATES. Exactly, Look! They must
   Have seen Cleisthenes today!
   That's why they've become . . . women!

STREPSIADES. Hail, mighty goddesses, all-powerful queens!
   And if you will deign to sing
   For anyone today, will you sing for me?

CHORUS. We welcome you, old veteran—one of the Old School
   Seeking for wisdom among the words of the new!
   And you, high priest of the subtlest rubbish, tell us
   What you desire. For among all the windbags
   Of the present day, it is to you we listen
   For your wisdom and learning—you who go strutting
   Barefoot along the street, your eyes darting,
   And under our proud protection prepared to endure
   Whatever mischance or evil may befall you.

STREPSIADES. O Earth! How beautiful a sound! How marvellous,
   holy, and solemn!

SOCRATES. These are the only goddesses! All the rest is nonsense.

STREPSIADES. By Earth! Isn't Zeus a god? The greatest god on
Olympus?

SOCRATES. What Zeus? There's no Zeus. Why do you talk such
drivel?

STREPSIADES. Really! Who sends the rain then? Explain that to
begin with.

SOCRATES. Why, *they* do. I can give as convincing proof as possible.
When have you ever seen it raining without clouds?
If *you're* right, one fine day he must rain from a clear heaven.

STREPSIADES. You've a point there, I admit, and very well made,
by Apollo!
I always believed before it was Zeus pissing through a sieve.
Then who sets off the thunder that makes me tremble?

SOCRATES. Their rolling through the air causes the thunder.

STREPSIADES. What daring of thought! How?

SOCRATES. When they're distended with water
And blown willy-nilly along through the sky, they jostle
And lurch against each other and clash in collision.

STREPSIADES. Ah, but who makes that happen? If it's not Zeus,
who is it?

SOCRATES. Not Zeus at all, it's Vortex.

STREPSIADES. I've never heard of Vortex.
Has he supplanted Zeus? But you haven't given a hint as
To how the noise is made.

SOCRATES. I have! I said they were brimful
Of water, didn't you hear me? And then they clang together.

STREPSIADES. It's hard to believe. How can I?

SOCRATES. I'll use your body to prove it.
Have you never stuffed yourself with stew at the Panathenaia
And heard your stomach rumble?

STREPSIADES. By Apollo, yes, a terrific
Commotion immediately. A regular stew-thunder.
First it goes Da . . . Da . . . Then louder, Datta . . . Damyadvam,
Then when I burst with a clatter it goes Damyatta, Damyatta.

SOCRATES. Then since a considerable noise issues from one small
stomach,
How from the boundless air other than mighty thunder?
The very words show the degree of difference. Fart. Thunder.

STREPSIADES. What about flashes of fiery lightning? Please instruct
    me.
  It shrivels one man to a cinder and simply tickles
  Another and leaves no mark—Surely Zeus fires the lightning
  At perjurers?

SOCRATES.   You were a musty old fool when Cronos was young.
  Fires it at perjurers? And yet he's never hit Simon,
  Cleonymos or Theoros—the pick of the perjurers!
  But he hits his very own temple and Sunium, Cape of Athens,
  And the biggest oaks. Would you say *oaks* were perjurers?

STREPSIADES. I couldn't think that, no! Then where does a thunder-
    bolt spring from?

SOCRATES. When a dry wind is whirled up in mid-air and enveloped
  In a cloud, the cloud swells up like an expanding bladder
  Till it bursts at pressure, hissing so fiercely that it ignites
  From its own compression and violence.

STREPSIADES.   By Zeus, that's just what happened
  To me at the feast! I was cooking a haggis for my relations,
  And I'd forgotten to prick it and it swelled and suddenly burst and
  Got me plumb in the eye and burnt my face!

CHORUS. Old Seeker after wisdom, if your powers of memory serve
    you
  And you summon your whole spirit to concentrated study
  You'll be the luckiest of Athenians, of all Greeks.
  Never grow slack, or weary, or flinch from the weight of your
    burden,
  Never slaver for supper; cut out wine, and the gymnasium,
  Eschew all follies, be sure this is the only solution
  For a wise man; to learn to use
  His tongue as a weapon to win him
  Whatever he choose.

STREPSIADES. If it's a matter of resolution, doing without sleep,
  And living on next to nothing, you'll find me
  Tough as an anvil to hammer.

SOCRATES.   Now please get
  Our pantheon into your head; we accept
  No other gods but Chaos, the Clouds, and the Tongue.
  These three and these alone.

STREPSIADES.   If I met other gods
   In the streets, I wouldn't even give them a nod,
   Let alone a libation, incense, or an offering.

CHORUS. Then tell us clearly what you want us to do.
   You honour us and revere us, you are resolved
   To learn wisdom—we, for our part, must not fail *you*.

STREPSIADES. Goddesses, it's only a very small thing I want:
   Simply I want to be streets ahead of everyone
   When it comes to argument.

CHORUS.   Very easily granted.
   Henceforward in the Assembly nobody
   Shall get more important measures passed than you shall!

STREPSIADES. No, no great measures, I don't want that at all.
   Just *little* ones, to pervert the course of justice
   Enough for me to escape my creditors.

CHORUS. Of course! That's only a trifle. Put yourself
   Without reservation in the hands of our agents.

STREPSIADES. I'll do what you say, I trust you,
   For I'm in a terrible jam.
   What with horses and ponies
   And wife-trouble, I'm fair bust.
   I'll surrender them my body
   To batter with hunger and thirst,
   To boil, freeze, flay, if that's
   The way I can dodge my debts.
   I'll master being a brassy
   Smooth-tongued, reckless, shameless,
   Go-getting, sophistical faker,
   Sharp in the law, a crook,
   A quibbling cunning pliable
   Liar, a bum, a proper old lag,
   A filthy trouble-making
   Dish-licker; I'll be delighted
   If I'm called all this to my face—
   If they like, they can mince me to sausage-meat
   For the students to eat for supper.

CHORUS. He certainly isn't feeble—he seems
   To have a firm resolve. Know then

You can win a sky-high fame
With what you learn from us.

STREPSIADES. What'll I get from it all?

CHORUS. For the rest of your life on earth
You'll be the most enviable
Of living men.

STREPSIADES.   Really?

CHORUS. You'll have a queue at your gate
Clamorous for advice
And consultation—you'll earn
A fortune with your replies.
A man of such ability
Can command any fee.
Socrates, take the old man's hand,
If you're going to teach him, begin
Trying out his intellect
And exercising his mind!

SOCRATES. Now tell me your way of life:
I've got to know; know what new
Technical gear to bring to bear.

STREPSIADES. Hey, now, what's in your mind?
You're not proposing to storm my walls?

SOCRATES. No, no, only ask some questions.
Is your memory good?

STREPSIADES.   It's a two-way memory.
If someone owes *me* I remember it.
If I owe someone, I'm a fool,
I clean forget it, somehow.

SOCRATES. Can you speak effectively?

STREPSIADES. Speak? No. Cheat? Yes.

SOCRATES. D'you think you can learn?

STREPSIADES. I'm sure I can.

SOCRATES.   So if I toss at you
Some metaphysical proposition
You could catch it in mid-air?

STREPSIADES. Snap at wisdom like
A dog at scraps?

SOCRATES.   The fellow's
   A barbarian lout!
   I'm afraid I may have to beat you.
   Now, if somebody *does* beat you
   What happens?
STREPSIADES.   I'm beaten. Then
   After a minute I get
   A witness, then I wait
   Another minute and then
   Summon him.
SOCRATES [*violently*]. Off with your cloak!
STREPSIADES. What've I done?
SOCRATES.   Nothing.
   Mufti's the rule here.
STREPSIADES. I'm not a plain-clothes detective, I haven't come
   With a warrant—
SOCRATES.   Off with it!   [Strepsiades *strips.*
   Stop talking nonsense.
STREPSIADES.   If I learn
   Really attentively and well
   Which student shall I be most like?
SOCRATES. The image of Chairephon.
STREPSIADES. Oh lord, only half-alive.
SOCRATES. Stop chattering. Follow me.   [*Leading him out.*
   Can't you go quicker?
STREPSIADES. Give me a honeycake first,
   It's like going into the cave
   Of Trophonios.
SOCRATES.   Come on!
   Stop hanging about the door.   [*Exeunt.*

CHORUS.   Go, and good luck to his courage!
               He deserves all he can, coming
               From the deepening twilight, eager
               To dip his ageing nature
               In these new dyes of wisdom!

   By Dionysus who brought me up, I intend to be
   Perfectly frank with you spectators—there's no other

Way to be judged a poet and win the prize. This
Comedy I consider the best of all my comedies,
And certainly it cost me the most blood and sweat,
So I wished you to be the first to sample it.
But the plays that defeated mine were so inferior
That I withdrew my play and began to question
Your critical judgement—for had it been as I thought it
My play could not have failed. But not even now
Do I really suspect your judgement, *at its best*—
For you liked my work from the very beginning approving
My characters 'Temperance' and 'Indulgence' in a play
I was too young to put my name to, a mere apprentice
Handing my first-born over to somebody else to care for;
But it was *you* who nurtured it truly and reared it,
And, ever since, you have given me your whole-hearted
Support and believed in my work.

                            Now comes my comedy,
Like Electra did to the tomb of Agamemnon,
To see if she can find, among you, a like recognition.
How modest and pure she is! She doesn't come on
Waving a property phallus to get a laugh
From the coarse children; she doesn't poke fun at bald-heads
Or flaunt her sex in an indecent dance;
There's no old man literally doing slap-stick
To bolster his rotten jokes. Nobody wildly rushes
On brandishing torches, there's no comical wailing—
This play relies on nothing but its merit!
—I'm what you know me, anything but a long-haired
Phoney, nor do I potboil the same theme twice.
I always come with new wit and original ideas,
All good and all 'perfectly unlike each other'.

It was when Cleon was all-powerful that I kicked him
In the guts; I never kicked him when he was down.
But look at these others—once Hyperbolos
Had given them their cue they knocked the daylights
Out of the wretched crook and his poor mother too.
Eupolis did it first in his play *Maricas*,
Pinching ideas from my *Knights* and making a mess of them,

Introducing a drunken old hag simply
To get in a Cordax dance— a thing Phrynichos
Did ages ago: at least he had a monster eat *his* old hag!

Then again, Hermippos attacked Hyperbolos
So all the others attacked Hyperbolos
—And lifted my image of eel-catching in the process.
A second-hand laugh at them won't exactly please me.
But if you think well of my invention and skill
Your critical acumen is assured for ever and ever.

> I summon Zeus, Lord
> Of gods, to my grand chorus;
> And the all-powerful wielder
> Of the Trident, the upheaver
> Of Earth and the salty sea;
> And our fame-bestowing Father
> Most holy life-giving Aether;
> And Apollo, charioteer
> Of the glittering circuit, peerless
> Among gods above and well-
> Beloved among earth-dwellers.

Wisest of spectators, direct your thoughts towards us.
You wronged us once and rightly we hold it against you.
Of all the gods we are the gods who have helped your city,
Helped you the most, yet we are the only gods
You do not sacrifice to nor pour libations to.

If you make some crazy fantastic plan,
We thunder at you, we sluice down rain.
When you chose that awful tanner Paphlagon,
Bane of the gods, as general, we bent our brows
In chasmal frowns—thunder and lightning clashed,
The moon veered from her course, the sun straight away
Drew his wick into himself and stated that if
You made Cleon general he wouldn't shine on you
Another day. *But that's just what you did do!*
There's a saying that when in this city bad counsel prospers,
The worse your mistakes are, the more the gods turn them
To equivalent good—and anyone can see
How this actually happens! So, if you accuse

Cleon of bribery and theft, put him in the pillory.
And then, as before, all the mistakes you've made
Will turn out fine for the State and for everybody.

             Phoebus, come as of old,
             Delian lord, holder
             Of Cynthia's up-jutting cliff;
             You virgin of Ephesus
             In your temple of pure gold
             Whom Lydian girls revere;
             O you our country's goddess,
             Athene, aegis-bearer,
             Our protectress; you, Dionysus,
             Master of high Parnassus,
             Glowing with torchlit revel
             And bacchanals from Delphi!

As we were getting ourselves ready to come down here,
The moon happened to meet us and bade us convey,
First of all, good wishes to Athens and her allies.
But then to say she was cross. You've made her suffer,
Though the help she gives you is never just in words
But in actual fact. She puts it to you like this.
It's night: you're suddenly called out on business
And you shout 'Boy! Don't bring a torch, the moonlight's
Quite strong enough!' And she helps you in various other
Ways, but you don't help her. You juggle with the calendar
So much she says the gods, all of them, curse her:
They turn up for a banquet and find there isn't one,
And feel defrauded and trail home hungry and angry
Because they haven't got the date of the banquet right,
According to the calendar. Then on some festival
When *you* ought to be in the temples sacrificing,
You're quarrelling in the courts and grilling witnesses;
And many a time we gods are fasting and mourning
The death of a Memnon or a Sarpedon, you
Are pouring libations and laughing at a feast.
We were so angry because of all this muddle
We saw to it that when Hyperbolos
Had got the office of Keeper of Holy Archives

His garland got blown off. . . . Perhaps he'll take
The hint and order all the rest of his life
According to the proper directions of the moon!

The scene is again outside the Logic factory.
Enter Socrates.

SOCRATES. By Breath-of-Life, by Chaos, by Air!
I never saw such a doddering fool.
He's clueless, gripless, hopeless, witless.
He can't grasp the simplest gambit
For a second before forgetting it.
I'll get him out into the light!
Strepsiades, bring your couch out here!

STREPSIADES [*inside*]. The bugs won't let me.

Enter Strepsiades, *carrying his couch.*

SOCRATES.   Yes, they will.
Now listen to me—

STREPSIADES.   I'm listening.

SOCRATES. Of all the thousand and one things
You've never learnt, what shall I teach you
First? Measures? Rhythms? Use of
Vocabulary?

STREPSIADES.   Measures, please.
The grocer gave me short measure
The other day.

SOCRATES.   I didn't meant that.
Poetry measures! Feet! Six or eight!

STREPSIADES. I never like more than a yard
Of anything.

SOCRATES.   Crass old ass!

STREPSIADES. But feet *do* make yards, I bet you.

SOCRATES. Oh, to hell with you! Perhaps
You'll get rhythm more easily.

STREPSIADES. Do I buy rhythm at the grocers?

SOCRATES. Will nothing civilize him? I'll try:
Is a dactylic rhythm best
For a war-song or a lullaby?

STREPSIADES. Count time on my fingers, eh?
I can do that.

SOCRATES.   Do it then!

STREPSIADES. Stuff it up with *this* finger now,
When I was a baby, *this* one.

SOCRATES. You're all thumbs, you old fool.

STREPSIADES. Old fool yourself! I simply don't
Want to learn this.

SOCRATES.   What do you want?

STREPSIADES. You *know*! False logic.

SOCRATES.   You must learn
Other things first: name me some males
Among quadrupeds.

STREPSIADES.   Me—from the country!
I'd be daft if I didn't know.
Ram, goat, bull, dog, fowl.

SOCRATES. You see! At once you're inaccurate.

STREPSIADES. How?

SOCRATES.   Which is male or female?

STREPSIADES. Come again?

SOCRATES.   Fowl and fowl.

STREPSIADES.   I see,
But what shall I say?

SOCRATES.   Call one
A hencock, the other a cock-hen.

STREPSIADES. A hencock! Fine, by Aether!
This bit of information alone
Is worth a troughful of barley. Bring him one,
I'll fill it to the brim!

SOCRATES. Him? There you go again—it's her.

STREPSIADES. Sorry, what's the matter?

SOCRATES.   Cleonymos.

STREPSIADES. Cleonymos. Where does *he* come in?

SOCRATES. 'Trough', 'Cleonymos'—male gender.

STREPSIADES. But he hasn't *got* a trough—
Well, not exactly. . . . He's got a nice
Round mortar and his bread is ground
By other people's pestles. What
Ought I to say in future?

SOCRATES.   A she-trough.
  A she-name like Sostraté.

STREPSIADES. A feminine trough?

SOCRATES.   That's right.

STREPSIADES.   I see.
  Miss Virgin Trough. Miss . . . Cleonymos?

SOCRATES. There's more to learn about people's names.
  Which are men's names? And which, women's?

STREPSIADES. I know *plenty* of women's.

SOCRATES.   Well?

STREPSIADES. Lysilla, Philinna, Cleitagora,
  Demetria.

SOCRATES.   Now any men's?

STREPSIADES. Thousands! Philoxenos,
  Melesias, Amynias . . .

SOCRATES. Those aren't masculine!

STREPSIADES.   Aren't men?

SOCRATES. Not a bit. If you met him,
  How would you greet Amynias?

STREPSIADES. I'd call 'Amynia'!

SOCRATES. Exactly! A woman's name.

STREPSIADES.   True!
  He's slinked out of the army. But why
  Must I learn what everyone knows?

SOCRATES.—Which is nothing. Onto that couch!

STREPSIADES. And do what?

SOCRATES.   Contemplate
  The state of your own affairs.

STREPSIADES. Not there, I *implore* you! If
  I must, then let me contemplate
  On the bare ground.

SOCRATES.   No!
  This is the only way.

STREPSIADES. Oh heaven, what a beating
  I'll take from the bugs today!   [*Lies down.*

SOCRATES. Now you must probe deep to the still centre:
  Let your whole life spin round you now,

And if you come to some dead end don't
Be baffled—simply direct your mind
To another channel. And *keep awake*!

STREPSIADES. Ow! Ow! Ow!

SOCRATES.   What's upsetting you?

STREPSIADES. I'm finished! I'm dead!
These Corinthian bugs
Have probed me deep!
From the four corners
Of the bed, they're stripping
My ribs, swilling
My blood, pulling
My balls off, tunnelling
Up my arse, they're killing me!

                                        [*Throws off the blanket.*

CHORUS. Don't take it too much to heart!

STREPSIADES. *Me*? [*Ironically.*] How could I? I've only
Lost all my money, lost
My colour, my blood, my shoes,
And to add to these trifles as
I hum to keep awake
I'm becoming almost a total
Loss myself.

SOCRATES.   You, there!
What are you doing? Thinking?

STREPSIADES. By Poseidon, what do you think?

SOCRATES. Come to any conclusions?

STREPSIADES. I'm wondering if the bugs
Will eat me whole.

SOCRATES.   You dolt!
May you be destroyed!

STREPSIADES.   My dear fellow,
I almost *am*!

SOCRATES.   Don't flinch!
Pull up the blankets, apply
Your mind to the problem of cheating
And duping the suckers whether
They're creditors or bugs.

STREPSIADES. I couldn't cheat them! How could anyone
    Apply his mind to cheating
    Under this crawling sheepskin?

                         [*He pulls it over him again.*

SOCRATES. I'll see what he's up to now.
    You there, are you asleep?

STREPSIADES [*emerging*]. Great god! How could I be?

SOCRATES. Got a grip on anything?

STREPSIADES.   No.

SOCRATES. Nothing?

STREPSIADES.   I've got my cock
    In my right hand.

SOCRATES.   Under you go,
    And think more quickly.

STREPSIADES.   Socrates,
    What shall I think about?

SOCRATES. What shall we aim at first?

STREPSIADES. I've told you a thousand times—
    How not to pay my debts.

SOCRATES. Down you go! Use your mind,
    Make a close analysis
    Of every point. Break it down.

                        [Strepsiades *lies down again.*

STREPSIADES [*scratching*]. Oh dear . . . oh dear . . . oh dear . . .

SOCRATES. Stop *shuddering*, please!
    If you get stuck shift
    Your ground to something else,
    Then back to the beginning
    And try everything again.

STREPSIADES. Not the bugs . . . oh, *dear* Socrates!

SOCRATES. What?

STREPSIADES.   I've got it, I've found a way
    To escape my debts.

SOCRATES.   Go on, tell me. . . .

STREPSIADES. Will you listen?

SOCRATES.   Go *on*, tell me!

STREPSIADES. If I employed a Thessalian witch
  I might conjure the moon down
  Overnight and shut her up
  In a round box, like a mirror,
  And keep guard over her.

SOCRATES. How d'you think that'd help you?

STREPSIADES. If the moon weren't there to rise
  And shine I wouldn't have
  To pay my debts. . . .

SOCRATES.   Why not?

STREPSIADES. We pay interest by the month.

SOCRATES. Excellent! Now I'll put you
  Another possibility.
  Suppose you lost a lawsuit
  And were liable to pay
  Five talents—tell me how
  Would you get out of that?

STREPSIADES. Oh dear! I don't know! I must think!

                              [*Goes under the blanket.*

SOCRATES. Don't always wrap your thoughts
  Close round you—give them air,
  Like maybugs children tether
  By the leg with a thread.

STREPSIADES. I've got a scheme!
  You'll have to admit it's brilliant.

SOCRATES.   What?

STREPSIADES. You must have seen at the druggist
  That gorgeous transparent stone
  You can generate fire with—

SOCRATES. A burning glass?

STREPSIADES.   That's it.
  Get hold of one of these,
  And when the clerk's writing out
  The charge I'll stand a bit off,
  In the direct line
  Of the sun's rays, and burn
  Every line out of it!

SOCRATES.   By the Graces!
Excellent!

STREPSIADES. I'm delighted!
I've burned five talents out!

SOCRATES. Now snap this up.

STREPSIADES.   What?

SOCRATES. How would you stop a case
That's going against you and likely
To be lost for lack of witness?

STREPSIADES. Easy as pie.

SOCRATES.   Well?

STREPSIADES.   Like this.
If there was one case
Before mine was called I'd go
And hang myself.

SOCRATES.   What *nonsense!*

STREPSIADES. They couldn't prosecute me
If I were dead. . . .

SOCRATES.   Clotted *nonsense!*
I won't teach you another thing.

STREPSIADES. Why not? *Do*, Socrates!

SOCRATES. What's the point? You forget
All you've been taught as soon
As I teach you. What was the very
First thing I taught you? Answer!

STREPSIADES. What was it. . . . Oh, what was it . . .?

SOCRATES. You forgetful, dim old booby!
Get out!   [*Turns away.*

STREPSIADES. Oh dear . . . oh . . . dear. . . .
I'm done if I don't learn
How to use my tongue. . . . Clouds,
What ought I to do?

CHORUS. If you've a son, send him
To learn, here, instead of you.

STREPSIADES. Oh yes, I've a son all right,
A real little gentleman,

But he doesn't want to learn.
Oh . . . oh . . . what shall I do?

CHORUS. Is he obedient?

STREPSIADES. Well . . . er . . . He's well-built,
He's in the flower of his strength,
He's got blue blood in his veins,
But . . . . Well, I'll go to him and by heaven,
If he won't play, I'll turn him
Out of the house (if he's still
In the house)! [*To* Socrates.] You go inside
And wait for me a moment. . . .

[*He goes into his own house.*

CHORUS [*to* Socrates]. Don't you understand yet, how it's only us
Of all the gods who provide you
With all you need? The old dunce
Is infatuated with your school—
He's eating out of your hand:
So soak him quick, and to the full,
Make your hay while his sun shines!

Strepsiades *and* Pheidippides *come out of their house.*

STREPSIADES. By Holy Mist, I simply won't have you
Stay here a moment longer. GET OUT
To your uncle Megacles and eat *him*
Out of house and home!

PHEIDIPPIDES.   Whatever's wrong?
Poor old da! By Zeus on Olympus
You've gone out of your mind!

STREPSIADES.   Zeus!
Zeus on Olympus—you're utterly hopeless;
You, at your age, believing in Zeus!

PHEIDIPPIDES. What's so funny?

STREPSIADES.   It's fantastic
When a young man like you believes
Such outdated claptrap. Listen to me,
I'll give you a clue or so to grow you
Up, if you understand me. But kindly
Don't tell anyone else—

PHEIDIPPIDES.   Well?

STREPSIADES. Swear by Zeus.

PHEIDIPPIDES.   I swear by Zeus.

STREPSIADES. There! You see how good it is to learn.
    Pheidippides, *there is no Zeus!*

PHEIDIPPIDES. Who's God then?

STREPSIADES.   Vortex. He drove Zeus out.

PHEIDIPPIDES. What rot!

STREPSIADES.   It's true.

PHEIDIPPIDES.   Who says it's true?

STREPSIADES. The Melian. Socrates. Chairephon.
    He knows how to measure the jumps of fleas.

PHEIDIPPIDES. And you're dotty enough to trust these clots?

STREPSIADES. Please! Don't insult these brilliant servants!
    They're so economical. They don't shave,
    Don't go to the baths to wash like you—
    And wash me clean as a corpse in doing it.
    Now, you must come and learn for me.

PHEIDIPPIDES. What's worth learning from dopes like them?

STREPSIADES. Dear boy, whatever wisdom *is*
    In the whole world, what wisdom *is*!
    You'll see how sluggish and slow you are—
    But wait a moment; I'll soon be back.   [*Exit.*

PHEIDIPPIDES. What am I to do? He's off his nut.
    Shall I have him certified, or alert
    The undertakers?

                    Re-enter Strepsiades.

STREPSIADES.   You see this?

PHEIDIPPIDES. A barnyard fowl.

STREPSIADES.   Precisely. And this?

PHEIDIPPIDES. A ditto.

STREPSIADES.   You make me laugh.
    In future, kindly distinguish a hencock
    From a cock-hen. Be accurate.

PHEIDIPPIDES. A hencock? So these are the tremendous
    Secrets these modern atheist Titans
    Vouchsafe their votaries?

STREPSIADES [*seriously*].   —Oh, there's much
  Much more, but I'm too old—
  I forget what I'm told as quick as I learn.

PHEIDIPPIDES. That how you lost your cloak?

STREPSIADES.   I haven't
  Exactly lost it—I've thought it
  Out of existence.

PHEIDIPPIDES.   Same with your sandals?

STREPSIADES. They were a necessary
  Expendable, as Pericles used to say.
  But come with me, do what I tell you now:
  You can misbehave later. When you
  Were a little boy I used to spoil you
  And do what *you* asked—with the very first
  Obol I earned as a juryman
  I bought you a little pushcart
  At the Spring feast. . . .

PHEIDIPPIDES.   You'll regret this
  One day, but . . .

STREPSIADES.   Thank you, you're a good boy.
  —Hey! Socrates, come out—here's
  My son, I've won him over.

SOCRATES.   Poor innocent,
  And he knows nothing yet of the technique
  Of hanging up in a basket.

PHEIDIPPIDES.   If
  I hung you up you'd look like an old cloak
  With the moth in it.

STREPSIADES.   How dare you
  Insult the master-mind?

SOCRATES.   How affectedly
  He mouthed his silly words—how could *he*
  Learn to argue his way out
  Of a lawsuit or a summons
  Or a weak position in dispute?
  Yet for one talent Hyperbolos
  Mastered the lot.

STREPSIADES.   Don't worry; he'll learn.
　　He's very quick by nature. Why,
　　When he was just so high he made
　　His own toy houses, he carved boats,
　　He knocked up miniature carts from leather,
　　Cut frogs from pomegranates—
　　You'd really have loved them. So please teach him
　　Your two systems of Logic—the true and better,
　　The false and worse, where the false
　　Defeats the true; and if you can't
　　Teach *both*, teach him the false.

SOCRATES. I'm going in now. Let him hear them
　　Argue it for himself.   [*Exit.*

STREPSIADES. Remember he must be able
　　To confound all truth and justice,
　　Of whatever sort, completely.

　　　　　　　　Enter True Logic; False Logic *following*.

TRUE LOGIC. Come out and show yourself
　　To the audience, brash as you are.

FALSE LOGIC. Anything you like—I'd prefer
　　To beat you in front of a crowd.

TRUE LOGIC. You beat me? Who are you?

FALSE LOGIC. Logic.

TRUE LOGIC.   But False Logic!

FALSE LOGIC. Though you say you've the better case,
　　I can beat you.

TRUE LOGIC.   By what tricks?

FALSE LOGIC. Finding new arguments.

TRUE LOGIC. You couldn't flourish if
　　There weren't so many fools.

FALSE LOGIC.—Wise people, you mean.

TRUE LOGIC. I'll destroy you and your lies.

FALSE LOGIC.   How?

TRUE LOGIC. Saying what's just and true.

FALSE LOGIC. I can easily counter that:
　　I assert that such a thing
　　As pure justice doesn't exist.

TRUE LOGIC. Doesn't *exist*?

FALSE LOGIC.   Where does it reside, then?

TRUE LOGIC. With the gods.

FALSE LOGIC. With the gods?
And Zeus put his father in chains
And got clean away with it.
How was that?

TRUE LOGIC.   Blasphemy!
I feel sick. A basin, quick!

FALSE LOGIC. You stupid old diehard!

TRUE LOGIC. You unprincipled pig!

FALSE LOGIC. You crown me with roses. . . .

TRUE LOGIC.   You lickspittle!

FALSE LOGIC. And lilies. . . .

TRUE LOGIC.   You parricide!

FALSE LOGIC.   And
You don't even know you
Shower gold on my head!

TRUE LOGIC. Such a charge used to be lead.

FALSE LOGIC. But now it's an honour.

TRUE LOGIC. You're too bold.

FALSE LOGIC.   You're too old.

TRUE LOGIC. Now, none of the young generation
Wants to attend the schools,
Because of you and your like—
But one day the people of Athens
Will wake up to how you've taught them
To be fools.

FALSE LOGIC. How squalid you look!

TRUE LOGIC.   I'll admit you look smart
Yet you *were* a beggar,
Whining 'I'm Telephos',
Fumbling in your wallet
For stolen crumbs of
Pandeletos' wit
To mumble and chew.

FALSE LOGIC.   Alas, for the wisdom you mock!

TRUE LOGIC. Alas, for the folly of Athens
    That allows you to ruin the young!

FALSE LOGIC. *You* teach this boy, you—
    Older than Cronos . . .

TRUE LOGIC. If he wants to be saved
    From learning empty patter . . .

FALSE LOGIC [*to* Pheidippides]. You, come here to me! *He's* mad!

TRUE LOGIC. Don't you dare touch him!

CHORUS. Stop all this scrapping and bickering.
    You, sir, expound your ancient traditions;
    And you, the latest up-to-date methods;
    And let him listen and make up his mind
    Which of your schools he'll choose to attend.

TRUE LOGIC. I'll do that.

FALSE LOGIC.   I agree too.

CHORUS. Who'll speak first?

FALSE LOGIC. I'll give him the honour with pleasure,
    And whatever lines of argument
    He takes, I'll cap them with subtle new
    Twists and if he's got a word to say
    I'll set my arguments on his face
    And eyes, like hornets, and sting him to death!

CHORUS. Now these two exponents reliant upon the dexterity
    And brilliance of their words, will demonstrate their skill:
    We'll see who's the better. Meanwhile this modern wisdom
    Of our followers is in jeopardy.
    Sir, you that have crowned
    Older generations with so many virtues, plead
    The cause dear to your heart: acquaint us with your views.

TRUE LOGIC. I shall expatiate on the discipline
    Of olden times as it used to be pursued,
    When I taught Justice to thrive and Temperance
    Was revered.
                And this was our first of maxims:
    A boy must hold his tongue among his elders.
    He must pass through the streets to the music schools
    Soberly and in concert with the boys

Of his own district stripped even when
The snow was falling. Once there, they must stand
Firmly with thighs apart and learn the old songs:
'Pallas the dread destroyer of cities', 'The
Far-Ringing War-Cry'—keeping clear solemn tones
As their fathers before them; and if any dared
To use tremolo or shakes like Phrynis does,
In his flowery new fashion, he would have got
The cane as being a foe to the Muse. And if
They sat in the wrestling school they sat with thighs
Outstretched in a decent posture, modest to the view,
And if they stood they smoothed the indented sand
To leave no mould for pederastian eye.
No one used oil below the navel—thus
Their parts were delicate, their hairs like peach down.
None cooed and minced towards a lover, none
Flaunted his pretty charms before his fellows.
Greed was abhorred, it was taboo to snatch
Radish tops, aniseed, or parsley before your elders,
Or to nibble kickshaws and giggle and twine one's feet.

FALSE LOGIC. Fustian musty nonsense dating
From obsolete festivals,
Stuffy gold cicalas, and anthems
By Kekides about blood!

TRUE LOGIC. This teaching built the men of Marathon!
But you teach them immediately to swathe
Their bodies in cloaks, so that I am enraged
Whenever I see them dancing at the games,
Holding their shields over their cocks, not caring
A fig for Athene. Therefore, be bold, young fellow,
And plump for me who have the better method.
So, you shall learn to hate the Agora,
And shun the baths and feel ashamed of smut;
And learn the proper riposte if you are mocked,
And to get up and give your seat to your elders,
And not to behave towards your parents rudely,
But to do nothing base and make your life
The model for a perfect epitaph.

Learn, too, never to have resort to brothels,
For if you become a regular, some courtesan
Will toss you an apple in the public street
And your whole reputation will be lost.
Don't answer your father back, or call him an old fogey,
Mocking his age—for it marks the honoured end
Of a lifetime's concern for your own welfare.

FALSE LOGIC. If you fall for that stuff you won't be
    Man enough even to stand
    Up to the sons of Hippocrates:
    They'll call you a soft sissy.

TRUE LOGIC. You will become the star of the gymnasium,
    Not swopping dirty stories and dirty gossip
    In the Agora as they do now; you won't be
    Dragged into court by a blackmail-mealy-mouth,
    You'll go to the Academy and in friendly rivalry
    Under the olive trees, race with some virtuous
    Friend of your own age chapleted with white reed,
    Fragrant with poplar-scent, a man untrammelled
    In spirit under the leaf-shedding lime, delighting
    In Spring when the plane rustles to the elm. . . .

                    Follow my precepts, steep
                    Your mind in them and keep
                    Clean breast and shining skin,
                    Broad shoulders, seemly tongue,
                    Strong thews, a modest cock;
                    But if you copy what
                    The up-to-date have got—
                    Mean shoulders, narrow chest,
                    Loud tongue and weak thews,
                    A giant of a cock, and endless
                    Measures to argue through—
                    You'll fall into the perverse
                    Mood of calling all
                    That is good bad, and, worse,
                    All that is bad, good;
                    And soon he'll fill you as full
                    Of filth as Antimachos!

CHORUS. You practise a beautiful lofty form of idealism!
   How sweet is the prudent blossoming of your words.
   Oh, lucky were they who lived in the days of old.
   [*To* False Logic.] Now as to this—you with your finicking Muse
   Must find new arguments to offset this master
   Who has put his case so nobly; you'll need to split
   Every hair of your wit or he'll defeat you utterly,
   And you'll become a public laughing-stock.

FALSE LOGIC. I've split my guts with frustration,
   So craving to put *my* side.
   If students call me weaker or false
   It's just because I was first
   To put valid counter-arguments
   Against laws and old customs.
   It's worth more than a thousand to me
   To prevail with my False Logic.
   Listen to me. I'll show how to knock
   His sort of education
   Sideways! So you mustn't have baths?
   Why not? Give me your reason.

TRUE LOGIC. It's very bad for a man, it enervates him.

FALSE LOGIC. Stop there! I've got you! You can't get out.
   Of all Zeus's sons tell me
   Who was 'the finest hero' in arms,
   And doing the most labours?

TRUE LOGIC. Why, Heracles. There's nobody better.

FALSE LOGIC. The 'baths of Heracles' are hardly
   Cold springs—yet who was braver?

TRUE LOGIC. This is it exactly. The sort of quibble
   These young slops like to use, and so the baths
   Are full and the wrestling schools are all empty.

FALSE LOGIC. So you attack market-place debates.
   I approve them. Were it wrong,
   Homer would never have made Nestor
   A market-lounger—like all
   Our wisest men. I turn to the art

Of speaking, which he avers
Is wrong for young men. I've shown it's not.
Next he says you must be chaste.
Both these concepts are quite misconceived.
What good has anyone got
Out of being chaste, I'd like to know?

TRUE LOGIC. It's often happened. Peleus won a sword!

FALSE LOGIC. A sword! *What* a prize! The lampmaker—
Hyperbolos—has made more
Talents out of crookery than I
Care to think of, but never
A sword, he has *never* got a sword!

TRUE LOGIC. But Peleus, by his chastity, won Thetis.

FALSE LOGIC. And she left him at once, didn't she?
He wasn't sexy enough
In bed—women enjoy lovemaking.
You're antediluvian!
[*To* Pheidippides.] You see what's in this chastity-lark?
All the fun you'll be without?
Nice boys, women, games of cottabos,
Savouries, drinking, laughing—
What sort of life is it without them?
Then take our natural needs:
You make love, you're caught, you're arrested:
You're done for if you can't speak.
But follow my example, follow
Your feelings—do as you please,
Be gay, think nothing is immoral!
If you're caught in the wrong bed,
Tell the husband you've done nothing wrong!
Cite Zeus. *He* wouldn't resist
Love and lovely women. You're mortal—
Could you succeed where Zeus failed?

TRUE LOGIC. But even so, suppose after trusting you
He's still convicted and gets a seducer's sentence,
How can you prove to him he's not a seducer?

FALSE LOGIC. Why should I bother? What's wrong in it?

TRUE LOGIC. But is there anything worse?

FALSE LOGIC. Suppose I can prove there is,
   Will you admit defeat?

TRUE LOGIC. I'd have to. Well, what?

FALSE LOGIC.   Answer me this: what sort of men
   Are our public prosecutors?

TRUE LOGIC. Convicted buggers.

FALSE LOGIC.   And our tragic playwrights?

TRUE LOGIC. Convicted buggers.

FALSE LOGIC.   You're right. And our orators?

TRUE LOGIC. Convicted buggers.

FALSE LOGIC. You agree you've been talking nonsense?
   Now what about most of the audience?
   Look at them well.

TRUE LOGIC.   I am.

FALSE LOGIC. Well?

TRUE LOGIC. Most of them . . . yes . . .
   Him . . . and him . . . and him . . .
   And that long-haired b——

FALSE LOGIC. So what?

TRUE LOGIC. I lose. Oh my dear fellow-buggers,
   By heaven, take my cloak!
   I must change sides and come
   Over to you.

                                             [*He does so.*

                    Re-enter Socrates.

SOCRATES. Now what'd you like?
   To remove your son at once
   Or shall I teach him?

STREPSIADES. Teach him, beat him, sharpen him up—
   One edge for small matters
   Of Law, and one for greater.

SOCRATES. Very well. We will make him
   A first-rate sophist.

STREPSIADES.   As pale
   And miserable as they come!

                    [*Exeunt* Socrates *and* Pheidippides.

CHORUS. Go then, but we can't help thinking you'll soon think
    better.
  Now we propose to tell the judges how they'll prosper
  If they help this Chorus to win, as it certainly ought to.
  Well then, in early spring you want your fields made fertile?
  We'll rain on yours first, and keep all the rest waiting.
  We'll take the greatest care of your crops and vineyards,
  Safeguarding them from shrivelling drought and cloudburst.
  But if some wayward mortal fails to honour our godhead
  He'd better resign himself to the sort of ills he'll suffer.
  He'll get no wine nor any produce from all his holdings;
  Whenever his olive trees or his vineyards ought to blossom
  We'll crush them, our stings will strike with inexorable precision;
  Whenever we see him building we'll hurl down huge hailstones
  And smash every tile—and if his friends and relations
  Have come to a marriage feast we'll rain nightlong so heavily
  He'd rather live in arid Egypt than judge wrongly!

STREPSIADES. Five, four, three, two—
  And then the ghastliest day of all!
  I shudder at it; I loathe the thought:
  The day of the old moon and the new!
  And everyone I happen to owe
  Has sworn to put his deposit down
  And bring me to court and ruin me.
  And when I say 'Be reasonable,
  Defer, remit, don't ask for the lot,
  Dear friends', they say that at this rate
  They'll never get any satisfaction
  And curse me—call me a crook
  And demand action. Let 'em, I say!
  Little I care if only my boy
  Pheidippides has been properly taught.
  I'll go and knock on the school door!
  Hey! Hey! Hey! Boy!   [*Knocks.*

                Socrates *comes out.*

SOCRATES. Ah, my dear fellow, I embrace you!

STREPSIADES. And I you. But take this present first:
  It's right to give a teacher his due.

Now, about my son: has he properly learnt
The Logic you demonstrated a moment ago?

SOCRATES. He's mastered it.

STREPSIADES.   Here's to the comprehensive
Crookery school!

SOCRATES.   You can oil yourself
Out of any lawsuit you like.

STREPSIADES. Even with witnesses present
When I borrowed the money?

SOCRATES.   The more
The merrier—thousands if you like!

STREPSIADES. Then I shall sing at the top of my voice
'O weep, you obol-weighers, weep!'
You won't trouble my sleep again.
What a son I've got from this factory!
His tongue a two-edged shining sword,
Defender, saviour of my house!
Disaster to my foes!
Looser of all his father's woes!
My boy, my child, come out at once—
Your father's calling you!

SOCRATES. Here he is.

                    Enter Pheidippides.

STREPSIADES. My dear, dear lad.

SOCRATES. Take him and go!   [*Exit.*

STREPSIADES. How I rejoice
In the beauty of your pinched pallid face!
I see you've a fractious, contradictious,
Confutatious look, a what-
Have-*you*-to-say-next look, our native expression,
And I'm sure you can simulate
Injured innocence when it's you
Doing the injury—there's a real
Glint of Athens in your eye.
Now it's your turn: you nearly killed me,
It's up to you to save me.

PHEIDIPPIDES. What's the matter?

STREPSIADES.   The old and new day.

PHEIDIPPIDES. What day's that?

STREPSIADES. The day of reckoning,
When creditors put down their deposits.

PHEIDIPPIDES. Those who do will lose them:
How can one day be two?

STREPSIADES. Why not?

PHEIDIPPIDES. You might as well say
A woman can be old and young at the same time.

STREPSIADES. That's the law, though.

PHEIDIPPIDES. I think the meaning
Of the law's misinterpreted.

STREPSIADES. You tell me.

PHEIDIPPIDES. Old Solon was
A lover of the people at heart.

STREPSIADES. What's that to do with the old and new?

PHEIDIPPIDES. He fixed the summonses for *two* days: for the old
and new.

STREPSIADES. But why did he add the old?

PHEIDIPPIDES. On the old day the debtors
Could get rid of their creditors—if they couldn't,
They could fight it out on the next day.

STREPSIADES. Why do they take the deposits on both the old and new,
And not just on the new?

PHEIDIPPIDES. I think they aim to behave
Like gourmands, they want to have
These deposits as soon as possible,
And therefore gormandize them
On the first day.

STREPSIADES [*to his unseen creditors*]. Look at you, dumb fools!
Why do you stay like stone, sheer sitting targets
For us clever ones—a mere lot; a flock
Of sheep; a pile of empties? Pathetic
I must sing an encomium to our luck,
Me and my boy:

Happy, splendid Strepsiades!
How clever you are, you
And the clever boy you've got!

          Kind friends say it, jealous
          Neighbours whisper it,
          When you win all your suits!
Now, my dear boy, come in, I must give you a feast.

                                          [*Exeunt.*

            Enter Pasias, *with* Witness.

PASIAS. Is it right, man, for a man
  To forgo his own, I ask you? Never!
  Better refuse at once, look you,
  Than get tangled up like this
  When to get my money, *my* money, back,
  I have to hoick you along to be my witness,
  Because of this quarrel with my neighbour; but
  Never while I live could I shame my country, is it?
  I shall summon Strepsiades.
  Come out, man, Strepsiades!

                Enter Strepsiades.

STREPSIADES.   What's up?
PASIAS. The old and the new day.
STREPSIADES [*to* Witness].   I call you to witness
  He has named *two* days. What's
  Your business?
PASIAS.   Twelve good minas
  You borrowed from me, indeed,
  To buy that dapple-grey horse!
STREPSIADES. Horse? D'you hear, sir, horse?
  Everyone knows I abominate
  Anything to do with horses.
PASIAS. By Zeus you swore, man, and all the gods,
  Pay me you would.
STREPSIADES.   Well, by Zeus,
  Pheidippides hadn't learnt
  Irrefutable logic then.
PASIAS. Is it bilk me you mean to try?
STREPSIADES. What was the point of my paying
  For him to learn it then?
PASIAS. And dare you deny an oath by the gods?
STREPSIADES. What gods?

PASIAS.   Gods, is it? Zeus, Poseidon,
  Hermes . . .

STREPSIADES. By Zeus, I'd give
  Three obols for the pleasure.

PASIAS. Shocking! May you be struck!

STREPSIADES. You tun-belly, you'd better
  Be rubbed with salt.

PASIAS. Are you making a butt of me?

STREPSIADES. He'll hold a good six gallons.

PASIAS. By mighty Zeus and all
  The gods, you won't escape me!

STREPSIADES. You and your gods. Really,
  Swearing by Zeus is a mockery
  To enlightened people.

PASIAS.   The time
  Will come you'll pay for those wicked words.
  But will you pay *me* or not?
  Tell me before I go.

STREPSIADES.   Be patient and
  I'll give you a clear answer.   [*Exit.*

PASIAS. What do you think he's going to do?

WITNESS. Get the cash and pay up, I suppose.

          Re-enter Strepsiades *with trough.*

STREPSIADES. Now where's this rapacious dun?
  What's this?

PASIAS [*misunderstanding*]. He's my witness, man.

STREPSIADES. Calling a trough 'he'—
  And you ask for money?
  Give money to a man who
  Doesn't know the sex
  Of a trough? Not an obol!

PASIAS. You won't pay me, is it?

STREPSIADES. Not if I know it. Now,
  Make yourself scarce! Quick!

PASIAS. May I drop dead if I don't
  Go and put down my deposit
  And summons you this instant!

STREPSIADES. Why lose more than your twelve minae?
I shouldn't like you to suffer more
Just for miscalling a trough.

[Exeunt Pasias *and* Witness.

Enter Amynias *groaning.*

AMYNIAS. Oh . . . oh . . . oh . . . oh . . .

STREPSIADES. Hullo, who's making this wailing? One
Of the jolly gods in Karkinos' play?

AMYNIAS. Do you want to know who I am?
Someone hopelessly wretched . . .

STREPSIADES. Keep it to yourself then!

AMYNIAS. Oh, bitter fate!
Oh wheels of my chariot broken!
Oh Pallas, you have destroyed me!

STREPSIADES. Why, has Tlepolemos been at you?

AMYNIAS. Don't mock me, sir! Have your son repay
The money I lent him. I'm in a bad way,
In every way.

STREPSIADES.   What money?

AMYNIAS.   What he borrowed.

STREPSIADES. It seems to me you *are* in a bad way!

AMYNIAS. I was driving my chariot and I fell out . . . .

STREPSIADES. You drivel as if you'd fallen off a donkey.

AMYNIAS. Drivel, when I *demand* my money?

STREPSIADES. You can't be quite in your right mind.

AMYNIAS.   Sir?

STREPSIADES. My guess is you've had a brainquake.

AMYNIAS. *My* guess is you'll get a summons,
If you don't pay up.

STREPSIADES.   Tell me, then, do you think
It's new water Zeus pours down when it rains?
Or that the sun sucks it back, and it's the same rain again?

AMYNIAS. Damme, I don't know and I don't care.

STREPSIADES. Don't care about such phenomena, and think
You have a right to claim your money? Really!

AMYNIAS. If you're hard up, you could pay me interest.

STREPSIADES. What sort of creature is interest would you say?

AMYNIAS. One that grows day by day and month by month
  More and more silver as time goes by . . .
STREPSIADES.   Well put,
  But do you think the sea is fuller than it was?
AMYNIAS. No, just the same. It's not in its nature to increase.
STREPSIADES. And all the rivers pouring into it
  And it not growing more, and you think
  Your silver should grow more? Out!
  Bring me a goad!
AMYNIAS.   Witness! Help!
STREPSIADES. Off you go! Trot, old hack!
AMYNIAS. This is an outrage!
STREPSIADES.   Gee up!
  I'll stick this into your quarters,
  Old dray-horse—ah, that's better!
  I meant to give you a boost,
  You and your wheels and your chariot!

               [*Exeunt*, Strepsiades *driving* Amynias.

CHORUS. See what comes of embarking on a career
  Of crime: this wicked old man
  Has aimed at bilking his creditors;
  But I say this now,
  Though he seems to be prospering
  On his crooked course,
  It'll suddenly take
  A turn for the worse.
  For I think he'll find that all he long ago
  Planned for his son to learn—
  To be able to get the better of truth
  In any dispute,
  By any means, however foul—
  Will soon rebound
  On his own head
  And he'll wish him dumb!

    Re-enter Strepsiades, *with* Pheidippides *beating him.*

STREPSIADES. Help! Help! Oh! Oh!
  Neighbours, cousins, citizens!
  Help me, I'm being beaten up—

Wow, oh my head! Wow, oh my jaw!
Do you hit your own father?

PHEIDIPPIDES.   Yes, father.

STREPSIADES. See, he admits he hit me!

PHEIDIPPIDES.   Yes, father.

STREPSIADES. You parricide!

PHEIDIPPIDES. *Do* go on! Say what you want to,
The more you curse the more I like it.

STREPSIADES. You filthy pansy!

PHEIDIPPIDES.   A spray of roses!

STREPSIADES. You hit your father?

PHEIDIPPIDES.   Yes, by Zeus.
And I'll prove I was right.

STREPSIADES.   Prove you're right
To hit your father?

PHEIDIPPIDES.   I'll put it to you
And win my case.

STREPSIADES.   You'll win your case?

PHEIDIPPIDES. With the greatest ease.
Whichever system you like.

STREPSIADES. What system?

PHEIDIPPIDES.   The False or the True.

STREPSIADES. By Zeus, I've had
You properly taught to refute all justice,
If you can prove it's right and proper
For son to beat father.

PHEIDIPPIDES.   I think I can
Prove it so utterly, so convincingly
You won't have a word to say.

STREPSIADES. Very well, let me hear you.

CHORUS. You'll have to think hard and quick, old man,
If you want to defeat him.
If he hadn't a cast-iron case he'd hardly
Be so completely brazen.
D'you see how confident he looks?
He's got all the answers.

But tell us Chorus how the fight first
Began. You owe us that at least.

STREPSIADES. I'll tell you from the beginning the origins of the
   quarrel.
   Remember, I took him into the house to give him a blow-out?
   Well, I said, 'Fetch your lyre, and sing me that air of Simonides—
   The *Golden Fleece* one'; but he turned on me very rudely
   And said that singing at meals was an archaic habit
   Like an old woman-servant droning away at the grindstone.

PHEIDIPPIDES. The moment you told me to *sing* instead of eating
   I was perfectly right to beat you—you weren't entertaining
   A cicala to dinner.

STREPSIADES. See! That's exactly what he said to me,
   And he said Simonides was a lousy poet anyway,
   It was hard to keep my temper, but I managed it, and I asked him
   To take a sprig of myrtle and recite a passage of Aeschylus.
   Can you believe it, he answered: 'I think of Aeschylus
   Simply as being historic—the very first of the poets—
   But as for his *work*, it's turgid, bombastic, and incoherent!'
   Can you imagine how my heart began to hammer?
   But I *still* kept my temper and said, 'Then give me a sample
   Of some outstanding passage in one of your modern poets!'
   Then he began that piece of Euripides, that disgusting
   Piece where a brother and sister lived in . . . well . . . ugh! incest.
   I let him have it then, I gave him a piece of my mind and
   As you can guess we went at it hammer and tongs, but it didn't
   Stop at abuse, we came to blows and he bashed me and nearly
   Crushed the life out of me!

PHEIDIPPIDES.   And wasn't I perfectly right to?
   You insulted Euripides, our greatest poet.

STREPSIADES[*furious*].   Our *greatest*
   Poet—here, wait a minute! No, he'll only beat me again.

PHEIDIPPIDES. He will. And rightly!

STREPSIADES.   Rightly? You haven't a shred of respect for
   The father who brought you up. Why, before you could speak
   I knew if you gurgled 'Bru-bru' you wanted your feeding bottle,
   And if you went 'Mam-mam-mam' I knew it was bread you
      wanted—

You hardly had time to say 'Kakka' before I grabbed you
And held you outside the door and
                    Now, when I yelled and screamed
                    I needed to go so badly
                    You hadn't even the grace
                    To let me get outside
                    But almost choking I had
                    To go where I was.

CHORUS. I think the hearts of the young are eager
   To hear his answer
   For if he can manage entirely to whitewash
   Such monstrous conduct
   There won't be an inch of skin left on
   The old men's bodies!

   Now do your stuff, use every new trick of your trade
   To seem to speak the truth; try to persuade us.

PHEIDIPPIDES. It's fine to be able to use these clever new methods
   To flout the establishment and give it
   A real upheaval. When I had a one-track
   Mind that ran on horses I was lucky if
   I could string three words together without some *gaffe*,
   But now my Master's put a stop to all that,
   And I know the form of the subtlest syllable.
   So I think I can show I was right to beat my father.

STREPSIADES. Oh, go back to horses! I'd rather pay for
   A four-in-hand than a left-and-right to the jaw.

PHEIDIPPIDES. Shut up! Kindly allow me to pick up
   The reins of my argument. Ready? Question one.
   You beat me when I was little, didn't you?

STREPSIADES. I did! But always for your own good.

PHEIDIPPIDES.   Exactly!
   Then isn't it right I should do the same for you
   'For your own good'—if 'good' and 'beating' are
   Synonymous. Why should your body be
   Bruiseless and mine not? I was born free, wasn't I?
   'Children weep: why shouldn't fathers weep?'
   If you argue this is how children learn, by beatings,

I'll answer: by consent, old age is second childhood,
But since it has the advantage of experience,
If it makes mistakes, surely they should be punished
Twice as severely?

STREPSIADES.   Nowhere does the Law
Permit such suffering to fathers.

PHEIDIPPIDES.   Who
Made the law but men like you and me
In common discussion in the old days?—So
What's wrong if in common discussion now
We totally reverse it? We'll be decent:
You can take as cancelled all the beatings you gave us
Before the law was altered: no *quid pro quo.*
But look at game cocks—look at all *Nature*:
Sons fight fathers. The only difference is
Animal-fathers don't make laws.

STREPSIADES. If you are going to take a game cock as your model,
Why don't you roost on a perch and peck dung?

PHEIDIPPIDES. There's no true parallel. Socrates would explain.

STREPSIADES. Then don't keep hitting me . . . or, simply, you're in
the wrong.

PHEIDIPPIDES. I don't see why!

STREPSIADES.   If *I'm* right to beat you,
You're right to beat *your* son. . . .

PHEIDIPPIDES.   Only
I haven't got one; then you'll die, and *I* shan't
Have any redress for your having beaten me:
I'll have been *cheated*!

STREPSIADES.   You know, my old friends,
I think he's made a point and we ought to concede it.
If we behave badly, why shouldn't we be beaten?

PHEIDIPPIDES. Now, take another point.

STREPSIADES.   I'm not sure I can.

PHEIDIPPIDES. You mayn't resent your own suffering so—

STREPSIADES. Can you teach me to like what I've had?

PHEIDIPPIDES. Perhaps, if I say I'd beat mother, too?

STREPSIADES. Your mother? What do you mean?
  This is worse than worse!

PHEIDIPPIDES.   Suppose
  By the same sort of argument
  I could prove I was right?

STREPSIADES.   Do that and
  You can take a running jump
  Over the cliff and Socrates, too,
  And all your confounded Logic!
  Oh Clouds, Clouds, what have you done to me?
  I pledged myself body and soul to you. . . .

CHORUS. It's wholly your own fault—you *asked*
  To be put on the primrose path.

STREPSIADES. But why did you aid and abet me?

CHORUS. If we find someone on the way to evil
  We lead him to the brink, and leave him—
  To repent and think. . . .

STREPSIADES. It's a heavy censure, Clouds,
  But a just one. I shouldn't have schemed
  To defeat my creditors.
  Now let's destroy this loathsome Chairephon
  And Socrates—they've cheated *us.*

PHEIDIPPIDES. *I* wouldn't dream of lifting a finger
  Against my teachers.

STREPSIADES.   Come, my boy,
  You must show reverence to our Father Zeus.

PHEIDIPPIDES. Our father Zeus! *My* father's a fool!
  Does Zeus exist?

STREPSIADES [*solemnly*]. Zeus our God exists.

PHEIDIPPIDES. He doesn't. He's been chucked out!

STREPSIADES. He does. I've been a fool to believe
  In Vortex—a mere image of clay.

PHEIDIPPIDES. Oh stuff it up! Talk your guff
  To yourself. You're the fool.   [*Exit.*

STREPSIADES. Oh, I've been mad! Mad
  To renounce the gods, for Socrates!
  Hermes, kind Hermes, do not

Destroy me utterly,
Be lenient to me in this maze
Of blether I've lost my soul in.
Advise me, shall I take them
To court, or not?

[A pause—he listens.

No! I agree, no lawsuits.
Oh yes! I'll go this instant
And fire their house. Quick!
Xanthias, quick! Bring me
A ladder and your pitchfork!

Enter Slave *with these things.*

Now, if you love your master
Climb up to the roof
Of this Logic factory
And break it up till it falls
In on the whole building!
Bring me a lighted torch
And I'll give the crooks a taste
Of *real* Truth and Justice!

[They set fire to the factory.

1 STUDENT [*within*]. Help! Help!

STREPSIADES. Come on, flames. Do your stuff!

Socrates and Students *come out.*

1 STUDENT. What are you doing?

STREPSIADES.   Doing?
I'm only arguing fire against your roof.

2 STUDENT. Help! Help! Who's set the house on fire?

STREPSIADES. Who stole my cloak?

3 STUDENT. Murder! Murder!

STREPSIADES.   That's just what I'm going to do
Unless this pitchfork tricks me,
Or I fall off the roof!

SOCRATES. What are you doing up there?

STREPSIADES. 'Pacing the air, conning the sun'.

SOCRATES. I'm *gasping* for air! I can't see for smoke!

Enter Chairephon.

CHAIREPHON. I'm being burnt to death!

STREPSIADES. You derided the gods. You subtle researchers,
  You spied on the face of the sleeping moon.

Enter Hermes.

HERMES. But where has it got you? Obliterated!
  For all your clever discoveries;
  But most of all for your blasphemies.

CHORUS. Let us get out! It is high time.
  Our chorus has played its part.

WASPS

The Wasps *seems to have won second prize when it was produced at the Lenaia in 422* B.C., *once more not under Aristophanes' name, though it was clear from the Parabasis, if not already, that he was the author.*

The publicly conducted running battle between Aristophanes and Cleon must have been almost a serial in instalments by the time of the *Wasps*, but although the play's principal characters are the father Philocleon ('Cleon-lover') and Bdelycleon ('Cleon-hater'), that master of mob oratory, still the most successful politician in Athens, is not singled out for attack in this play. The chief subject is rather the way in which the Athenian jury system was being abused to the advantage of Cleon and like-minded politicians of the Left.

Criminal and civil cases at this time were heard and judged, sentences pronounced, and damages assessed, by courts regularly consisting of 500 jurymen (Dicasts or Heliasts) together. Verdicts were given by inserting a pebble into an urn. Wax tablets were used for awarding a harsher or milder sentence by a longer or shorter stroke being scratched on them. Much of course depended on the effectiveness of advocates prosecuting or defending; their speeches were timed by a water-clock, but otherwise were scarcely inhibited.

Jurymen were chosen by lot, from Athenian citizens aged thirty or more, in a way which ordinarily prevented bribery or intimidation in particular cases. But by the ninth year of the Peloponnesian War, with younger men away or less able to attend, and with the economy of the city deteriorating, juries consisted increasingly of old men (often basically countrymen), not very smart (in any sense), easily persuaded, and naturally inclined against the rich, the sophisticated, and the urban aristocracy. Cleon's increase of pay for a juryman to three obols a day in fact provided a meagre living for such as Philocleon and the Chorus in this play. It was correspondingly a possible threat in any court case that the jurors' pay might have to be reduced if the state treasury were not kept sufficiently enriched from confiscations and fines from convictions. In the war between the Athenian democracy and the kingdom of Sparta, it was popular in Athens to make play with dirty words like 'tyranny' (or monarchy) for internal political reasons, and the slur of being Spartan in sympathy was more easily cast than thrown off. Aristophanes thus guys in the *Wasps* the same unscrupulous appeals to gullible mass-audiences in the law courts that he had already exposed in political life in general.

For though the jurymen are always, like wasps, stinging rich men for a fine, they are themselves well and truly conservative. The Chorus and

Philocleon are old soldiers, preferring simple clothes and food and the old airs and dances, reminding each other of unspectacular incidents of army life. They don't easily take to the ways of the urban smart set, in which Bdelycleon moves, with their upper-class sports like horse-racing and wrestling, their foreign fashions in clothes from Persia or even Sparta, their clever capping of each other's verses, and their craze for telling pointed stories. And when it is demonstrated to them that most of the money coming in to Athens from the annual tributary payments of her allies in smaller cities and islands is not being spent on their jury pay, they quickly drop their devotion to Cleon and the politicians of the 'people'.

Philocleon, however, has caught the jury-service bug so badly that he takes to trying cases in his own kitchen. But he fails signally to adapt to the elegant life and ends the play in a thoroughly old-style uproar of wine, women, and dancing.

CHARACTERS

XANTHIAS ⎱ *middle-aged*
SOSIAS ⎰ *slaves*
BDELYCLEON
PHILOCLEON, *his father*
BOYS
Three more SLAVES
GUEST
DOG
GIRL
BAKER WOMAN
ANGRY MAN
WITNESS
CRABS
CHORUS *of old justices* (*Wasps*)

It is almost dawn. Xanthias *and* Sosias *have been on guard all night outside the house of* Philocleon.

XANTHIAS [*cursing under his breath*]. Arrrgh!

SOSIAS. What's the matter now, misery?

XANTHIAS. —Trying to teach myself to sleep
   On guard, with my eyes skinned . . .

SOSIAS.   It's
   Your ribs'll be skinned if you do! You know
   What a cunning old cuss we've got inside.

XANTHIAS. Just what I aim to forget by having
   A quiet ziz. . .

SOSIAS.   Then have a go!
   I feel in a cosy sort of haze
   Myself.

XANTHIAS. Lit like a corybant?

SOSIAS [*producing flask*]. Not quite—but like the god,
   Bless him, as makes them that way.

XANTHIAS [*producing his flask*]. I go for him too, and a moment ago
   I was overcome by a sleep as strong
   As the Persian army—I nodded off
   And had an amazing dream.

SOSIAS.   Me too—
   Queerest I ever. But tell yours first.

XANTHIAS. Seemed like I saw an eagle, a huge brute,
   Sweep to the market-place and grip
   A brass shield in its claws and whip it
   Right up to heaven—but then it was
   Cleonymos that hopped it and dropped it.

SOSIAS. He's a real riddle, Cleonymos.

XANTHIAS. How come?

SOSIAS.   A chap will say in a bar:
   What is it that can drop a shield
   On land, by sea, or in the air?

XANTHIAS. Something awful's going to happen
   To me, having a dream like that.

SOSIAS. Stuff it—there's nothing to worry about.
  God's guarantee!

XANTHIAS.   But isn't it
  Awful to see anyone chuck
  His arms away?—But tell me yours.

SOSIAS. Mine's a dream and a half all right!
  About the whole ship of state—

XANTHIAS.   Tell me
  The lot right down to the bilge.

SOSIAS. In my beauty sleep I was,
  And I thought I saw a flock of sheep
  Wearing cloaks and carrying staves
  Meet in the Assembly on the Pnyx
  And there was a grab-all monster haranguing them
  In a voice like a pig being roasted alive.

XANTHIAS. Pho!

SOSIAS.   What is it?

XANTHIAS.   Stop, not another word!
  Your dream stinks of high, putrid leather.

SOSIAS. Then this disgusting monster got
  Some scales: slicing and weighing fat—

XANTHIAS. Slicing and parcelling up the State—

SOSIAS. And I saw Theoros sitting beside him
  But with the head of a crow and Alcibiades
  In his mincing voice remarked: 'Look
  At Theowos—who's he going to wook?'

XANTHIAS. Good old Alcibiades!

SOSIAS. But doesn't Theoros turning into
  A crow mean something ghastly?

XANTHIAS.   No,
  It's perfectly splendid.

SOSIAS.   Why?

XANTHIAS.   He was
  A man and then, like that, a crow.
  It means he's going to the crows,
  See? And a good riddance.

SOSIAS.   Mr. Diviner!
  I'd give you two obols—if I had them. . . .

XANTHIAS [*coming down-stage*]. I think it's time I explained matters
  To the audience; but I'd better put
  In one or two provisos first.
  Don't expect anything profound,
  Or any slapstick *à la* Megara.
  And we got no slaves to dish out baskets
  Of free nuts—or the old ham scene
  Of Heracles cheated of his dinner;
  No side-swipes at Euripides,
  And even if Cleon—somehow—has had
  The luck to shine we won't shred him
  To bits again. Our little story
  Has meat in it and a meaning not
  Too far above your heads, but more
  Worth your attention than low comedy.

  Do you see that chap asleep on the roof?
  Big, hefty, isn't he? He's our master,
  And he's locked his father in the house
  —Our job's to see he don't get out.
  The old man's got a weird disease:
  You couldn't know it, you'd never guess it
  If I didn't tell you. Well, have a go!   [*Points into audience.*
  Amynias there, Pronapes' son—
  What does he say? Dice-lover? No.

SOSIAS. Thinks everyone's the same as him?

XANTHIAS. No, but that 'lover' is a chief part
  Of the disease. What, Sosias,
  Are *you* telling Derkylos that he's
  A *drink*-lover?

SOSIAS.   Not on your life!
  That's a *gentleman's* complaint.

XANTHIAS. Nicostratos from Scambon guesses
  It's sacrifices or it's strangers.

SOSIAS. No, no, Nicostratos, he doesn't

Sniff around strangers like that dirty
Old mongrel Philoxenos.

XANTHIAS. Stop this nonsense. You'll never guess.
Keep quiet now if you want to know:
I'll tell you what the old man's disease is.
He's a law-court lover—no one to touch him.
Judging's his passion; he's broken-hearted
If he doesn't sit on the front bench.
He hardly sleeps a wink all night
And if he even as much as nods,
His mind weaves dreams round the water-clock.
And he's so inured to clasping the voting
Pebbles tight he wakes with his thumb
Pressed to his first two fingers—like
A man at the new moon offering incense.

Then if he sees 'Lovely Demos' scribbled
Up on a doorway (you know, Pyrilampos'
Pretty boy), *he* writes 'Lovely vote-box'
Below it. Why, he even insisted
When it crowed in the evening his cock
Had been got at to call him late
By officials whose accounts were overdue.
Straight after supper it's 'Bring my slippers!'
And he dashes to the court and drowses
Stuck to the doorpost like a limpet.
He's so bad-tempered he convicts
Every single time and stumps back home
With wax in his nails—just like a bee.
And he's so scared he might run short
Of pebbles and not be able to cast
His damning vote he keeps a beachful
Here in the house. Well, that's his mania,
And the more you advise him to turn it up
The worse he gets. So he's locked up
And we're here to see he can't get out.
His poor son—it's upset him terribly.
At first he reasoned with him gently,
And tried to wheedle him into not

Putting his cloak on and going out.
No use. So next he had him bathed
And purified. No use. He tried
Initiating him as a corybant.
What happened? The old devil upped
And, sacred drum and all, he burst
Into court and began judging as he was.
When these rites didn't do the trick
We sailed to Aegina to have him sleep
A night in the temple of Asclepios—
By daylight he was back at the bar.
So in the end we shut him up,
But he wormed out by the drainpipes.
We stuffed up every hole with rags,
Then he hammered pegs into the wall
And hopping like a jackdaw hopped it!
So now we've got the whole house swathed
In nets and act as warders. The old man
Is called Philocleon—and rightly.
His son's Bdelycleon—and he's . . . well,
He's better not crossed nor argued with . . . .

> [*The two slaves look at each other, drink, and relax.*

BDELYCLEON [*from above*]. Xanthias! Sosias! Wake up!
> [Xanthias *groans.*

SOSIAS. What's up?

XANTHIAS. He is.

> Bdelycleon *appears on the roof.*

BDELYCLEON.   Quick, one of you!
Father's got into the kitchen somehow
And he's scrabbling round like a mouse. . . .
See that he doesn't siphon himself
Out of the bath waste. Sosias!
Lean your great carcass against the door.

SOSIAS. Right, sir!

BDELYCLEON.   Good god! Whatever's that racket
In the chimney? Hey! Who are you?

PHILOCLEON [*inside chimney*]. Smoke going up.

BDELYCLEON.   What sort of smoke?

PHILOCLEON. Fig-wood.

BDELYCLEON.   I see. Acrid enough.
  But you're *not* going up, to pollute
  The air—it's down for you, down you go!
  Where's the chimney cover? Right; and I'll weight it
  Down with this log. Oh god, there's no one
  Anywhere feels as low as I do—
  They'll call me a bastard of Smoky Joe's.

SOSIAS. He's heaving at the door.

BDELYCLEON.   Then heave
  Back at him, heavier! I'm coming!   [*Descends.*
  Look out for the bolt and bar—he'll bite
  The pin through if he can.

PHILOCLEON [*inside*].   Confound you!
  What are you doing, you filthy brutes?
  I've got to get out and judge Dracontides.
  I couldn't let *him* be acquitted.

BDELYCLEON. Would that be such a terrible Disaster?

PHILOCLEON. Why, I went to the oracle
  At Delphi once, and the god foretold that
  If I acquitted *anyone*
  I'd shrivel and die.

BDELYCLEON.   Apollo save us!
  What a forlorn hope.

PHILOCLEON.   Let me out,
  Please let me out, or I shall burst.

BDELYCLEON. No, by Poseidon! Never.

PHILOCLEON.   Then,
  I'll gnaw the net through.

BDELYCLEON.   You've got no teeth!

PHILOCLEON. Blast it to hell! How shall I kill you?
  Bring me a sword, quick—no, no,
  A heavy damages-assessment.

BDELYCLEON. He's on the edge of doing something
  Really appalling.

PHILOCLEON.   No, I'm not . . .

I simply want to go and sell
The donkey, and its panniers . . . .
It's the new moon—it's market day.

BDELYCLEON. Couldn't *I* sell them?

PHILOCLEON.   Not like I could.

BDELYCLEON. Agreed. I could do better—but
Get the donkey out!

XANTHIAS.   He's artful, isn't he?
And he really thinks he's hooked you, too.

BDELYCLEON. With that bait? Did he really think
I'd swallow that? I saw through him
In a flash, but still I think I'll go
And get the donkey out. Then he can't
Try *that* one on again.   [*Goes to the stable door.*
Old moke [*To the donkey.*], why are you moaning? At being sold?
Hup there! What heavy weather! Why
Are you wheezing? Someone might think
You had a new Odysseus under you. . . .

Enter donkey with Philocleon *underneath.*

XANTHIAS. But—there *is* somebody underneath!

BDELYCLEON. Let's have a look. . . .

XANTHIAS.   Here he is!

BDELYCLEON. What's this? May I ask who *you* are?

PHILOCLEON. Noman.

BDELYCLEON.   Noman. Where d'you come from?

PHILOCLEON. Ithaca. By Bolted out of Prison.

BDELYCLEON. Noman—out of nomansion. Look
Where he'd got to, the old crook. Pull him out!
Looks like a writ-server's nag.

PHILOCLEON. If you don't let me alone, we'll fight.

BDELYCLEON. Whatever about?

PHILOCLEON.   The donkey's shadow.

BDELYCLEON. You're just a crooked wicked cheat!

PHILOCLEON. *Me* wicked? Just you wait—I'm good!
You'll see one day when you taste the stuffed
Paunch of an old judge.

BDELYCLEON.   Get inside
  And stuff yourself and the donkey!

PHILOCLEON [*yelling*].   Help!
  Help—judges! Cleon! Help! Help!   [*Exit.*

BDELYCLEON. Yell yourself sick—once you're locked up.
  You two, pile stones against the door,
  Shoot the bolt home, pin it fast
  And reinforce it with this beam—
  Then roll the mortar block against the lot.   [*They do.*

SOSIAS. Good god! Where did that clod drop on
  My head from?

XANTHIAS.   Mice perhaps?

SOSIAS.   Mice?
  Not much! A judge-mouse scuttering
  Under the tiles.

BDELYCLEON.   This is too much!
  Is he turning into a sparrow? Is he
  Going to take off—where's the net? Shoo!
  Shoo! Back in! Shoo! By god it'd be
  Far easier to besiege Skioné
  Than a father like my father.

SOSIAS. He's really cooped up now, I reckon;
  He hasn't a hope of getting out.
  Couldn't we have a little drop. . .
  Of Sleep? Only the smallest sip?

BDELYCLEON. SLEEP? And his fellow-judges here
  Any minute now to pick him up?

SOSIAS. But it's hardly *dawn*, sir. . . .

BDELYCLEON.   Then they're late!
  They usually call him about midnight,
  Waving lights and singing bits
  Out of old Phrynichos to call him with.

SOSIAS. If they turn up, shall we throw stones?

BDELYCLEON. Don't be a fool! You might as well
  Stir up a wasps' nest as this lot.
  They're violent old splenetic men

With sharp stings at their loins and they snarl
And snap like showers of sparks.

SOSIAS. Don't worry! If I've got stones I'll soon
Get in amongst this swarm of judges.

*They retire to guard the door; Bdelycleon ascends to the roof.
Enter Chorus of old men, with Boys.*

CHORUS. Keep your best feet foremost! Comias, are you flagging?
By heaven things have changed! You once tugged at the leather
Tough as a watchdog's lead—now, Charinides goes better!
Hey! Strymodoros of Conthylé, best of our judges' ragbag—
Where have Euergides and Chabes of Phlyé got to?
Ah! Here come the dot-and-carries—looking as young as ever
They did when we mounted guard in Byzantium. Remember
How we pinched a baker's tray: split it, lit it, got a potful
For a real brew-up . . . . But hurry! Today's the trial of Laches:
Everyone says he's stuffed with money he's fiddled—Cleon
Whose word is our law bids: 'Come early and bring a three-day
Ration of rage to vent on his flagrant peculations.'
Press on, my colleagues, while the last of the night is with us,
But let's explore with our lanterns in case there are stones to trip
us.

BOY. Father! Father, look out for the mud!

CHORUS. Pick up a stick and trim the light.

BOY. I can do it easier with my fingers. . . .

CHORUS. You fool—you'll pull the whole thing out!
—And oil's so scarce. But you don't feel
The pinch when it comes to paying, do you?   [*Hits him.*
It's time you learnt some sense.

BOY.   You teach me
That way again and we'll put out the lamps
And go home and leave you to skate around
In the mud like snipe on a marsh.

CHORUS.   I've often
Taken it out of bigger men.
Oh heaven; I feel the squelch of mud!
It'll rain for four days—the gods
Will see to that—and look at the blobs

Of soot on the lamps: sure sign of rain.
Ah well, it's wanted—rain and north wind
For the late crops. But how is it
He hasn't come out of the house? He's usually
So quick to join us. He was never
A rear-ranker—he led us singing.
He loves singing. *We'll* stop and sing. . . .
If he hears my siren voice he'll come—
He'll *have* to come to the door.

[*Sings.*]

> Why does our old comrade
>   Neither appear nor hark?
> Is it he's lost his slippers
>   Or stubbed his toe in the dark?
> Has his ankle swelled or has a
>   Lump come up in his groin?
> He was always the strictest of us,
>   Alone he was never swayed
> By anyone's plea for mercy.
>   He grimly inclined his head
> Like this, and said
>   'You go and cook a stone.'
>
> Is it yesterday's doublecrosser
>   Whom we acquitted because
> He gulled us into believing
>   What a patriot he was,
> Swearing he was the first to
>   Unmask the Samian plot?
> Does he toss in pain and fever
>   Over this luckless matter?
> (He was ever that sort of stickler)
>   Sir, don't be a vain regretter—
> For we've got a rich greasy traitor
>   From Thrace to stock the pot!

[*To* Boy.] Come on, my lad, get on, get on!

BOY. If I asked you for something, father,
   Would you give it me?

CHORUS.   Why of course
  I would, my lad. Tell me
  What do you specially want me
  To get you? I think you love
  Knuckle-bones, don't you?

BOY.   No,
  Daddy, it's figs I want.
  They're far nicer.

CHORUS.   Not on your life!
  You can hang yourself first—see?

BOY. Then I won't guide you a step
  Further—see?

CHORUS.   And out of
  My miserable pittance I have to
  Buy bread and fuel for three,
  And tasty extras, and now
  You ask me for figs. . . .

BOY.   Daddy,
  If the Archon declares the court
  Won't sit, where shall we get
  Our dinner from? Have you got
  Anything to fall back on
  Or are we utterly sunk?

CHORUS [*moaning*]. Oh, oh . . . Don't know *where*
  Dinner's to come from.

BOY.   Mother!
  Why did you bear me, to feed
  On nothing but legal scraps?

CHORUS. Poor little empty purse—
  What a useless ornament!

BOY. What's left us but to weep?

PHILOCLEON[*from inside*]. I'm wasting away hearing
  Your voices through this crack.
  But I'm not in a mood for singing.
  What shall I do? I'm kept
  Prisoner by these brutes.
  I crave to come back and do
  Some really vicious work

At the voting-urns, but I can't
Get out to you. Oh! Zeus,
Terrible Thunderer, turn me
Suddenly into smoke
(As substantial as the boasts
Of Proxenides, as full
Of sound and fury as
The braggart son of Sellos).
Lord, pity me, grant my prayer
Or pulverize me now
With your blinding bolt and gather
My ashes and blow them into
Some bitter throat-burning brew,
Or make me the stone
They count the verdict votes on.

CHORUS. Who is it keeps you locked up? Tell us,
    You're speaking to friends.

PHILOCLEON.   My own son.
    But *don't shout*—he's just up there
    Asleep on the roof. Lower your voices.

CHORUS. But why does he do this? What motive
    Has he got?

PHILOCLEON. He refuses to let me judge
    Or sentence anyone—he wants to
    Keep me in clover here. But I
    Simply don't want to be.

CHORUS.   The loathsome
    Shadow-Cleon! So he dared to smear you
    For telling the truth about the ships—
    He'd never have had the guts unless
    He'd been a conspirator.
                    But it's time
    To think up a new way of getting
    Down here without him noticing.

PHILOCLEON. You do the thinking! I'll do anything
    You say. I just can't wait to do
    The round of the court with my vote.

CHORUS. Is there no crack you could wriggle or worm your way
    through,
  Then wrapped in rags creep out like many-counselled Odysseus?
PHILOCLEON. Every crack's stuffed up—there's not room for a gnat.
  You must think of something better! I can't run out like milk.
CHORUS. When you were in the army—remember—you pinched
    some spits
  And quickly got down the walls, when we were taking Naxos.
PHILOCLEON. Of course I remember—but things are a trifle
    different.
  When I was young I could steal, I was strong and able-bodied,
  No one was guarding me, I could flee wherever I chose to;
  But now there are men with weapons stationed at every corner
  On the watch for me. There are two down there on the door
  With spits—as if I were a cat running off with the joint.
CHORUS. You'll have to think up a plan as quickly as possible;
  It's dawn, my dear fellow . . . dawn.
PHILOCLEON. The best I can think of is to gnaw the net
  And may the huntress queen forgive my trespass.
CHORUS. That's spoken like a man who's bent on safety.
  More power to your jaw!
PHILOCLEON [*chewing*].   Mmmph . . . got it! Clean through!
                          [*He is seen at the window.*
  For heaven's *sake* don't shout. We must be cautious,
  Bdelycleon mustn't notice.
CHORUS. Keep calm. Don't be afraid.
  If he makes any fuss
  I'll put him in such a panic
  He'll run for his life, I'll teach him
  Not to mock our sacred statutes.
  Now fix a rope to the window
  And tie it securely under
  Your arms—work yourself
  Into a fine frenzy,
  Then lower yourself down.
PHILOCLEON. Hey! If I'm caught on the rope
  And they haul me back, what
  Will *you* do? Tell me now.

CHORUS. Summon our utmost strength
  And fight so hard that no one
  Could possibly hold you. As for
  Us, there'll be no holds barred.

PHILOCLEON. I'll do it then. I trust you.
  But listen, if I'm injured
  Carry me off and bury me
  Under the bar of the court.

CHORUS. You'll be all right. Don't worry.
  Keep a stiff upper lip, dear fellow,
  And pray to the gods of our fathers.

PHILOCLEON. O Lycos, master, hero, neighbour, you
  Who joy in the tears and groans of the accused,
  Choosing to dwell near by with that end in view,
  You who of all the heroes willingly
  Resort with those who weep—now pity me,
  Save me, the nearest neighbour to yourself.
  And never, I swear, I'll never piss or break
  Wind by your shrine again. . . .   [*Begins to descend.*

BDELYCLEON [*shouting from the roof*]. Up, you! Wake up!

SOSIAS. What's happening, sir?

BDELYCLEON. Voices: all round me.

SOSIAS.   Is the old man
  Squeezing out of a hole?

BDELYCLEON.   No!
  He's on a rope, letting himself down.
  Zeus blast him!

SOSIAS.   What are you up to,
  Or down to, you old fiend?

BDELYCLEON.   Quick!
  Get to the other window. Bash him
  With the harvest boughs. Maybe he'll turn
  If he feels the sting—of an olive branch.

PHILOCLEON. Help! All of you down on the cause-list!
  Smikythion, Tisiades,
  Chremon and Pheredeipnos—help!
  It's now or never before I'm lugged
  Back in. . . .

CHORUS.   The young fool!
  He's certainly stirred a wasp-nest now.
  Why are we holding back our fury?
  Out, out, with the bitter-fiery
  Stings of our punishment and strike!
  Quick, boys, hold our cloaks, then run
  And shout the news. See Cleon knows,
  Make him aware this man's an arch-
  Enemy of our city: he proposes
  To stop all lawsuits. . . .

BDELYCLEON.   My dear man,
  Listen to facts, stop bellowing.

CHORUS. By heaven, I'll bellow to heaven.

BDELYCLEON. But I shan't let him go!   [*Descends from the roof.*

CHORUS. Why this is shocking! Shameless
  Naked tyranny! City,
  Beware—and you, Theoros,
  God-hated as you are,
  And all you other toadies
    Set over us.

XANTHIAS.   By Heracles!
  Look at their stings—d'you see, sir?

BDELYCLEON. I do. They finished off Philippos,
  Gorgias' son. . . .

CHORUS.   And we'll finish
  You in a moment. Right!
  Close ranks! Keep in order!
  Turn in on him everybody
  Stings at the ready—keep
  Your rage at boiling point.
  See that he has no doubt
  What sort of swarm he's roused.

XANTHIAS. It'll be rough if we fight, sir.
  The sight of their stings turns me
  Into a jelly.

CHORUS.   Then let him go!
  If not, I warn you you'll envy
  Tortoises for their shells.

PHILOCLEON. On, men, flint-hearted wasps!
   You lot, fly in and sting them
   Right up the arse—you others,
   Get at their eyes and fingers.

BDELYCLEON. Midas, Phryx, Masintyas!
   Come out and help quick.

                    Enter three more Slaves.

   Hold him fast—give him up
   To nobody. If you don't
   You can starve in chains. There's nothing
   To fear—these are empty threats.

CHORUS. If you don't let him go,
   This is what you'll be stuck with!

PHILOCLEON. O Hero, O Lord Cecrops the Dragon-tailed,
   Do you see how these barbarians handle me—
   Me—and I taught them once to weep full measure!

CHORUS. Isn't old age the worst of evils? Of course it is.
   See how they hold their old master by force, forgetting
   How he bought them caps and coats and sleeveless vests and
      tunics
   And saw to their feet in winter, preventing them from freezing.
   But they've wiped the memory of all his philanthropy out.

PHILOCLEON. Let me go, you—you filthy animal
   Have you forgotten how I caught you stealing grapes,
   Tied you to an olive and flogged your bottom raw
   Till everyone envied you? But you don't seem to be grateful.
   You let me go, you lot, before my son can get away.

CHORUS [*to* Bdelycleon]. We'll soon give you the justice
   You deserve—short, sharp, and painful!
   You'll know who we are then,
   Fierce, righteous, steely-eyed.

BDELYCLEON. Drive these wasps from the house!

XANTHIAS. I'm hard at it!

BDELYCLEON.   Sosias!
   Smoke them out—out you go!
   Go to the crows, won't you?
   Beat them out, stink them out

With a whiff of Aeschines,
Sellartios' son.

SOSIAS.   We're getting them
Well on the run now!

BDELYCLEON. But you'd never have got them out
So easily if they'd tasted
The vitriolic verses
Philocles used to write!

CHORUS. Even the poor can see now
How stealthily, behind their backs,
Tyranny's come sneaking in—
And you, with your long snaky locks,
Want to ban the laws
The city has made
And be absolute ruler of our nation
Without any excuse
Or justification
But simply because you choose.

BDELYCLEON. Can't we discuss matters and come to terms quietly
Without this brawling and bawling?

CHORUS.   Terms with an anti-
Democrat? A self-confessed lover of tyranny?
A renegade backer of Brasidas? You with your woollen-edged
Spartan-copying cloak and your unbarbered beard?

BDELYCLEON. By god, I'd rather be shot of my father entirely than
        sail
Such choppy seas all the time.

CHORUS.   My lad, this is only
The thin end of the wedge (there's a nice metaphor for you).
Wait till the Prosecutor gives you the lash of his tongue,
And calls witness after witness. . . .

BDELYCLEON.   Can't you go somewhere else?
Must we have this shouting match till Olympus-come?

CHORUS. To the last drop of my blood! I'll never condone anyone
Bent on tyranny.

BDELYCLEON.   Tyranny! Tyranny! Quack! Witnesses! Witnesses!
You've nothing else in your heads. Whether the charge is serious
Or some piddling misdemeanour—it's tyranny! Tyranny—

For fifty years the word wasn't in the vocabulary,
Now it's common as salt fish—on everyone's lips in the market.
If anyone buys an expensive bass and doesn't want anchovies
They say 'He's a snob, he's obviously stocking a tyrant's larder.'
If you ask for garlic to give some kick to your fish the
Greengrocer's silly girl says with a wink 'Reelly?
So you want garlic, do you—it's tyranny you're after
Or d'you expect the Athenians'll pay you garlic as tax' . . . .

XANTHIAS [*chips in*]. You're right! I went to my special at the
    brothel yesterday;
  Midday it was, and because I asked *her* to ride my fancy
  She flies at me: 'Do I want old Horsy Hippias back?'

BDELYCLEON. That's just the sort of nonsense they love to hear.
  And because I want my father to be quit of
  This dirty-keyhole-smutty-blackmail-backstairs-libellous sort of
    life
  And live in style like Morychos, you crack me down and label me
  'Conspirator', 'after tyranny'.

PHILOCLEON.   And quite right too!
  I wouldn't swop caviar for the life you're stopping *me* from.
  I simply don't fancy eels or mullet—but I relish
  A nice little lawsuit tastily dished up.

BDELYCLEON.   By god you ought to
  By now! You've had time enough. But if only you'd keep quiet
  And *listen* I think I could show you how wrong you are.

PHILOCLEON. *Wrong*, to be a judge?

BDELYCLEON.   A laughing-stock, you mean!
  Everyone sees, but you, how you are taken in
  By the crooks whose slave you are.

PHILOCLEON.   A slave? What drivel.
  I'm master!

BDELYCLEON. That's what *you* think. You're not. You're everyone's
    slave.
  Now, tell me what cut *you* get, from the whole sum of tribute
  Our empire pays us.

PHILOCLEON.   I certainly will. Will *you*
  Accept my friends here as arbitrators?

BDELYCLEON.   I will,
  And for me too. Let him go, all of you
                    [They do. Exeunt Xanthias *and* Sosias.

PHILOCLEON. Bring me a sword—if I'm defeated I'll fall on it.

BDELYCLEON. Suppose you disagree with the verdict?

PHILOCLEON.   May I never again
  Pledge myself in a cup of undiluted pay.

CHORUS [*to* Philocleon]. You'll have to produce a brand-
  New trick out of the bag—
  A real knock-out, none
  Of our usual routines will do.

BDELYCLEON. Bring me a note book, quick!
  I must keep your points.   *[A slave brings him one.*

CHORUS. Everything's at stake, so
  Stick to your own game—
  Don't try to play him at his,
  For your and all our sakes;
  He'll do his best to beat us
  (Heaven forbid such a thing),
  Don't give him an opening.

BDELYCLEON. I'll make brief notes of his main points.

PHILOCLEON. But what will *you* say, friends,
  If he wins the argument?

CHORUS. We'll simply be knocked out,
  No good any more, mocked at
  In the streets as nid-nod doddering
  Tools in the State processions,
  Form-proffering fools.
  But now, since you propose to expatiate upon
  The whole nature of our powers—you must bridle your tongue,
    mount
  And ride the race of your life.

PHILOCLEON.   Right from the starting gate
  I'll leap into the lead and prove we are second to no one.
  Who is more lucky or blest or fêted or feared than a judge is,
  Old though he is? He's early to rise—but already some brawny
  Hefty big fellow is waiting, looking out for him at the court.

So I come, and he offers a horny hand (that has dipped to the elbow
In pilfering public funds) as tenderly as a lily
And bows and scrapes and pleads in a simpering piteous whimper
'Pity me sir if ever you made a bit on the side when
You was on Government service or catering for your regiment. . . . '
He'd never even have known of my existence unless he'd
Been up before me before, and I had somehow acquitted him.

BDELYCLEON. Note one. Suppliants, rumbling of.

PHILOCLEON. Then when I've been soft-soaped, and my temper greased,
I go into court and do nothing I've seemed to promise.
I know every tone of voice that builds for an acquittal;
Is there a trick, an inflection we justices haven't heard?
Some of them snivel their poverty, piling the woe on till
I've *almost* a fellow-feeling. Some of them tell us stories—
A crack from Aesop, a joke to loosen our tight lips,
And if it doesn't, his next line is to drag in his children,
Dear little boys and girls, and I sit all ears to hear them.
They grovel and whine, and their father, as if in front of a god,
Implores me, all of a tremble, to release him from further questions.
'Oh sir, if you love the bleat of the sacred lamb have pity
On my poor little boy, but if you like what little girls have
My sweet little daughter squeals as prettily as a piglet.'
So we loosen the strings of our wrath . . . the turn of a peglet.
Isn't this true power? And true contempt of money.

BDELYCLEON. Note two. Awareness of graft; money, contempt of.
Now give me some positive pleasant example of
The exercise of your powers in ruling Greece.

PHILOCLEON. Well, when the—er—elder boys are being examined
For enrolment as citizens it is our special privilege
To inspect their balls. . . .
                                Then if Oiagros the actor
Gets into a case, he'll never get out of it till he's spoken
The bit we think the best bit of the *Niobe*.
Then if a flautist wins his case he must fix his mouth-strap

And play for us as we go when the court rises.
Again, if a father makes a will on his deathbed leaving
His daughter to a friend, we don't give a fig for the seal
Or the cap over it—we dispose of her to whoever's
Got round us best. And for all this, WE CANNOT BE CALLED TO
ACCOUNT.

BDELYCLEON. You've really got something there—the only thing so
far.
But it must be wrong to violate the seal of an heiress.

PHILOCLEON. And when there's a really big or difficult case
The Assembly and the Council prefer to refer it to us.
Then Euathlos and the great shield-shedding Smarmyonymos
Swear they will never betray but always fight for the people—
And you know no counsel has a chance unless he declares
The court shall be discharged after the first verdict.
Even Cleon, the champion shouter-downer, hardly niggles at us
But cossets us personally and flicks off the flies. Have *you*
Ever done that sort of thing for your father, may I ask?
And Theoros, a man no less distinguished than Euphemios,
Whips the sponge from his bottle and polishes our slippers.
And *you* deprive me and keep me from keeping up with
Standards of living like this—and *this* you swore
To prove was hard labour and no less than slavery.

BDELYCLEON. Go on, you old wind-bag! You'll have to stop in the
end.
And then I'll show you what sort of power you have.
An arse reverts to its nature however much you wash it.

PHILOCLEON. But the nicest part of it all—and heavens, I nearly
forgot it—
Is when I come home with my pay and everyone crowds round
me
Because of it. My daughter washes my feet and anoints them
And she cuddles me close and then with 'Darling darling papa'
Kisses the obols out of my mouth with her pretty tongue;
Then my dear wife fusses round me wheedling me with cakes,
She sits beside me and pets me and whispers, 'One little
nibble'.
And I love all this. I don't have to depend on you or

That sour house-boy to see if, muttering under his breath,
He'll deign to bring me breakfast.
                                        But if things don't go smoothly
I've got my dissolver of evils, my salve, my defence, my shield,
If *you* don't pour me a drink I've got this long-eared pitcher
To tilt at my ease and he lets go a great braying fart at
Your little mimsy goblet as I slosh and swill him down.
My power's no less than Zeus's!

                We're treated on a par!
                If the court's in an uproar
                Everyone passing murmurs,
                'They're thundering—like Zeus!'
                And if my eyes flash lightning
                Rich nobles blench and squitter.
                You—you're afraid of me too,
                But may I drop dead this moment
                If I'm afraid of you!

CHORUS. That was a splendid speech.
    So cogent and closely argued—
    Have you ever heard a better?

PHILOCLEON. And he thought he'd easily usurp my laurels
    Although he knows I'm an old hand at this.

CHORUS. He moved from point to point
    So exquisitely fitly
    And omitted nothing—I seemed
    To sit in a haze of pleasure,
    As if I had been transported
    To the Islands of the Blest.

PHILOCLEON. Look how he's fidgeting and hemming and hawing.
    [*To his son.*]—I'll make you whine like a whipped cur today!

CHORUS. My lad, you'll have to take
    Some brilliant avoiding action—
    We're not exactly indulgent
    To young men who get across us.
    So you'd better look out for a brand-
    New millstone tough enough
    To blunt our rage, or an argument
    As tough or tougher. . . .

BDELYCLEON. It's a tougher job than a comic poet can cope with,
To heal a disease endemic to this city.
But oh dear father, lordly son of Cronos—

PHILOCLEON. Don't 'father' *me* like that! Just you get on and tell
me
How I'm a slave or I'll kill you (though I have to cut
Good holy meat from my diet).

BDELYCLEON.   Just *listen*, dear little dada,
And wipe the wrinkles off your forehead. Ready? Consider
The total tribute from the cities—count it up on your fingers
And not with voting pebbles; then think of the heaps of taxes,
The one-per-cents, the deposits-in-court, the mines, the markets,
The harbour-dues, fines, and rents—more than two thousand
talents.
Got it? Now, out of all this, think of the judges—only
Six thousand of you as yet. How much of it comes to you?
One hundred and fifty talents.

PHILOCLEON.   Not a tithe of the city's income!

BDELYCLEON. That's it.

PHILOCLEON.   And, tell me, what happens to all the rest
of the money?

BDELYCLEON. It goes to the crooks who swear they'll 'never betray
the rabble
But always stick up for them'. And you swallow this
And really believe you rule! While they blackmail our allies:
'Give us fifty talents quick, or we'll reduce your town to rubble.'
And you suck at a crumb of rule and think yourselves happy and
glorious.
The allies aren't fools, you know—when they see you lot
And the rest of the city riff-raff get bloated on a vote-box,
And nothing to follow, they soon reckon you just an empty token,
A nothing-worth, and upon the crooks in power they pour
Jars of pickle, wine, cheese, carpets, sesame, cushions,
Cloaks, crowns, drinking bowls, cups, necklaces—the lot.
But to *you*, their *rulers*—for all your toil by land and sea they
Don't give as much as a head of garlic to flavour your fish.

PHILOCLEON. They don't and that's a fact. Why, I've just had to
send out

To Eucharides to buy three for myself. But stop
Being so tedious; come to the point and tell me straight
Why I'm a slave.

BDELYCLEON.   Isn't it the uttermost form of slavery,
While all these crooks and their henchmen are powerful and in
    the money,
That *you* have to put up with three obols—a mere pittance,
Though earned by land and sea in the extremities of battle?
But what astounds me most is the way you let yourselves
Be bossed about. That sissy son of Chaireas prances
In with his mincing walk and stands with his legs straddled
And demands *you* to come to the court at daybreak and 'whoever's
A minute late won't get his obols'. But *he's* as late as he chooses
And gets his drachma retainer as counsel; and add to that
If his palm's well greased by some defendant, he winks at a
    colleague
And they fix the case and play like men two ends of a saw.
But you don't even notice—you're all eyes on the pay-clerk.

PHILOCLEON. Do you mean, they do *this* to *me*? What mud are you
    stirring up?
You maze my mind—you're getting me all in a muddle.

BDELYCLEON. You know, you could all be rich! I cannot conceive
How you're kept shut up in the dark by these racketeers,
You—ruling so many towns, from Pontus to Sardo—
And all you get is three obols and that's doled out a drop
At a time like oil from wool: a bare minimum to live on.
They want you to be poor; and I'll tell you why. It keeps you
In your place—you know who's boss. So if one of them sets you
On to a private enemy, you do as they tell you
And grind him to powder. If they wanted to make life easy
For the people it wouldn't be difficult. A thousand
Cities pay tribute; let each city feed twenty Athenians,
Then twenty thousand Athenians would live in clover on hare
And beestings and cream—fare fit for the victors of Marathon.
But now you simply bum round the pimp with the pay-packet.

PHILOCLEON. Oh heaven, my hand's numb! I can't get a grip on
    the sword.
I'm weaker than water.

BDELYCLEON.   Whenever there's a scare on, oh yes,
They promise Euboeia and fifty bushels of wheat per head:
What have they actually given you but a mere *five* bushels?
—After having to establish your citizenship almost
Letter by letter; and then it was rationed quart by quart.

> That's why I locked you up
> 'Cause I wanted you decently fed;
> And not be the sucker of any more
> Loud-mouthed boys in the racket.
> And I'll make the best provisions
> For you, on no conditions
> But *one*—you must never again
> Take a suck at a pay-packet.

CHORUS. He was a wise man who said
Don't make your mind up till you've heard
Both sides. You, my boy, seem to have won
In a canter—you've drawn the fangs
Of my anger. Crack! There goes my staff of office!
[*To* Philocleon.] Now listen, my old friend, don't be a fool:
Give in; accept; accept; don't jib, or be perverse.
I wish *I* had a relation
Who took such care for my future.
It's obvious one of the gods
Is all for you—accept
Your luck in the same spirit!

BDELYCLEON. I'll give him whatever's best
For his time of life—a bowl
Of lentils to spoon up;
A nice soft cloak, a rug,
And a pretty slave to massage
His manhood—if he's stiff.
Hey! What's the matter—he's
As dumb as a hooked fish!
I don't like the look of this.

CHORUS. He's mulling it all over.
He knows what a fool he's been,
And wouldn't have been if
He'd listened to you from the start.

Now's his moment of truth.
He's bracing himself to be wise
And live the rest of his days
Following your advice.

PHILOCLEON [*groaning*]. Ooooooh . . . Oooooh . . .

BDELYCLEON. Whatever's the matter?

PHILOCLEON. You—you offer me cloaks, rugs,
   Girls to . . . Things like that. . . Ugh!
   What *I* love is the herald's
   'Who's not voted let him stand up'.
   Let me be last of the voters,
   But oh let me stand by the boxes!
   Oh my poor soul! Where is it?
   Poor shivering shadow, appear! Oh gods,
   O Heracles, give me the chance
   To totter to court and convict
   Cleon of theft!

BDELYCLEON.   Father,
   Do take my advice—

PHILOCLEON.   I will,
   In everything but . . .

BDELYCLEON.   Well?

PHILOCLEON. In not being able to judge.
   I'd rather go straight to hell.

BDELYCLEON. I give up! Since this *is*
   What you obviously want,
   Don't go *there*—stay here.
   Do your judging at home.

PHILOCLEON. Don't be a fool. How?

BDELYCLEON. Same routine. Suppose
   The house-girl has left the door
   Open without permission:
   You fine her a single drachma.
   That's what you did there.
   It's easy enough to plan;
   If it's fine you can judge in the sun,
   If it rains—indoors; if you don't

Get up till noon, no one
Will shut you out from the bar.

PHILOCLEON. I like the sound of that.

BDELYCLEON. Then if counsel's too long-winded
You needn't get peckish and
Take it out on the prisoner.

PHILOCLEON. D'you think I can judge as well
On a full stomach?

BDELYCLEON.   Better.
Isn't it said, where there's false
Or tricky evidence judges
Ought to chew the matter over
And digest it?

PHILOCLEON.   Yes. You convince me.
But where do I get my *pay*?

BDELYCLEON. From me.

PHILOCLEON.   That's excellent!
I won't have to split it with
Anyone else. That idiot
Lysistratos did the dirty
On me in the meanest way.
We'd got a drachma between us,
And he went to the fishmonger
To get it changed and brought me
Three mullet scales and I thought
They were obols and so I pouched them.
Ugh! The revolting stink!
I spat them out and threatened
To have him up—

BDELYCLEON.   So what?

PHILOCLEON. Said I had the crop of a cock:
I'd soon digest hard cash.

BDELYCLEON. So you see how much better off
You'll be here?

PHILOCLEON.   I'm not so blind
As that. But where are you going?

BDELYCLEON. To get the paraphernalia.   [*Exit.*

PHILOCLEON. My heavens! The oracle's
　　Come true; it's a common saying
　　The Athenians would end up trying
　　Lawsuits in their own homes,
　　Each have a miniature court rigged
　　Up in his own porch
　　Like a little shrine of Hecate.
　　Well, well . . . Everyone with his law court . . .

　　　　　　　　Re-enter Bdelycleon.

BDELYCLEON. What's that? Look, I've brought
　　All the stuff—and a few extras.
　　Here's a pisspot—you may need it.
　　I'll hang it up on this peg.

PHILOCLEON. Good idea! Old men are weak in the bladder.

BDELYCLEON. Here's a fire and a pot of soup,
　　Whenever you feel empty!

PHILOCLEON. So if I feel feverish
　　I can take a sup of soup
　　And still get my pay. Splendid!
　　But what's the point of the cock?

BDELYCLEON. To crow and wake you if
　　You happened to nod off
　　Half-way through the evidence.

PHILOCLEON. Everything's fine so far,
　　But I want one thing.

BDELYCLEON.　　　　　What?

PHILOCLEON. Could I have an image of Lycos?

BDELYCLEON [*producing a small statue*]. Our noble lord in person.

PHILOCLEON. O Master, how grim you look!

BDELYCLEON. He's almost . . . like Cleonymos.

PHILOCLEON. He's got no shield, at any rate.

BDELYCLEON. The sooner your lordship's seated
　　The sooner I can call a case.

PHILOCLEON. I've been ready for ages. Get on.

BDELYCLEON. Let's see . . . What first? What
　　Have the slaves been up to lately?
　　Thratta burned out a pot.

PHILOCLEON. Hi! Wait a bit. This is awful,
  Do you want to give me a fit?
  How can you bring a case
  Without a bar for the court?
  Of all our holy appurtenances
  It's the one we can't do without.

BDELYCLEON. We haven't got one.

PHILOCLEON.   I'll slip
  Indoors and fix something up.   [*Exit.*

BDELYCLEON. He's got it badly—what
  A strange obsession this is!

SOSIAS [*inside*]. Go to the crows, you brute you!
  Keeping a dog like this.

          Enter Sosias *with two dogs.*

BDELYCLEON. What's wrong?

SOSIAS.   This Laches—Labes—
  This whatsit of a dog got
  Into the larder and scoffed
  A whole cheese, a Sicilian cheese.

BDELYCLEON. We'll make him the first case.
  You prosecute.

SOSIAS.   Not much!
  This other mongrel, Cleo— . . . this
  Other dear little doggie
  Would love to—if there's a charge.

BDELYCLEON. Bring them both in.

SOSIAS.   Yessir!

        Re-enter Philocleon, *carrying part of fence.*

BDELYCLEON. What's this?

PHILOCLEON.   Bit of the pig-pen.

BDELYCLEON. Isn't that a sacrilege?

PHILOCLEON. Not a bit—I'll begin
  As I mean to go on. But call
  The case—I'm feeling crusty.

BDELYCLEON. I must get the cause-lists first
  And the depositions.

PHILOCLEON.   Confound it!
  These delays are driving me raving mad.
  I'm itching to put down 'Guilty'.

BDELYCLEON. Right then!

PHILOCLEON.   Call the case!

BDELYCLEON. I'm ready, sir.

PHILOCLEON.   Who's first?

BDELYCLEON. What an utter fool I am.
  I forgot to bring the urns!

PHILOCLEON. Where are you going?

BDELYCLEON.   To get them.

PHILOCLEON. Don't bother. I've got these stewpots.

BDELYCLEON. Fine, then we've got everything
  We need—except a water-clock!

PHILOCLEON. What's my pisspot, if *it* isn't?

BDELYCLEON. What wit! You coarse old so-and-so!
  Here, someone! Xanthias!
  Fire, myrtle boughs, and incense.
  We must be holy first
  And pray.   [Xanthias *fetches them.*

CHORUS. And we with prayers and libations
  Shall pray for your lasting concord
  Since you have put behind you
  Your strife and come from the issue
  In cleanly and goodly fashion.

BDELYCLEON. Keep holy silence all!

CHORUS.   Phoebus, Pythian Apollo,
            Bless all that is toward
            Outside these doors today
            And suffer our erring footsteps
            No more to stray but follow
            The paths of peace.
                  Io Paian!

BDELYCLEON. O Lord and Master who keep my door and courtyard
  Look with favour upon these newborn rites
  Which on behalf of my father we institute today.

May he be purged of his choler and severity
And the gall in his heart inmixed with a little honey.
                    Let him show clemency
                    And pity more the accused
                    Than the accuser: let him weep
                    At the confessor's plea
                    And pluck the nettle anger
                    Out of his heart for ever.

CHORUS. We join our voice with yours,
  Cognisant fully of all that has gone before,
  And our old hearts rejoice
  In a young man such as you
  So steeped in love of the people
  As no one else we know.

BDELYCLEON [as herald]. If there's a justice at the door let him
    enter!
  No one may be admitted once proceedings have begun!

PHILOCLEON. Where's the prisoner? He'll get it hot and strong.

BDELYCLEON. I'll read the charge. A dog from Cleon's kennel
  Accuses Laches—Labes—of Aixone
  In that he did alone by himself devour a cheese,
  A Sicilian cheese: for which offence we demand as
  Penalty: one collar of fig-wood.

PHILOCLEON.   Not if I know it!
  It's death—a dog's death—if I find him guilty.

BDELYCLEON. Here's the accused!   [Points to dog.

PHILOCLEON.   What a nasty
  Brute—why he looks a thief.
  Can't deceive me with that
  Snarl of a smile. Where's the accuser?

DOG. Wf! Wf!

BDELYCLEON. Here he is.

SOSIAS [aside]. Spit and image of Labes—
  And as good at licking dishes . . .

BDELYCLEON. Silence! Now up dog
  And state the charge.

PHILOCLEON [aside].   I'll just
  Have a taste of these lentils.

SOSIAS. Sir, it's a monstrous bit of
    Dirt on me and the sailors.
    Went in a corner he did,
    A dark corner, and bolted
    A whole Sicilian cheese.

PHILOCLEON. Phaugh! No doubt of that—
    He's just belched in my face.

SOSIAS. Nor he wouldn't give me a sliver,
    Though I asked him. Call that a friend?
    And me the watchdog too,
    And not a scrap.

PHILOCLEON.   Nor me!
    Not a share to anyone.
    He's as hot as this soup, the swine!

BDELYCLEON. Look here, father, I won't
    Have you prejudge the case.
    Hear the other side.

PHILOCLEON.   My dear boy,
    The evidence shouts aloud!

SOSIAS. Don't you acquit him! He's
    Gone round and round the cheese dish;
    Pared off the rind, he has,
    Of every city, the greedy
    Gluttonous sneak-thief, fair glued
    To them.

PHILOCLEON. —And I haven't enough
    Glue to mend my pitcher!

SOSIAS. Then give him the works—it's a saying:
    One bush can't foster *two* thieves.
    And me, I might bark and get nothing,
    And then never bark no more.

PHILOCLEON. What an indictment! He's
    An incorrigible old lag!
    Don't you think so, cock? He does.
    Hand me my water-clock.

BDELYCLEON. Get it yourself. I'll call
    My witnesses. Those for Labes,
    Stand forward! Cup, pestle,

Cheese-grater, pot, brazier,
And all the sooty lot!
[*To* Philocleon.] Will you *never* finish piddling?

PHILOCLEON. I'll finish him today.

BDELYCLEON. *Do* stop being so snappy
To all the prisoners.
[*To the prisoner dog.*] Now, sir, your evidence.

[*Silence.*

Are you tongue-tied? Speak up.

PHILOCLEON. He's nothing to say.

BDELYCLEON.   Nonsense.
Just a passing fit, like Thucydides
At his trial—a temporary lock-jaw.
Here, gangway! I'll speak for him!
Sirs, it's difficult to answer
For a dog that's been slandered,
But I'll try. He's a good dog
And keeps the wolves off.

PHILOCLEON. He's a thief and conspirator.

BDELYCLEON. He's the best dog we've got now,
Controlling as many flocks
As you order him to. . . .

PHILOCLEON.   What good
If he swipes the cheese?

BDELYCLEON.   He fights
For you, guards the door, he's top-dog!
And if he swiped the cheese
Forgive him. He never learnt
His manners.

PHILOCLEON.   I wish he'd never
Learnt to write rigmaroles
To bore us like this.

BDELYCLEON.   I'll call
My witnesses. Cheese-grater!
Speak out. You were mess-caterer.
Answer plainly. Didn't you grate
Fair shares for all the soldiers?
He says he did.

PHILOCLEON.   He's lying.

BDELYCLEON [*sob-stuff*]. Sir, pity these sweated labourers!
    Labes, here, lives on fish heads
    And scraps and he's on the go
    From dawn to dusk, but this other—
    He's a house-dog—curled up sleek
    On the mat and whatever anyone
    Brings in, demands his whack,
    Or he'll bite.

PHILOCLEON.   Oh dear! What's coming
    Over me? I feel soppy!
    On the point of giving in!

BDELYCLEON. Have pity, pity, father.
    You wouldn't have him destroyed.
    Where are his dear little puppies?   [Sosias *brings them*.
    Come, you poor whimpering creatures,
    And whine and weep and howl.   [*The puppies do*.

PHILOCLEON. Get down, get down, get down, get down!

BDELYCLEON. I will, but I know how false
    A hope a judge's 'get down'
    Can be—but I *will* get down.

PHILOCLEON. Confound it! Swilling soup
    Isn't a good idea—I'm
    Only in tears because
    I'm awash with soup.

BDELYCLEON.   Then you won't
    Acquit him?

PHILOCLEON.   It's hard to decide. . . .

BDELYCLEON. Look, father—don't be hard-hearted.
    Take this pebble, shut
    Your eyes, and pop it in the
    Second urn. *Do* let him off!

PHILOCLEON. I don't know how to. 'I never
    Learnt my manners'. . . .

BDELYCLEON.   Here, then
    I'll lead you the nearest way.

PHILOCLEON. Is this the nearest?

BDELYCLEON.   Yes.

PHILOCLEON. Very well . . .   [*He puts the pebble in the wrong pot.*

BDELYCLEON.   I've foxed him! He never
  Meant to. [*To* Philocleon.] I'll do the count.

PHILOCLEON. How's it going?

BDELYCLEON.   Wait a minute!
  Labes . . . is . . . acquitted.   [Philocleon *collapses.*
  Father, whatever's the matter?

PHILOCLEON. Water . . . water . . . water . . .

BDELYCLEON. Pull yourself together.

PHILOCLEON. Was . . . he . . . *really* acquitted?

BDELYCLEON. Yes.

PHILOCLEON.   Oh god, it's the end.
  I'm finished. Done for.

BDELYCLEON.   Don't
  Take on so. Here, get up!

PHILOCLEON. I can never look myself
  In the face again. Acquitted!
  A man acquitted. What
  Will become of me? Dear gods,
  Forgive me, it wasn't *me*.
  It's not in my nature, I
  Did it against my will.

BDELYCLEON. Don't upset yourself so. I'll
  Look after you, take you everywhere—
  Lunch, dinner, parties, theatres;
  One long round of pleasure
  For the rest of your life—and no one,
  No Hyperbolos shall ever
  Make a fool of you again.
  So let's go in, and begin.

PHILOCLEON. Very well. Let's go in.   [*Exeunt.*

CHORUS. Go where you please, and be happy
  Wherever you go!—But you,   [*Addressing the audience.*
  Countless thousands in front of me now,
  I want your full attention!
  Don't let my words go
  In at one ear and out at the other

(As it does with some I could mention)
—That wouldn't be like *you*.
So apply your minds now, to an honest genuine statement.
The poet's got a bone to pick with you spectators.
He says you've wronged him—he's given you plenty of pleasure
In previous plays, though at first, being too shy and modest,
He was anonymous, hid his light under a bushel
And, like a ventriloquist, made his jokes through the mouths of
Any number of others. Now he's come right into the open,
His muse is bridled and bitted—he's ready to risk his own neck.
And though he's had more honour for this than any before him
He swears that his head's not swollen. He's never abused his
    position,
Got drunk and pawed at the pretty boys as they have learnt their
    wrestling;
But the buggers who *did* got short shrift if they came and
    objected
To his mockery, offering hush-money. He kept his nose clean.
His muse is clean, straightforward—never a ponce or a pander.
From the very beginning he left inoffensive decent people
Alone and went for the big crooks with a Heraclean power,
And boldly entered the lists against the yellow-fanged monster
Whose blood-shot eyes glittered bright as that strumpet Kynna's.
And round its head a hundred lickspittle toadies slobbered
And it roared like a river in spate, stank like a seal, had
The dirty balls of a troll and the back end of a camel,
But did your poet blench at the sight? Did he take bribes?
    Never.
He fought and he fights for you. And for you he's wrestled
(Only last year, he says) with shivering wraiths and spectres
Who stole by night to throttle fathers and choke grandfathers
And crept into bed beside the most innocent harmless people
Whispering affidavits, writs, proofs, oaths, counter-oaths
Till they leapt out of bed screaming and ran for the police.
Yet having this champion, this cleanser of his country,
You dropped him flat last year, just when his original brilliant
Ideas should have borne fruit: you let them wilt and wither,
Simply failing to grasp them. Yet the poet swears by Bacchus
And Bacchus and Bacchus you never heard a comedy better.

He says the blame is yours—you hadn't the mental equip-
ment!
But the discerning will always pick the potential winner
However he loads the dice against himself by his daring.

> So, in future, dear friends, cherish
> Poets who aim to break
> New ground in theme and technique;
> Put their plays in your cupboards
> Like the spices you keep your clothes with
> And you'll wear sweet wit-scented
> Clothes all the year through.
> In the old days we were strong in the dance,
> Strong in battle,
> Strongest of all as men.
> Alas, that was long ago!
> My hair grows whiter than a swan
> But from our ashes we must blow
> Some youthful sparks, for we,
> Old as we are, are better I say
> Than the crimped long-haired lounging
> Pansies of today.

Now if any of you spectators, knowing our mettle,
Is puzzled by seeing us wasp-waisted and wonders
What's the point of the sting, I'll easily tell you
'Though you hadn't a clue before'. We are the only
Aboriginal inhabitants—the native race of Attica,
Heroes to a man, and saviours of this city
In many a battle when the barbarians invaded us,
Infesting the city and pouring in smoke and fire upon us,
Intent upon rooting out our nests by force—not likely!
Seizing up spears and shields we made sally after sally,
Steeped in a bitter fury, standing shoulder to shoulder
And biting our lips with anger. The sky was benighted
By arrows, but with the gods on our side we had them routed,
For, before we fought, an owl had winged her way over the
army.
Then we pursued them closely, prodding their baggy back-
sides,
And they fled in panic, stung in the jaws and on the eyebrows.

It's still a widespread barbarian saying 'There's nothing fiercer
Than an Attic wasp'—with reason!
> We were fierce, afraid of nothing on land,
>> And in our triremes
> We were masters of the seas;
> We didn't care whoever
> Turned the wittiest phrase
> Or greased his way into favour,
> It was who was the best oar.
> And we socked the Medes and made them flinch,
> *We* exacted the tribute that's still being paid
>> And the young pansies pinch.

So we swarm together, as if in nests,
Some to the civil, some to the criminal
Courts, some to the Odeon, some
On the walls in a huddled mass, bent
Double and hardly moving, like
Grubs in their cells. We can adapt
Ourselves to any sort of life—
Sting anyone and then live on them!
But we've a lot of layabout drones;
They've got no stings—they stay and eat
The fruits of the tribute and never do
A hand's turn. It makes us bitter
To see them pilfer our pay, and they've never
Handled a lance or an oar or raised
A blister in their country's service.
So for the future we suggest
No citizen without a sting
Qualifies for his three obols.

> *Re-enter* Bdelycleon *and* Philocleon.

PHILOCLEON. No, no! I'll *never* give up this cloak,
Not while I'm alive—it saved my life
When the great north wind won us that battle!

BDELYCLEON. You don't seem to know what's good for you.

PHILOCLEON. It's not the sort of thing for me—
Too smart. Only the other day
I stuffed myself with sprats and had
To pay three obols to the cleaner.

BDELYCLEON. Give this a try! After all, you've promised
   To do all I suggest for your good.

PHILOCLEON. What do you want me to do?

BDELYCLEON.   Take off
   That rag and put *this* on, and wear it
   With *style*, father.

PHILOCLEON.   What's the point
   Of begetting and bringing children up
   When all they want is to choke one?

BDELYCLEON. Come! Take it and put it on. Stop quacking.

PHILOCLEON. Good heavens what's this horror?

BDELYCLEON.   Some people
   Call it a Persian cloak, others a fleecer.

PHILOCLEON. I'm not surprised. But I thought it was
   A Thymaitian rug.

BDELYCLEON.   You've never been
   In Sardis or you'd know—but you don't.

PHILOCLEON. I haven't. I don't. It looks to me
   More like Morychos' mantle.

BDELYCLEON. It was woven in Ecbatana.

PHILOCLEON. Woven? It looks like guts—have their oxen
   Got guts of wool?

BDELYCLEON.   Oh *really*, father!
   It's fabulously expensive stuff,
   And genuine folk-barbarian woven—
   A talent's worth of wool at least!

PHILOCLEON. It's a fleecer all right then.

BDELYCLEON.   Stand still, do,
   And put it on.

PHILOCLEON.   Poof! It's *stuffy* enough!

BDELYCLEON. Put it *on*!

PHILOCLEON.   Not me. Why don't you simply
   Wrap me up in an oven?

BDELYCLEON.   Then I'll
   Put it on you. There. [*To* Slave *carrying away old garments.*] Off
      you go.

PHILOCLEON. Have you got a meat-hook handy?

BDELYCLEON.   Why?

PHILOCLEON. To pull me out before I'm roast alive.

BDELYCLEON. Now take off those revolting slippers,
  And put on these smart Spartan sandals.

PHILOCLEON. Wear enemy footgear? Me? Pah!

BDELYCLEON. Pop in your foot. Push into it
  Spartan-style.

PHILOCLEON.   It's monstrous of you
  To make me tread on enemy soil.

BDELYCLEON. Now the other foot.

PHILOCLEON.   No, one
  Of its toes detests Spartans.

BDELYCLEON.   Both on, please!

PHILOCLEON. So I'm left in my old age without
  Even a chilblain—it isn't fair!

BDELYCLEON. Right. Now walk like a rich pansy. . . .
  No! Like this . . .

PHILOCLEON.   Watch me, then. Tell me
  Which of your rich pansy friends
  I look most like.

BDELYCLEON.   Like a bandage
  Round a boil.

PHILOCLEON [with distaste]. I'm simply longing
  To waggle my fanny . . . is that the expression?

BDELYCLEON. Oh leave it alone! Can you hold
  Your own in intelligent conversation?

PHILOCLEON. Of course I can.

BDELYCLEON.   Show me how.

PHILOCLEON. I know plenty of stories—say, how
  Lamia farted when they caught her.
  And what Cardopion and his mother . . .

BDELYCLEON. No, no; not myths—human affairs.
  Everyday life.

PHILOCLEON.   Oh, I see! I know
  A good one. Once upon a time
  A cat and a mouse . . .

BDELYCLEON.   You ignorant oaf,
  As Theogenes said to the muck-shoveller,
  Do you mean to drivel about cats
  And mice in civilized company?

PHILOCLEON. What'd you have me say?

BDELYCLEON.   Something
  Serious—how you went with Androcles
  And Cleisthenes on a special mission.

PHILOCLEON. But I never did. The only mission
  I ever went on was escort duty
  To Paros at two obols a day.

BDELYCLEON. Then, oh—say how you saw Euphudion
  Beating Ascondias all ends up
  In a Pancration—despite
  His age and grey hair. Praise his muscular
  Arms, his *iron* physique, his *breast*plate chest.

PHILOCLEON. But you mustn't *use* a breastplate in
  The Pancration.

BDELYCLEON.   It's just their way
  Of speech. But tell me another thing.
  If you were drinking with strangers which
  Of all your exploits when you were young
  Would you tell them?

PHILOCLEON.   My most brilliant . . .
  Why, when I pinched Ergasion's
  Vine-poles.

BDELYCLEON. Vine-poles! You're killing me.
  Say how you hunted a boar or a hare,
  Ran a torch-race—something daring!

PHILOCLEON. I know! When I was very young
  I challenged the runner Phayllos, and beat him
  By two votes—in an action for defamation.

BDELYCLEON. Oh, turn it up! But lie down and learn
  How to be social and convivial.

PHILOCLEON. Lie down? How?

BDELYCLEON.   Gracefully.

PHILOCLEON. Like this?

BDELYCLEON.   No, not like that.

PHILOCLEON.   Then how?

BDELYCLEON. Just flex your knees, and simply *melt*
Into the cushions—praising a vase.
Then quiz the ceiling and drop a phrase
About the *wonderful* curtains. Right:
Water for our hands—table laid—
Dine—wash again—then the libation . . .

PHILOCLEON. Zeus! It's all make-believe. I thought . . .

BDELYCLEON. The flute-girl's played—your fellow-guests
Theoros, Aeschines, Phanos, Cleon,
Some stranger beside Akestor—could you
'Cap the catches' with them?

PHILOCLEON.   Couldn't I?
No backwoods bumpkin better.

BDELYCLEON.   Very well.
Suppose me Cleon. Harmodios' tune:
      'No one in Athens has ever seen—'

PHILOCLEON. 'Such a first-class—crook as you have been.'

BDELYCLEON. Would you really say that? He'd shout you down!
He'd smash you! Have you run out of the country!

PHILOCLEON. If he tries, here's another for him:
     'You're mad for power—you climb to the bridge
     Of the Ship of State and think,
     "It's rocking, *I* can steady it"
     —And it's *your* weight, making it sink.'

BDELYCLEON. And suppose Theoros, sitting at Cleon's
Feet, takes his hand and begins like this:
       'O heed the example of Admetos,
       Love Good and you will find—'

PHILOCLEON.   'Playing the fox is the dirty trick
       Of a double-crossing friend.'

BDELYCLEON. Then maybe the next'll be Aeschines,
Sellos' son; he's quick and witty.
    'Cleitagoras and I
    When we were in Thessaly
    We cut a caper.
    You should have seen the power and the riches—'

PHILOCLEON. 'Somebody asked me which is
              The chap with the cash, and I said
              "They're both millionaires—on paper."'

BDELYCLEON. Yes, I think you'll pass on that.
  Right! Let's dine at Philoctemon's.
  Boy! Chrysos! Pack up the dinner!
  Now for a real booze-up.

PHILOCLEON.   No, no.
  Wouldn't do at all. I know the result
  Of drinking: breaking things up, brawls;
  Then a terrible hangover and a fine.

BDELYCLEON. Not if you drink with gentlemen.
  They'll go to whomever you've beaten up
  And get you off. Or you'll tell some crack
  From Aesop or Sybaris, picked up
  At the party, so the whole thing's
  Laughed off and he goes home happy.

PHILOCLEON. I'll learn up plenty of those—if I
  Can get away with whatever I do.
  Off we go! Nothing shall stop us now!   [Exeunt.

CHORUS. I've often considered myself clever,
  But never gauche like Amynias—
  Leogoras used to have him to dinner,
  Now he gnaws an apple for lunch
  Or a pomegranate, as empty
  As Antiphon. And when he
  Went to Pharsalos as envoy
  He lived alone with the slaveys,
  The poorest of the bunch.
  Lucky Automenes! How astonishingly lucky
  You are to have been the father
  Of sons of such infinite brilliance!
  Firstly the wisest, the uni-
  versally loved, the singer
  And harper—in everyone's favour.
  Second the actor whose acting
  Is out of this world, he's so clever.
  And thirdly the most original—

Ariphrades: learning from no one,
But out of sheer native genius
Inventing an unmentionable
Quite new vice in the brothels.
There are some who said that I was reconciled
With Cleon. It's true he had me in a tight
Corner and gave it me hot—he's not a tanner for nothing. . . .
And the louder I yelled the louder the bystanders
Laughed and hung about to see what sort of joke
I could screw out of my afflictions—and maybe
Seeing the situation I *did* lay it on a bit;
But now the vine-pole's tricked the vine again.

Enter Xanthias.

XANTHIAS. Gods! Tortoises aren't half lucky!
Them with their backs and ribs
Well and truly plated to keep them
From being hammered—but me,
I'm black and blue all over.

CHORUS. What's wrong, boy? You're a bit
Old for a boy, but it's right to
Call you 'boy' if you're beaten.

XANTHIAS. It's the old man—plastered!
Worst of the lot—and we got
Hippyllos, Antiphon, Lycon,
Lysistratos, Theophrastos,
And a school with Phrynichos,
But he was the most impossible.
Directly he'd stuffed himself
He got frisky and bucked around
Farting and braying with laughter
Like a donkey full of corn,
And beating me, 'Boy! Boy! Boy!'
Like I was one, and when he saw him
Lysistratos said 'Old pal,
You're as lively as new wine.'
And *he* yelled back '*You're* like
A tatty grasshopper,
Or Sthenelos after he'd

Been sold up.' They all roared
Except Theophrastos who made
A face—he being a gent.
And the old bastard says to him
'Who do you think *you* are
With your airs and graces, you
Sucker-up to the rich.'
And so he took the mickey
Out of them all in turn
And talked smut and behaved
Like nobody's business—then
He rolls home stinko hitting . . .   [Philocleon *is heard singing.*
I'm getting out before
He beats me up again!   [*Exit.*

> *Enter* Philocleon *with a* Girl *and waving a torch about.*

PHILOCLEON. Way 'Hey' and up she rises!
Up . . . down . . . up.
Some of you follows fellowing me
Will be sorry. If you don't push off
I'll toast you with this torch.

> *He is followed by a* Guest.

GUEST. You'll pay for this tomorrow!
And you've no excuse, you're not
Even young—we'll take you to court.

PHILOCLEON. Ph! Do your worst, you old women!
Don't you know I hate the sound
Of the word (hic) court. *This*
Is what I like—you can have
Your voting-boxes and justices.
Out of my way—my vote's
For this pretty little poppet
I've got in tow. Hang on darling!
I know it's a bit old
And frayed—but it'll do you.
Did you see how cunningly
I sneaked you away and saved you
From those nasty-minded drunks?

So you owe it to thank my cock
In the usual manner—you won't though!
I know you, you'll lead me up
Your garden path and then trick me
And laugh—I know you've done it
To all of them. Now, darling,
Be a good girl and when
My son's dead I'll get you freed
To be my mistress, eh, my little pussy?
At present I haven't got
Control of my affairs—I'm too young.
I have to be carefully guarded.
My son's my guardian. He's a tartar
And a skinflint—hard as winter.
He's afraid I'll go to the bad,
And I'm his only father.
Look, he's coming—he's after us.

                              Enter Bdelycleon.

Here, lovie, hold these torches
And I'll have a go at him
As he did at me before
I was initiated
Into *these* mysteries . . .

                    [*What they are his gesture makes clear.*

BDELYCLEON [*furious*]. You . . . You . . . dirty old . . . So you *want*
    Bed do you? What you'll get
    Is a nice, mature, single COFFIN,
    And smart for it too.

PHILOCLEON [*laughs*].   I'll give you
    As good as I get—if you want it!

BDELYCLEON. Don't laugh! Where's the flute-girl?

PHILOCLEON. What flute-girl? Are you dotty,
    Or have you come from *your* coffin?

BDELYCLEON. Why, Dardanis—she's there
    Beside you!

PHILOCLEON. Nonsense. A torch
    I lit on the market-place
    For the gods.

BDELYCLEON.   A torch?

PHILOCLEON.   A torch.
  Can't you see from its pattern and colour?

BDELYCLEON. What's this dark triangular
  Bit in the middle?

PHILOCLEON.   The pitch
  Running out . . .

BDELYCLEON.   And *this* side:
  It's a female bottom—

PHILOCLEON.   No, no,
  Just a bulge in the torch.

BDELYCLEON. Bulge, my foot. Come along
  With me, my girl.

PHILOCLEON.   What
  Are you going to do?

BDELYCLEON.   Take her
  Off your hands—and your hands off her!
  You're too old anyway.   *[Leads the* Girl *off.*

PHILOCLEON. Now listen to me!
  Once I was watching the games
  And I saw Ephudion fighting
  Ascondas, and, though he was old,
  He got him where he wanted.
  So look out or I'll give you
  A lovely black eye. . . .

BDELYCLEON.   By god,
  You've learned *that* lesson well.

                 Enter Baker Woman.

BAKER WOMAN. God help us! [*To* Bdelycleon.] *You* help.
  Here's the old so-and-so
  Ruined me, swatting about
  With his torch—bowled over ten
  Of my best one-obol loaves,
  And another four.

BDELYCLEON.   Do you see
  What your drinking's done? Suits
  And more suits.

PHILOCLEON.   Nonsense, boy.
  I'll make it up in a flash
  With a jolly story.
BAKER WOMAN.   Not with Myrtia,
  Sostraté's daughter—Anchylion's daughter—
  Not bloody likely. You wrecked my bread!
PHILOCLEON. Listen, woman, you'll like this.
BAKER WOMAN. Not much I won't.
PHILOCLEON.   —One evening
  As Aesop walked home from dinner
  A drunken bitch barked at him
  And he said, Bitch, bitch.
  Instead of that nasty noise
  You'd better be buying flour.
BAKER WOMAN. So it's insult too. I summon you,
  Whoever you are, to appear
  At the market court and pay for
  The damage to my goods—
  Chairephon be my witness.
PHILOCLEON. Here, really you'll like this—
  Lasos and Simonides
  Were finalists in a choral
  Competition, and Lasos says,
  'I'm hanged if *I* care.'
BAKER WOMAN.   Really.
  But *you* will.
PHILOCLEON.   And Chairephon's
  Your witness, like shivering Ino
  Just going to hurl herself
  To death, off Euripides' feet.   [*Exit* Baker Woman.
BDELYCLEON. Oh heaven, here's someone else,
  And he's got a real witness.
              Enter an Angry Man *with a* Witness.
ANGRY MAN. I charge you with criminal
  Assault.
BDELYCLEON. Oh *don't* do that.
  By the gods, I'll make it all right!
  Just name your figure, and no questions.

PHILOCLEON. I admit I assaulted him.
  I'll pay up without a murmur.
  Here, will you leave it to me
  To fix the damages—or will you?

ANGRY MAN. I don't want no trouble. *You* say.

PHILOCLEON. A man from Sybaris fell
  Out of his carriage bang
  On his head and was badly injured.
  (He wasn't a good driver.)
  And a friend who saw it all said,
  'Each man to his own trade'
  —So you go to the doctor.

BDELYCLEON [*aside*]. Typical!

ANGRY MAN [*to* Witness]. Remember what he said!

PHILOCLEON. Hi! Don't go off in a huff.
  —A woman once bust a jug
  In Sybaris. . . .

ANGRY MAN.   I call you to Witness.

PHILOCLEON. —Just what the jug did!
  But the woman said 'Why bother
  About witnesses; if you had
  More sense you'd call for a rivet.'

ANGRY MAN. You can have your little joke—
  Till the judge calls the case!   [*Exit with* Witness.

BDELYCLEON. By heaven, you can't stay here!
  I'll carry you in.

PHILOCLEON.   Why?

BDELYCLEON. If we don't we'll soon be lost
  In a cloud of witnesses!

PHILOCLEON. They say, at Delphi, Aesop—

BDELYCLEON. Blast Aesop.

PHILOCLEON.   —was charged with stealing
  A sacred cup, but he told them
  How a beetle . . .
                        [Bdelycleon *seizes him and drags him in.*

BDELYCLEON. I'll *do* you and your beetles!   [*Exeunt.*

CHORUS.   I envy the old crust
             His luck: what a change
             From his simple austere ways.
             A whole new range of living
             Soft sensual easy days.
             Maybe he won't like it.
             It's often hard to adjust
             The psyche to such a break,
             But people have managed to make it
             If only they've really stuck to
             The advice they agreed to take.

             As for the young man
             He deserves the highest praise
             From us and from everyone
             Who has good at heart. Philocleon's
             Son is a paragon
             Of filial love and wisdom.
             No son since time began
             Has been so single-minded,
             So doting towards his father
             In proffering life as he'd rather
             He led it and how to find it.

             The scene changes to inside the house.

                    Enter Xanthias.

XANTHIAS. By Dionysus, an evil spirit has gone
     Through our house like a whirlwind. The old
     Man after hours of drinking heard
     The flute, and he's danced all night for joy
     The old steps of Thespis—nothing'll stop him.
     And he says he'll have a tangle
     With these newfangled tragedians any moment.

                    Enter Philocleon.

PHILOCLEON. Who's at the door?

XANTHIAS.   More
     Trouble.

PHILOCLEON. Unbolt it—this
     Is how that routine begins.

XANTHIAS. How madness begins.

PHILOCLEON. Rib-wrenching, pipe-opening, joint-cracking.

XANTHIAS. Go and drink hellebore.

PHILOCLEON. Phrynicos used to crouch like a cock.

XANTHIAS. And where are your spurs?

PHILOCLEON. Then kick to the sky
   And do the splits.   [*He does.*

XANTHIAS. Look out!

PHILOCLEON.   My joints are getting
   More supple in their sockets.

                    Enter Bdelycleon.

BDELYCLEON. Oh god, what madness!

PHILOCLEON. I challenge the lot.
   If a poet thinks he can dance, let him
   Have a go against me!
   Does anyone dare?

            Enter small figure dressed as a Crab.

BDELYCLEON.   Here's one.

PHILOCLEON. What little twit is that?

BDELYCLEON.   The middle
   Son of Karkinos.

PHILOCLEON.   I'll middle him
   With a knuckle-dance—he doesn't know
   A thing about rhythm!

                Another Crab *enters*.

BDELYCLEON.   Here comes his brother.

PHILOCLEON. I'll have him for dinner.

BDELYCLEON. Nothing but crabs, ugh!

PHILOCLEON.   What's this
   Creepy-crawly—a shrimp or a spider?

BDELYCLEON. It's a mini-crab and it writes
   Mini-tragedies.

PHILOCLEON.   Oh Karkinos,
   Proud father of such a brood
   Of almost invisible children!
   I must really gird up my loins—

You be mixing a dressing
For when I beat and eat them.

CHORUS. Now all of you please move a little back,
So they can twirl at their ease!
Oh great-named sons of the sea's
Wandering citizen, dance on the shore
Of the unplumbed salt estranger!
Swivel your feet, do a Phrynichan kick;
Let the audience clap as your legs jerk up,
Tie your stomachs in knots and spin like tops!
See how the Ocean Ranger
Creeps in to rejoice in his dancing three!
But come, if you like it, dance with me,
Join with the Chorus; no one before
Has danced, danced out a comedy!   [*All dance.*

PEACE

Aristophanes presented his Peace *to the world for the first time at the Great Dionysia in* 421 B.C. *It won second prize.*

The play takes up as reprises several of the subjects of the four earlier plays that have survived, in particular the most important theme of the need for peace. This time, so far from the one-man peace treaty Dikaiopolis sought from the Spartans in the *Acharnians*, it is peace for the sake of Athens and her allies, for Sparta and hers, for all Greece in fact, that Trygaios mounts his flying dung-beetle to travel to heaven to ask from Zeus and the Olympian gods of all the Greeks. The two chief leaders on either side, the Athenian Cleon and the Spartan Brasidas, had both been killed in the Battle of Amphipolis the year before—so that War (who has occupied heaven, from which the other gods have decamped in disgust with the Greeks) has lost both the pestles with which he liked to pound Greek cities in his mortar. Though nearly all Greeks want peace, Trygaios finds that no community or group except the farmers (who form the Chorus of the play) really try hard enough to haul the goddess Peace up again from where War has buried her. But the farmers do succeed, and the celebrations of the return of Peace on earth therefore make a grand finale in a rustic wedding feast.

In fact, the Peace of Nikias between Athens and Sparta—which was to last for fifty years, but didn't—came into being within days of the production of the *Peace*.

For the rest, familiar Aristophanic jibes are made at profiteers from the war (including this time the makers of weapons), the purveyors of oracles and prophecies, Cleon (though not too harshly, since he's dead), informers; a version of the paltry origins of the war is given again, and its genuinely disastrous effects in poverty and food shortages (especially for the Megarians) described; Aristophanes points too to the militaristic ethos, after thirteen years of virtual hostilities, and its influence on children, such that they only know war songs to sing.

Rival writers come in for cracks, as ever; especially Euripides for his ragged or sick characters—and the beetle itself is a joke on the winged horse Pegasus in his *Bellerophon*. But fair words are said of Sophocles. In the Parabasis it is now Aristophanes the bald and bold who is confident that he has deserved well of the Athenians both as citizens and as playgoers.

Some new fun is made too at the expense of the gods. Perhaps because of the war—or the Sophists—religious reverence has diminished in Athens, and there must be less food for sacrifices (Hermes is positively hungry). But the fuller development of this theme is to come in the next play we have, the *Birds*, seven years later.

CHARACTERS

FIRST SERVANT
SECOND SERVANT
TRYGAIOS, *a vine-dresser*
His DAUGHTERS
HERMES
WAR
TUMULT
PEACE
PEACE-AND-PLENTY
PEACE-WORK
HIEROCLES, *an oracle-monger*
SICKLE-MAKER
CREST-MAKER
SPEAR-BURNISHER
BREASTPLATE-SELLER
TRUMPET-MAKER
HELMET-MAKER
BOY, *son of Lamachos*
BOY, *son of Cleonymos*
CHORUS *of farmers*

The scene is the courtyard of Trygaios' *house. There is a pen with a door, right. Two* Servants *are standing, centre, looking towards the pen.*

1 SERVANT. 'Ere, 'ere you! Quick as you can! Grub, for the
    dung-beetle!

2 SERVANT. 'Ere y'are.

1 SERVANT.   Give 'im the cake; the dirty . . . ugh!
    What I'd *do* to 'im.

2 SERVANT [*ironic*]. May 'e never suck sweeter—

1 SERVANT.   You fool! Punch up another:
    Ass-droppings is what you want—

2 SERVANT.   Here's a *horse*-d'oeuvres, then . . .

1 SERVANT. Cripes, where's the last you brought? 'As 'e been an'
    ate it?

2 SERVANT. Grabbed it and dribbled it with 'is forefeet—then
    scoffed it.

1 SERVANT. Get cracking then; more! More!

2 SERVANT.   Gawds, help me, you muck-rakers,
    Or I'll choke to death.

1 SERVANT.   Come on! 'E's after another:
    A 'fairy'-cake 'e says—'e likes it minced special.

2 SERVANT. Well, there's one thing at least: no one will accuse me
    Of tasting what I prepare—like them classy chefs do.

1 SERVANT. More! More! Keep at it.

2 SERVANT.   Not me, by Apollo!
    I can't stand this muck no more. I'm gettin' the cess-tub
    An' I'll chuck in the ruddy lot.

1 SERVANT.   —And your sweet self after it—

2 SERVANT. 'Ere! Anyone! Where can I get a nose without nostrils?
    Is there a dirtier job than mashing muck for a dung-beetle?
    Now a pig or a dog picks it up where it falls; no nonsense.
    But this 'ere brute's so cocky, 'e turns up 'is nose at
    Anything not done dainty, like for a lady.
    Now, I'll take a peek inside, with the door just ajar, 'cause
    I wouldn't like 'im to see. . . . Finished, you b——eetle?
    Go on, gobble and gorge, you bloated greedy-guts,

May you burst before you knows it! Look! 'E's like a wrestler,
Got it gripped in 'is molars, and weaving with 'is 'ead, like
He was plaiting a tug's hawser—you gluttonous golloper,
What god are *you* the ward of? 's not Aphrodite,
No, nor the Graces, neither.

1 SERVANT.   Whose d'you think, then?

2 SERVANT. Zeus, the Thunder-Dropper. Couldn't be elsewise.
Now, I suppose some slick young pleased-with-'imself puppy
Will say 'What does this mean? What's this beetle in aid of?'
And maybe some Ionian beside him'll answer
'Indeed, but it's *Cleon*, man; *Cleon* for certain,
So shamelessly as he feeds on the filth of our city' . . .
Well, I'll go in and give the beetle a booze-up.   [*Exit.*

1 SERVANT. And I'll stay and explain to the young men and children,
The old men and maidens, the V.I.P.s and the
Superexcellentissimos—
                    He's mad as a hatter,
My master. Mad; mad. Not *war*-mad like you are,
But in a quite *new* way. All day he goggles
At the sky with his mouth gaping, railing at Zeus. 'Zeus,'
('E says) 'what d'you mean to *do*? Put down your broom, Zeus,
Don't make a clean sweep of all the people in Greece!'

TRYGAIOS[*within*]. Oh . . . Oh . . . Oh . . .

1 SERVANT.   There 'e is now!

TRYGAIOS [*within*]. O Zeus! What will you *do* with us!
Before you know what you're at, you'll have extracted
The last drop of blood from our cities. . . .

1 SERVANT.   That's it. The madness
I just been talking about. That was a sample:
But *do* you know what 'e did? When first 'e went barmy,
Muttered, 'e did, to 'isself, '*If only somehow
I could actually get to Zeus*'—then 'e 'as very lightweight
Ladders constructed, and tries to climb up to 'eaven!
—Till 'e falls off and gets a crack on 'is onion.
Now, yesterday 'e goes off—*I* don't know where 'e gone to—
And comes back with this ruddy great brute of a beetle,
Makes me groom it like a 'orse; 'e pats it like a pony,
'My little Pegasus,' 'e croons, 'my thoroughbred flyer,

You got to fly me up to Zeus *himmediate*.' . . .
See? Now I'll just have a squint, and see what it's up to . . . .

[*Looks in the pen.*

Oooooh! Help! Everybody, help! Master's mounted the beetle!
They're off! They're up! Oh help! they're in the air!

Trygaios *appears in the air above the pen, astride the beetle.*

TRYGAIOS [*to the beetle*]. Charily, gingerly, gently, my jackass!
Don't strain too strongly right from the start, don't
Trust your thrust before your joints are juicy,
Sweaty, and limber from loosening your wings, and
Don't breathe your back-fire breath in my face, or
I'd prefer you were stalled, below, in your stable!

I SERVANT. Master! Master! 'Ave you gone off your rocker?

TRYGAIOS. Quietly! Quietly!

I SERVANT.   —What's the reason?
Where are you flying? And why are you flying?

TRYGAIOS [*with pomp*]. I fly on behalf of all Greeks! I am planning
A daring and novel *démarche*—

I SERVANT.   —But what are you after?
Come down to earth, are you out of your senses?

TRYGAIOS. Silence! Don't utter a word of ill omen.
Just give me a cheer. (—Oh, and *please* tell people
To brick up the privies and sewers, and keep their
Arses indoors.)

I SERVANT.   —I'm hanged if I'll be quiet
Unless you tell me where you're intending to fly to.

TRYGAIOS. Where else but to Zeus in heaven?

I SERVANT.   What's in your mind?

TRYGAIOS. I want, I *must* ask him what he proposes to do with
All the peoples of Greece.

I SERVANT.   And if he won't tell you?

TRYGAIOS. I'll take him to law for betraying Greece to the Persians—

I SERVANT. You'll do *that*, by heaven, over my dead body!

TRYGAIOS. There's no other way . . .

I SERVANT [*calling*]. Ooooh ooh ooh, children! Children! Your
    father's
Leaving you in the lurch,

Slipping off slyly to 'eaven without so much
As a good-bye kiss—'ere, you poor little wretch,
Plead with 'im—

Enter Trygaios' *two* Daughters.

1 DAUGHTER [*about fifteen*]. Father, father, is this true,
This rumour that's round the house,
That you're leaving us, *you*, father,
To fly in the face of fortune?
If you love us, tell us.

TRYGAIOS. Well, it is true, my dears, and I'm truly sorry to see you
Begging for bread and calling me 'dad' when I haven't a farthing,
No, not a bean in the house, not a sausage *what*soever;
But, *if* I come back; IF I have done as well as I should do,
You shall have a big cake:—and a black-eyeful of sauce to go
with it!

1 DAUGHTER. But how will you go? A ship can't sail in the air.

TRYGAIOS. I shan't sail, dear. My 'wingéd courser' shall carry me—

2 DAUGHTER. But what is the point of harnessing up a beetle
If you want to go to the gods?

TRYGAIOS.   According to Aesop,
It's the one flyer that reached them.

2 DAUGHTER.   What stupid nonsense
You talk! A stinking monster like *that*, to the *gods*?

TRYGAIOS. It got there to spite the eagle and smash its eggs.

1 DAUGHTER. But oughtn't you to ride some grander flyer like
Pegasus
And appear to the gods in a more tragic style?

TRYGAIOS. Then I'd have to take double rations. Now what I eat
will
Fatten my steed—

2 DAUGHTER.   But suppose he falls in the wet
And watery sea: how will his wings get him out?

TRYGAIOS. Ah! I've a portable rudder; and my beetle's a water-
Boatman from Naxos.

2 DAUGHTER.   What port will you put in at?

TRYGAIOS. Beetle Bay. It's on the Piraeus.

1 DAUGHTER.   You'd better look out
  You don't fall and cripple yourself, and provide a plot
  For Euripides. You'll become a tragedy . . .

TRYGAIOS. I'll attend to all that.
                             [*Exeunt* Daughters *and* Servant.
  [*To audience*]. But now farewell all you
  For whom I attempt this feat:
  I beg you for three days, mind
  You don't fart;
  For if he gets wind of your wind,
  He'll toss me head over heels
  And dive to earth for a meal.

  Come along, Pegasus, cantering contentedly
  With golden-studded clattering bridle
  And both ears pricked as we go on our journey!   [*They fly off.*

  What are you doing? What are you doing?
  What is this nose-dive towards the latrines?
  Pull out and climb from the earth on your pinions,
  Full speed ahead for the palace of Zeus, and
  Keep your nose *away* from your provender!

  What are you doing down there on the Piraeus?
  Man, you're destroying me—you, by the brothel,
  Bury it, heap it with earth, put a wreath on it,
  Souse it in myrrh. If I suffer today, the
  City of Chios shall pay for your lack of
  Control—a fine of five talents, I warn you!
  This is no longer a joke, I'm afraid. Hi!
  You scene-shifter, carefully, carefully,
  There's a whistling wind round my navel already,
  Please look after me—or I'm bound to feed my beetle.
                        [*As he speaks the scene is changing.*
  Nearly there now. That must be the palace.

      Outside the palace of the gods in heaven.

  Whoa back! Who's doorman? Will nobody answer me?

               Hermes *comes out.*

HERMES [*angrily*]. Smells like man . . . .
   Wonder where from?

                                                      [*He sees the beetle.*

   By Heracles! What hippo-harpy is this?
TRYGAIOS. A beetle horse, Hermes.
HERMES.   You repulsive, you shameless,
   You disgusting, you extra-repulsive,
   Double-dyed-disgusting-damned-whatsyername—
   Well, *say something*!
TRYGAIOS.   You've said it.
HERMES. Nationality? Country? Speak up!
TRYGAIOS.   You've said it.
HERMES. By Mother Earth, tell me or die!
TRYGAIOS. Trygaios, an Athenian, an expert vine-dresser,
   Neither a sycophant nor a lover of argument.
HERMES. Why have you come?
TRYGAIOS.   To bring you this *meat*. . .
HERMES [*all smiles*]. And how did you get here, my poor dear fellah?
TRYGAIOS. (So now I'm not so double-dyed-disgusting!)
   Hermes, you're greedy. Please, go and call Zeus!
HERMES. Zeus? What a hope. The gods have all gone.
   You're nowhere *near* them. Left yesterday, *they* did.
TRYGAIOS. But where on earth—?
HERMES.   —Earth my eye!
TRYGAIOS. But where?
HERMES [*singing*].   —To a happy land, far far away—
   The very absolute top of the vault of heaven.
TRYGAIOS. Why are you here, then, all by yourself?
HERMES. I look after their little particular et ceteras:
   Pots, pans, plates, jars—
TRYGAIOS.   But *why* have they gone?
HERMES. Can't *stand* you Greeks. So they've installed
   WAR in their place—handed you over
   To him; he can do whatever he chooses.
   Them, they've gone up as high as they can
   So they won't have to witness your bloody battles
   Nor attend to your prayers—

TRYGAIOS.   But *why* have they done this?

HERMES. So many times, *they* were for Peace,
    You were always for War. Why, if the Spartans
    Were a little on top they'd immediately say,
    'We'll teach the Athenians a lesson.' And then
    If you had the luck, and the Spartans came crawling
    With proposals for peace, *you* at once yelled
    'O Athens! O Zeus! They're trying to trick us!
    We can't allow this. They'll come again soon,
    If we hang on to Pylos.'

TRYGAIOS.   That's *just* how we talked!
    You've got it exactly.

HERMES.   —So I wouldn't know
    If you'll *see* Peace again.

TRYGAIOS.   Where has *she* gone?

HERMES. War's walled her up deep in a pit.

TRYGAIOS. Where?

HERMES.   Under here—you can see all the boulders
    He's piled in the mouth. No one will ever
    Extract her—

TRYGAIOS.   But what is he planning for *us*?

HERMES. Search me. Last night, he brought in a colossal mortar—

TRYGAIOS. A mortar? What for? A mortar?

HERMES. To pound up the cities of Greece, I suppose.
    But I'm off—   [*A tremendous noise.*
                 I think he intends to come out.   [*Exit.*

TRYGAIOS. Heavens above! I'll get out of the way;
    I don't like the sound of this mortar of War's. . . .

                        Enter War.

WAR. Humans, O humans, you long-suffering and wretched
    Fools! What a pain in your jaws you'll get in a minute!

TRYGAIOS. O Lord Apollo! What a monster that mortar is!
    O gods, what a grim sight—even to *look* at him!
    Can this be War in person—the tough one, the terrible,
    We fly from in fear? What will he do with us?
    Make us into salad?

WAR. *You'll* do—just right for leeks—you city of Prasiai—
  If you were wretched before, it'll be ten times more painful:
  Today you'll be pulverized!

TRYGAIOS.   What does that matter
  To *us*? It's simply a bit of bad luck for the Spartans!

WAR. Megara, my garlic, Megara! Now, once and for ever,
  You shall be ground up small and pounded into mincemeat!

TRYGAIOS. Oh god, what pungent tears he's put in for Megara.

WAR. Sicily, ah, my cheese, alas for you, Sicily!
  You shall be grated to ruins—

TRYGAIOS.   Poor rind of a city!

WAR. Now to pour in some Athenian honey—

TRYGAIOS.   I say, there,
  Use some other brand! Be careful of our honey,
  It's expensive stuff—

WAR [*shouting*].   BOY! BOY! Where's my boy: TUMULT!

                        Enter Tumult.

TUMULT [*meekly*]. You called me?

WAR.   Hanging about doing nothing?
  Take that!

TUMULT. Ow—Ow . . . Did you season your knuckles with garlic?

WAR. Go in and get me a pestle!

TUMULT.   But, master, we 'aven't got one,
  We've only just moved in . . . .

WAR.   Then hop it quickly and borrow one—
  Ask the Athenians!

TUMULT [*going*].   I'll go—or I'll catch it—going!   [*Exit.*

TRYGAIOS [*aside*]. What are we going to do? My dear fellow
    mortals,
  You can see what peril we're in. If he comes back with a pestle,
  War will pound our cities to dust . . . O Lord Dionysus,
  May he die rather than . . .

                      Re-enter Tumult.

TUMULT.   Ooooh, *sir* . . .

WAR.   Haven't you got one?

TUMULT. Would you believe it, sir? The pestle what the Athenians
   'Ad; well, they've been and *lost*? *Cleon* they said was the ticket,
   That tanner-bloke what upset all Greece—but they've *lost* 'im!

TRYGAIOS [*aside*]. O mighty mistress Athene! He's done something
      good at last!
   Good riddance, good luck to the State! He's gone before they
      can mix
   This bitter salad—

WAR.   Then go and get one out of the Spartans.

TUMULT. Going, sir!

WAR.   Quick about it!

TRYGAIOS [*aside*].   Oh my friends, *what* are we to suffer?
   Now is the crucial moment. If there's a Samothracian
   Grouper present, let him pray the gods to avert this cata—
   Or, at least, to *divert* the feet of this—

                         Re-enter Tumult.

TUMULT.   Oooooooh, sir . . .

WAR. Well, what's the matter? Haven't you got one *yet*, boy?

TUMULT. *But 'e's dead too, sir*—The Spartans' pestle 'as snuffed it.

WAR. What the hell?

TUMULT.   No, Brasidas. The Spartans
   Lent him to pals in Thrace and 'e's gone and got killed at Amphi-
      polis—
   In the same battle as Cleon.

TRYGAIOS. Thank all the gods! Mortals, take heart! All may be well!

WAR. Pick up this paraphernalia, take it away,
   I'm going inside to prepare a pestle, myself!   [*Exit.*

TRYGAIOS [*joyfully*]. Oh now is the time to sing the song of the
      Persian, Datis,
   That he sang at noon before Marathon (proud he knew Greek
      so well),
   'Oh Lordies, how I'm rejoiced, I'm liked it, I'm merry-makered.'

   You Greeks, oh isn't it great to be rid of plots and battles?
   —Before another pestle dishes us, come let us wrestle
   And pull Peace out of her pit, who is so beloved by all.
         You farmers, merchants, labourers,
         Craftsmen, aliens, visitors,

Islanders, come quick!
Bring crowbars and ropes as quick as you can,
For we've got the chance to make use of our luck,
Come one and all, to a man!

Enter Chorus *of farmers.*

CHORUS. Quickly, everybody, comrades! Willingly, immediately,
Now, if ever, Panhellenic let us help each other out,
And free ourselves from battles and blood-boltered misery—
The day has dawned we can indulge our hate of Lamachos!

Tell us what to do, direct us, we shall never rest until
With our levers and our crowbars we have haled into the light
Peace, the greatest of goddesses, the glorious lover of the grape!

TRYGAIOS. Quiet, please! Or in your riotous rejoicing in the job
You'll kick up such a racket you'll rekindle War again!

CHORUS. How *can* we help rejoicing when for once the order wasn't
'Report with three days' rations.'

TRYGAIOS. But for heaven's sake be careful of dear Cleon 'down
below';
Or full of sound and fury, just as when he was alive,
He'll burst from hell to bar you pulling Peace out of her pit—

CHORUS. Once the darling's in my arms there's simply nobody could
part us.   [*They give a cheer.*

TRYGAIOS [*horrified*]. Quiet! Quiet or you'll wreck us with this
howling hullaballoo,
He'll hurtle out and trample us to bits—

CHORUS.   Then let him rip!
Trample, trip, and trouble! *We* don't care, we're far too happy!

TRYGAIOS. What's the matter? Stop your dancing. Don't you *see*
you'll ruin us?

CHORUS. It isn't that I *mean* to, but an impulse of delight
Makes my ankles independent—look, they're at it by themselves . . . .

TRYGAIOS. For the moment, please STOP dancing!

CHORUS.   See, I've stopped . . .

TRYGAIOS.   That's what you *say*,
But you *haven't*—

CHORUS [*unheeding*]. Just another, just *one* other step . . . no more . . .

TRYGAIOS. *One*, then, but not another; *not-one-other-step-at-all*!

CHORUS [*guileless*]. We *won't* dance if it'll *help* you . . . .

TRYGAIOS.   —So you say—but HAVE YOU STOPPED?

CHORUS. One last twiddle of the ankle and we're finished with the right leg—

TRYGAIOS. Very well—but that's enough, and kindly don't offend again!

CHORUS. But the *left*, it's only fair to let the left leg have its fling—
We must caper, cheer, and chuckle, for we've chucked our shields away,
And it makes us feel far friskier than sloughing off old age!

TRYGAIOS. But it's *not* the moment *now*, when the whole thing's in the balance—
First get her out, *then* celebrate as loudly as you like.
        Then's the time to laugh and cheer,
        To go sailing, stay at home,
        To take the pretty boys to bed,
        Or laze in bed alone;
        To sit and watch the festivals,
        Give parties, and play cottabos,
        Indulge yourselves and raise the roofs
        And shout *Io! Io!*

CHORUS. Oh heaven, may I have the chance to live and see that day!
        When I think of what I've suffered—
        Beds of straw and suchlike horrors—
        Living rough, like Phormion:
I'll never be a bitter crusty peevish judge again
Intolerant and testy as I was before the war,
        But you'll see me soft and gentle,
        And much younger than I was,
        When I get release from this;
        For we've almost lost a lifetime
        Worn to pieces wandering weary

From parade-ground to parade-ground toting shields and trailing
    spears.
              So, brief us what to do
              To receive your commendation,
              Since we've got the luck to have you
              To direct our operations.

TRYGAIOS. Well, then, let's see which way to lever these boulders.
                [*They begin to pry up the rocks.*
                 Hermes *rushes out.*

HERMES [*in fury*]. You perisher, you louse! What are you up to?

TRYGAIOS. Nothing. Nothing. It's quite all right—I assure you.

HERMES. Dead, destroyed, doomed!

TRYGAIOS.   When my number comes up, yes—
    And you're the god of luck: you should know it's a lottery—

HERMES. You shall die, you disgusting scum!

TRYGAIOS.   What day?

HERMES.   At this very instant!

TRYGAIOS. But I'm not prepared in my mind, and I haven't my
    ration
    Of bread and cheese to take with me—

HERMES.   You're utterly done for!

TRYGAIOS. How can I have such luck—and know nothing about it?

HERMES. What? Don't you know that Zeus has imposed the death
    penalty
    On anyone caught in the act of digging up Peace here?

TRYGAIOS. So I *must* die, must I?

HERMES.   Yes.

TRYGAIOS.   Then lend me three drachmas.

HERMES. What for?

TRYGAIOS.   To buy a pig. I must join a religion
    Before I die.

HERMES [*shouting*]. Zeus! Zeus! O Thunder-Dropper . . .

TRYGAIOS. Hermes, don't give us away, I beg and beseech you—

HERMES. How can I hold my tongue?

TRYGAIOS.   By eating the meat I
    Brought you so kindly—

HERMES.   But I'll catch it from Zeus if I
  Don't shout up and report what you're going to do here.
TRYGAIOS. *Don't* shout, dearest Hermes. Friends, what has come
      over *you*,
  Standing there dumb?—You tongue-tied idiots,
  Speak up, *say* something. *He* will, if *you* won't.
CHORUS. Hermes, if you've ever guzzled one of our prime sucking
      pigs,
  Sacrificed to *you*, dear master, you will never never never
  Dream of giving us away, or look with anything but favour
  On our work—
TRYGAIOS.   O Hermes, hear—how they're sucking up to you!
CHORUS.   Do not take against our prayers
                And prevent us freeing her:
                Sweet, supremely open-handed,
                Lovingest of gods, O hear—
  If it's true you are disgusted with fire-eaters like Peisander,
                Then with holy sacrifices
                And magnificent processions
                We shall worship *you* for ever.
TRYGAIOS. Hermes, listen to them, I beg you, *do*.
  They've never honoured you more than now.
HERMES.—Never been bigger thieves.
TRYGAIOS.   I'll tell you a dead secret.
  There's a tremendous plot against the gods.
HERMES. Go on. I've an open mind.
TRYGAIOS.   Well, for years the moon
  Has been conspiring with the crooked sun
  To betray Greece to the barbarians—
HERMES.   What for? Why?
TRYGAIOS. We sacrifice to *you*, the barbarians sacrifice
  To them; and so of course they want you dead
  So they can get all your rites for themselves instead.
HERMES. So *that's* why the sun's been robbing the days
  And the moon nibbling bits of its disk off!
TRYGAIOS.   Yes,
  That's it. But, dear Hermes, *you* help us, collaborate
  In pulling out Peace and we'll put on the Great

    Panathenaia just simply for *you*,
    And all the rites of the other gods too:
    The mysteries of Demeter; the feast of Zeus;
    The ritual wake for Adonis; and all
    The cities freed from their ills, I swear they shall
    Sacrifice to Apoll— to HERMES the SAVIOUR,
    And there's far more besides; but first I will give you
    This *beautiful gold cup*, to pour a libation with.

HERMES. D'you know, I always get a queer sensation
    At the sight of gold. . . . It somehow makes me sort of sym-
       pathetic.
    Right! My lads, down to work! Take your picks; hoick the stones!

CHORUS. O wisest of all gods, we'll begin at once!   [*They do.*
    You be foreman; direct us; you'll see, we won't shirk.

TRYGAIOS.   Come then, take the cup.
                  Pour the due libations:
                  May the gods bless the work.

HERMES.   Holy silence! Pour libations!
                  Holy silence! Pour libations!

TRYGAIOS.   Let us pray.
                  Let us hope that this very day
                  May be harbinger of happiness
                  To all the cities of Hellas;
                  And whoever pulls on the ropes,
                  Of his own free will, may he never,
                  Never again have to bear
                  A shield on his arm. Amen.

CHORUS. Never, by Zeus! May he spend his life in peace
    With his wi—, with his mistress beside him,
    Poking the fire to a blaze.

TRYGAIOS.   And whoever prefers
    (Dionysus!) to be at war—may he never cease
    Picking arrow-barbs out of his elbows!

CHORUS. Oh mistress Peace, if any man mad for promotion
    Hates seeing you being restored,
    May he suffer in all his battles
    Like the back of Cleonymos.

TRYGAIOS. And if any spearmaker, or any retailer of shields
  Wants war to go on, simply so as to profiteer,
  Let him be kidnapped by thieves
  And forced to eat nothing but barley.

CHORUS. And if any bright would-be general
  Or would-be deserter slave
  Won't help us—let 'em be whipped
  And broken upon the wheel!

  But for us it's a good time coming!
  Hit the high notes! Strike up the music!

TRYGAIOS. Don't speak of striking or hitting—

CHORUS. No, it's singing and dancing we like!

TRYGAIOS. I will pour the libation.
  To Hermes, the Graces, the Hours,
  To Aphrodite, to Desire—   [*Pours.*

CHORUS. Not Ares?

TRYGAIOS. NOT Ares!

CHORUS. Not Enyalios? No war god?

TRYGAIOS. NOT ONE!

CHORUS. Come on then, everyone, haul on the ropes!

                                            [*They pull.*

HERMES. Heave ho!

CHORUS. Heave *harder*!

HERMES. Heave ho!

CHORUS. Harder *still*!

HERMES. Heave ho! Heave ho!

TRYGAIOS.   They're not all pulling their weight!
               You Boeotians! You're simply
               Going through the motions.
               Stop scrimshanking! Yank away,
               Or pay for it later.

HERMES. Heave *now*!

TRYGAIOS. Heave ho!

CHORUS [*cross*]. You should both help us, too!

TRYGAIOS. *Don't* I wrench and tug and sweat?

CHORUS. Then *why* are we getting nowhere?

TRYGAIOS [*mock-army*]. Lamachos, 'old boy', you're obstructing us,
   You're right in the way, and we want none
   Of your Gorgonizing or 'bull'—

HERMES. And look at those Argives! *They* don't pull
   They mock at your misery—and yet
   They're making their living from *both* parties!

TRYGAIOS. But the Spartans—they're heaving like hearties—

HERMES. Yes, but it's only the *prisoners*,
   And their fetters impede them rather.

TRYGAIOS. The Megarians do no good—they cling on
   With their teeth gritted like mangy old mongrels—
   We ought to feed them; they're utterly starving.

CHORUS. We're making no progress, none.
   Come on, we must *all pull together*!

HERMES. Heave ho!

TRYGAIOS. Heave *harder*—

HERMES. Heave ho!

TRYGAIOS. Heaven—*heave*!

CHORUS. We're just on the move!

TRYGAIOS. Some are pulling, others not.
   What do you mean, you Argives,
   You there, simply leaning—
   Stop going slow! Heave with a *ho*!
   Or you'll get it hot!

HERMES. Heave *now*!

TRYGAIOS. Heave *ho*!

CHORUS. We've got some malingerers—

TRYGAIOS. You who yearn for peace, *pull*!

CHORUS. But somebody's *still* a blackleg!

HERMES. Confound you Megarians, *you get out*!
   The goddess recalls you with utter hate;
   It's you who began it—you were the cause!
   Stop, you Athenians! Shift your position,
   You who do nothing but go to law,
   If you're really serious—back! Back a bit,
   Back to the sea, you're a maritime nation.

CHORUS. Let's do it alone, us farmers.

HERMES. It's certainly going better!

CHORUS. We're doing it, boys, he says so!
  Now, everybody; one more effort!

TRYGAIOS. The farmers have it, they're doing it, nobody else!

CHORUS [*puffing*]. Pull now—come on all—
        All together—doing fine—
        Don't give up—tougher still—
        That's the stuff—
        Heave ho and up she rises—
        All together—hell for leather—
        Heave—heave—heave—heave—heave.

Peace, *with her two attendants* Peace-and-Plenty *and* Peace-work,
    is heaved out of the pit amid cheers, puffings, and pantings.

TRYGAIOS [*in delight*]. O divine, divineyard Mistress,
  What word can I find to greet you?
  —Some word that can hold a million gallons of meaning,
  And I haven't a thing to hand.

  And you—I'm happy to meet you,
  O beautiful dog-star-day girl, O harvest-breasted
  Peace-and-Plenty!
                    —And you other shiner,
  Peace-work, mirror of Peace,
  Whose face is fairer still;
  At whose barest breath
  My heart flares: she's as sweet
  As myrrh—or exemption
  From military service!

HERMES [*cynically*]. Not like a knapsack, is she?

TRYGAIOS. Ugh! D'you want me to be sick?
  That frousty filthy contraption
  Of even filthier minds,
  That smells of onion-belch:
  [*Lyrically.*] But SHE of feasts and banquets,
  Festivals, tragedies,
  The songs of Sophocles, thrushes,
  [*With edge.*] And—snips of Euripides—

HERMES. You ought to be ashamed
   Lying about her so!
   For I'm certain she's got no use
   For the windy-wordy quibble-and-gabble
   Of that poetical b——

TRYGAIOS [*dreamily*].—Of ivy, and of vat-cloths,
   Of the bleating of sheep, and the shape
   Of women off to the fields,
   Of the kitchen-maid half-seas-over,
   And the wine-jar upside down . . .

HERMES.—And see how, reconciled,
   The cities talk to each other
   Happy and laughing again,
   Giving each other the glad
   Black-eye as you might say,
   (For they've got some still).

TRYGAIOS. Yes, and look at the audience.
   You can see by the set of their faces
   How each of them earns his living!

HERMES. Lord, look at that poor crest-maker,
   Tearing his hair out there!
   And the pitchfork-seller—oh! Thunder-Dropper—
   Farts in the swordsmith's face!

TRYGAIOS. That fellow's a sickle-maker,
   You can see how delighted *he* is;
   And that wretched spear-burnisher,
   He's getting a terrible ragging . . . .

HERMES. Come, now. It's the right and proper
   Time to announce to the farmers:
   THEY CAN ALL GO HOME!

TRYGAIOS. SILENCE! Everyone listen. The farmers may go home,
   And take their agricultural implements with them!
   Spears have had it, swords and javelins, chuck 'em on the nearest
      dump!
   We're back to good old-fashioned Peace!
   Go, singing paeans, to the fields!

CHORUS. Day delightful to all farmers, joyful day for all the just!
    Oh you vines and figs I planted when a little nipper, I
    So *long* to greet you, touch your tendrils, after such a lapse of
        time.

TRYGAIOS. Friends! But first salute the goddess, who has done
        away with crests
    And Gorgon shields. Then buy provisions; salted fish and all
        we need
    For the country—then it's home, and hurry hurry to our fields!

HERMES. Poseidon! What a posse! Big and burly men of metal!

TRYGAIOS. Their spades like spearheads glint! See that pitchfork
        catch the light—
    Perfect weapon to attack . . . the tangled vineyard and reduce it!
    Oh, I long to take my fork and break the back of every furrow,
    For I've been away so long . . . .

> And call to mind, my comrades,
> The good old days we lived in
> That once were ours in peacetime:
> Dried fruits and figs and myrtles,
> The bounties of the harvest,
> The vintages, the violets
> In clusters by the fountain,
> The ever-welcome olives—
> Oh, for all these former blessings,
> Here and now adore the goddess!

CHORUS. Welcome, welcome, our darling—and now you've come
    You can understand
    How we yearned for, craved for, burned for
    Our return to farm our land.
    Most belovéd, you were always our greatest benefactress;
    To all us farmers who
    Scrape an honest living
    There was none but gracious you
    To give a helping hand—
    In the days before the war,
    Oh the precious and delicious
    Little perquisites there were

(Which we didn't have to pay for!)
You were our staple food, and our safeguardian,
And so the vine and fig-shoot,
And *all* plants whatsoever,
Laugh with delight to see you!
But, kindest Hermes, tell us, will you, why she's been so long
away?

HERMES. Listen to my exposition if you want to know the facts:
Phidias was the first offender—carved himself and Pericles
On Athene's shield, remember?—and a public outcry followed,
And they put him into prison. It looked bad for Pericles.
He sensed the popular temper; saw that he might take the rap,
And shrewdly offered to the city, as a counter-irritant,
The anti-Megara Order—starting, with this scrap of paper,
Such a fire that every eye in Greece was stinging with the smoke.
The vineyard sobbed, the butt in fury broached upon the jar;
There was none to call a halt, and Peace in terror disappeared.

TRYGAIOS. *I* never knew how Phidias was involved in this affair—

CHORUS. Nor did *I* till now. What a *lot* we seem to miss!
(*That's* why she's so beautiful, she's Phidias' cousin.)

HERMES. Then your tributary cities saw you snapping like war-
mongrels
And, in terror of more taxes, bought the sympathy of Sparta
(What a price they paid for it), and Sparta being Sparta
Turfed out Peace without a qualm, and wilfully made war.
And they thought they'd profit from it—it was ruin for their
farmers
(Who were innocent), for commandos from *your* triremes wrecked
their fig-trees.

TRYGAIOS [*angrily*]. And didn't *they* deserve it? Didn't *they* cut
down *my* fig-tree
Which I'd planted from the pips, and lavished all my love upon?

CHORUS. And they bust my biggest corn-bin—by heaven, *they*
deserved it!

HERMES. —Then from the fields the labourers came in like refugees
Without a *grape-seed*, even, to suck; and hungry for their figs.
(And how could they discover they were being had for mugs?)
So they listened to the demagogues, who handed out the rations

—And *they*, though they could see you half starving, poor, and
   weak,
Pitched out Peace although she had a country-longing look.

Then they rounded on your allies with a whispering campaign—
All the richest were accused of being secretly for Sparta;
Then you tore them into tatters like a rabid pack of hounds.
Yes! All their dirty hand-outs, and the dirtier the better,
The sad war-fevered city swallowed with a bitter relish.

Then seeing what the informers worked, such friends as *still*
   you had,
Gagged their mealy mouths with gold, and *they* of course grew
   rich,
But Greece slid down to ruin and you never noticed it.
And most blameworthy of you all, I name—the tanner Cleon.

TRYGAIOS. Quiet, O master Hermes, quiet! Not a syllable, let him
   be—
Below in hell, or where you like, he's not our pigeon now,
He's *yours*, whatever name you call him:
While he lived he was a sod, a
Slimy-limy boasting bastard,
Calumniating agitator.
Call him all the names you choose,
But still he's yours for ever—yours!
[*To* Peace.] But tell me, Peace, dear mistress, why so silent?

HERMES. She'll never utter a word in front of *this* audience,
   She's suffered too much from *them*.

TRYGAIOS.   But wouldn't she whisper
   To you?

HERMES.   My darling, tell me, what's in your mind,
   You, who abominate armaments more than anything . . .
                              [*Peace whispers to him.*
Yes . . . yes, I can hear. You accuse them of *that*? I've got it.
[*To audience.*] Listen to me! She says that after the battle
Of Pylos she came to you with a crateful of treaties
And you *blackballed her three times* in full Assembly!

TRYGAIOS. We did. I admit we were wrong. But won't she forgive
  us?
  Our minds were entirely skinned by that stinking tanner.
                                    [Peace *whispers to* Hermes.

HERMES. She's asked me to ask you this. Who hates her most?
  And who hates fighting most, and so loves her most?

TRYGAIOS. Fatty Cleonymos—no doubt about it.

HERMES. What's he like as a soldier?

TRYGAIOS.   Well . . . an excellent record—
  But not—er—not like his—er—father (whoever *he* was)
  For if he goes into bed—er *battle*; immediately,
  He chucks his weapon away . . . .
                                    [Peace *again whispers.*

HERMES.   Here's another question.
  Who is the politician most in favour?

TRYGAIOS [*to* Peace]. Hyperbolos. He's the people's pet at present.
  Whatever's the matter, Peace, why hang your head?

HERMES. She's turning away in disgust because you've chosen
  So repulsive a leader—

TRYGAIOS.   But, you see, we don't propose
  Really to use him. It's just that lacking a leader,
  Being naked so long, the people have put him on
  For want, so to speak, of anything better to wear . . . .
                                    [Peace *whispers to* Hermes.

HERMES. She asks how this can benefit the State?

TRYGAIOS. We'll soon become *very* enlightened . . . .

HERMES.   How on earth?

TRYGAIOS. He's a *lamp*maker, isn't he? Before,
  We did our business in the dark; but *now*
  We'll be able to deliberate by lamplight!
                                    [Peace *whispers.*

HERMES [*laughing*]. The things she wants to know!!

TRYGAIOS. What does she want to know?

HERMES. All the good old things from before she went.
  First, how is Sophocles?

TRYGAIOS [*slowly*].   Well, he's *well* . . .
  But it's all very odd—

HERMES.   What's odd?

TRYGAIOS.   —He's gone and turned
Into Simonides!

HERMES [*shocked*]. *Simonides?*

TRYGAIOS. Yes. He's got so old and grasping—d'you know, he'd go
To sea in a sieve for cash.

HERMES.   I'm sorry to hear it.
And what about Cratinos, that old crackpot?

TRYGAIOS. Cracked his mortal pot—when the Spartans came—

HERMES. How?

TRYGAIOS.   Fainted clean away. He couldn't bear to see
A buttful of wine bust up and run to waste—
O god, and what other disasters, poor old City!
That's why we'll never let you go again.

HERMES [*summing up*]. Very well! Now *you*, sir, marry Peace-and-
Plenty,
Propagate your vines in love upon your farm.

TRYGAIOS. Come kiss me, Peace-and-Plenty, quickly let me kiss
you—
[*To* Hermes.] —But after such a time, will it do me any harm
To indulge myself in all the issue of the harvest?

HERMES. *Not* if you will take a dose of pennyroyal salts.
And quickly as you can take Peace-work to the Council,
For she was theirs before, and it's there she gets results.

TRYGAIOS. Lucky, lucky Council! To have you there, my darling,
There'll be *such* a party . . . .
                              But now, my friend, good-bye.

HERMES. Fare you well, dear mortal. Remember me.

TRYGAIOS.   Home, beetle!
Fly home, fly home, my beetle!   [*Looking about for his steed.*

HERMES.   He isn't here to fly.

TRYGAIOS. Not here? But where's he got to?

HERMES.   —Hitched to Zeus's chariot
He hauls along the thunder.

TRYGAIOS.   Poor wretch, what will he eat?

HERMES. Ganymede's own personal—ambrosia.

TRYGAIOS.   But how will
I ever get to Athens?

HERMES.   You'll get there quite all right.
Go along with Peace, here.

TRYGAIOS.   Stick close to me, dear ladies.
The young men, if I know them, are burning for your love,
Like soldiers with their weapons trained and at the ready,
They eagerly await our arrival from above.   [*Exeunt.*

CHORUS. Go and good luck go with you. We'll deliver these props
    in the meanwhile
To the scene-shifters to deal with, for plenty of crooks hang
    about in
The wings with an eye to the main chance, so keep 'em with care
    while
We expound to these people the drift of the play and whatever
Else may occur to us. First: it is perfectly just for the ushers
To eject any poet who tries to lard himself up to the audience
In his choric address—but if anyone's worthy of honour,
Give him honour where honour is due, and who so, more than
    your poet?
For didn't he stamp on his rivals for scoffing at rags and for ever
Trotting out lice for a laugh? And didn't he hate seeing Heracles
    handled
As a cheat and a starving vagabond? And didn't he rid you
Of that utterly boring slave who comes on, howling the house
    down,
And all so his feed of a fellow-slave can poke at his weals and
Say, 'Dermatitis, old chap? Has the whip made a raid on your
    ribs or
Broken the trees on your back?' Having got shot of such twaddle,
What did he do? You know! He remoulded the drama, magnifi-
    cent
Phrase and idea together and never a smutty story—
Nor did he ever make play with the insignificant amours
Of private men and women, but having the heart of a Heracles
Flew at the highest and mightiest, enduring the tannery stenches
And malevolent-minded threats, and fought the foul-mouthed
    abortion,

Whose glazed eyes gleamed with the glare of the predatory
    prostitute Kynna
And around whose head, in a ring, a hundred arse-lickers hollered,
Who stank like a seal, had the sweaty crotch of a Lamia,
And a hell-fire rump—and seeing this horror he never flinched,
But fought for you, and the empire, hanging on to the bitter end.

Now it's right to remember this and give me the prize;
For you know, when I won before, I never attempted to tamper
With the beautiful boys; or solicited round the gymnasia;
But immediately went off home and took my props,
Leaving little pain, having given much amusement,
And everything done with taste.

Yes, it's right for everyone, man and boy,
To be on my side—and to recommend
All the bald-heads to *vote for me*!
For if I win today,
And you're at a party, they'll say,
'Give *this* to the bald-head, *that* to the bald-head, don't
Grudge a *thing* to a man with a dome
Like the best of our poets.'
Muse who has driven War clean away, come and join me
    In the dance; if you love me:
Sing of the wedding of gods and of human banquets,
And the joys of the blessèd—your part from time immemorial . . . .
    But if Karkinos comes, and
   Asks you to dance, with him and his children,
    Don't listen to *him*, don't
    Budge and don't help him—
    But consider them all as
Domesticated quails, as crookèd-necked dancers,
As mannikins, as goat-turds, as mechanical showmen.
    And if he's told you that (beyond his hope) he
    Finished his play, *The Mice*, well the cat just
    Strangled it one evening!
Such are the chosen airs of the sweet-tressed Graces
    For the sensitive poet
To sing while the spring is soft in the swallow's murmur . . . .

And Morsimos can't get a play on, nor for that matter
    Can Melanthios, whose minny
  Voice I heard once, twittering sweet nothings
    When he and his brother
    Tried to train the chorus,
    Both of them hideous—
Gorgons, sweet-guzzling, skate-swallowing, harpies,
Terrors to old women, stinkers, fish-murderers:
    Having spat on them well and truly
      O Muse, dear, sit beside me
      And come to the banquet.

The scene changes back to earth. Enter Trygaios *with* Peace-and-
              Plenty *and* Peace-work.

TRYGAIOS. Phew! It was hard to get right to the gods!
My legs are like lead! [*To audience.*] D'you know, from the sky
How *tiny* you looked, but altogether wicked—
Close-to, even more so.

              Enter First Servant.

I SERVANT.   Master! You're back, then?
TRYGAIOS. So it is rumoured.
I SERVANT.   'Ow did it go, sir?
TRYGAIOS. Go? With pains in my legs! It's no joke of a journey.
I SERVANT. Excuse me, sir—
TRYGAIOS.   What?
I SERVANT.   —Did you see any other
Odd bodies floating around in the air but yourself?
TRYGAIOS. Not many except two or three spirits
Of dithyrambic poets—
I SERVANT.   Doing what?
TRYGAIOS.   —Flapping
Round trying to capture some rambling odes,
                [*Puts on a poetry voice.*
Those 'airy-fairy wimble-wamble raptures.'
I SERVANT. Then it's stuff, what they say?—
TRYGAIOS.   What is?
I SERVANT.   —When we snuffs it,
We turn into stars?

TRYGAIOS.   No, it's true.

1 SERVANT.   Well—who's *that* star?

TRYGAIOS. Ion of Chios. He once wrote a poem
Called *Morning Star*. So when he got there
That's what they called him—Morning Star.

1 SERVANT. And what are them shooters, 'ploughing a shiny
Furrow through 'eaven (as the poet 'as it)?

TRYGAIOS. Some of the *rich* stars, reeling home from supper
Holding up lanterns . . .
[*Becoming master.*]   But, take in this girl—
Her name's Peace-and-Plenty—fill the bath to the brim,
Heat up the water, get the bed ready,
And when you have done, come back again here.
Meanwhile, I'll deliver Peace-work to the Council.

1 SERVANT. Whee-whew! What pick-ups! Where did you get 'em?

TRYGAIOS [*with dignity*]. I brought them from heaven.

1 SERVANT.   Then I don't give a damn for
The gods, if they go in for brothels like we do.

TRYGAIOS. They're not *all* of them like that — only *some* of them
Live by it.

1 SERVANT. Now come along, dearie—er—what'll she eat?

TRYGAIOS. Nothing—she wouldn't care for our barley,
She's accustomed to lapping ambrosia in heaven.

1 SERVANT. I wouldn't mind seeing 'er lap. Come along!
                          [*Exit, with* Peace-and-Plenty.

CHORUS.   So far as I can see it,
                   The lucky old codger has
                   Done himself proud!

TRYGAIOS. And what'll you say when you see me dressed in my
best?

CHORUS.   O enviable, happy,
                   Old man in second springtime,
                   Scented like a flower!

TRYGAIOS. Ah! what'll you say when, beside her, I tickle her
breasts?

CHORUS. Well—luckier than Karkinos' twirling little beasts.

TRYGAIOS.   And perfectly right! For didn't I
                    Mount on a beetle's back and fly
                    To the rescue of all Greece,
                    So that everybody can
                    Go safe to the fields again
                    And sleep in peace together?

                    Re-enter First Servant.

I SERVANT. She's 'ad 'er bath—and what a figure!
    They've mixed the cakes, the sesame's kneaded,
    Everything's habsolutely ready,
    Except. . . .

TRYGAIOS.   Well, *what*?

I SERVANT [*leering*].   —That's up to you, sir!

TRYGAIOS. First, take Peace-work to the Council.

I SERVANT. Who? . . . —Is *she* the one we worked on
    At the festival at Brauron?

TRYGAIOS.   Yes—what *work* it was: to catch her!

I SERVANT. How *fresh* she looks—as if she 'adn't
    Been out o' bed since the previous Fair day!

TRYGAIOS. Now, I *wonder*: if there's any one
    Among you people I could *trust* to
    Hand her over . . .? [*To* Servant.] *What are you doing,
    Drawing* on her *thighs*, there?

I SERVANT [*innocently*].   Nothing:
    Only markin' out a pitch—where
    I could stick my tent-pole up, at
    The Isthmian games—

TRYGAIOS.   Will no one take her?
    Well, come here. I'll simply put you
    Into the audience—

I SERVANT.   Someone's waving!

TRYGAIOS. Who?

I SERVANT.   Ariphrades. He wants you
    To take her *his* way.

TRYGAIOS.   No, not likely!
    He'd swill her down in a single swallow . . . .

Come here, Peace-work. Put down your chattels.
I'll present you to the Council!

> [*He addresses the audience, as the Council.*

Members of the Council! Look this way!
Look at her, see who I've got for you—Peace-work!—
(What pleasures are in that name!)
What a victim for sacrifice!
See where you used to cook, what a smoky-black
Chimney she's brought, what a lovely array
Of utensils, and all for your use—as they were!
And tomorrow what charming games!
You can wrestle on foot, or all fours, you can roll her
Over and over, all sleek with oil,
Top, bottom, and sideways—a regular free-for-all.
Then the chariot-racing, the panting, the passing,
The overturning, the crash on the bend—
Oh receive her with kindness, gentlemen!
(How delighted you look, my friend—
You wouldn't be half so keen
If you didn't get anything out of it, though;
You'd have called it a *dies non*,
When nothing at all can be done.)

CHORUS.   A man like you is a blessing
                 To all the State for ever.

TRYGAIOS. You'll see what I am really worth—when the grapes are
     ripe!

CHORUS.   Everyone confesses
                 You to be our saviour—

TRYGAIOS. Say so when you down a rummer of new vintage wine!

CHORUS. But for the gods, we'll *always* deem you first in our esteem!

TRYGAIOS.   I, Trygaios, an Athenian!—
                 Indeed you owe a lot to me,
                 I've freed you from your troubles
                 (Both town and country people),
                 And I've neutralized Hyperbolos!

CHORUS.   Now what shall *we* do next?

TRYGAIOS.   Inaugurate her altar,
                 With little pots of pulse.

CHORUS.—Like a piddling little Hermes?

TRYGAIOS. Sh! Well, what about a bull?

CHORUS. A bull? No fear! We had enough
  Bull in the army.

TRYGAIOS.   A nice fat pig?

CHORUS.   Not likely!

TRYGAIOS. No?

CHORUS.   —And find ourselves becoming
  Like that swine Theagenes?

TRYGAIOS. Well, what then?

CHORUS.   —A blah-lamb.

TRYGAIOS. A blah-lamb?

CHORUS.   Yes, a blah-lamb!

TRYGAIOS. *Is* that an Ionic word?
  Surely it's Ionic?

CHORUS.   Yes!
  If some fool in the Assembly
  Starts to whip up war-talk,
  We shall simply speak Ionic—
  And shout Blah! Blah! Blah!

TRYGAIOS. Magnificent idea!

CHORUS. And, besides, we'll be so gentle
  And lamblike to each other,
  And *much* nicer to our allies . . .

TRYGAIOS. —Then get a lamb as quick as poss.
  And I'll contrive an altar
  On which to sacrifice!   [*He goes into his house.*

CHORUS. It's odd how everything goes
  According to plan when the gods
  And good luck are on your side—
  Everything comes to hand
  Just when it's needed.

                Re-enter Trygaios *with a table.*

TRYGAIOS. You never spoke truer word. Look, here's the altar.

CHORUS.   Then hurry while the fickle
              Frightening winds of war cease

Their tempests of slaughter,
For at the moment clearly
They're shifting, easing, veering
Towards a peaceful quarter.

TRYGAIOS. The basket of barley is ready, the chaplet, the knife, and
The fire, and nothing remains but to wait for the victim.

[*A lamb is brought in.*

CHORUS.   Then hurry hurry even more,
For if Chairis hears of this, he will
Slip in without a by-your-leave;
And pipe so hard, and puff so much,
That when you see him it's odds-on
You'll tip him—you'll have to!

TRYGAIOS [*to* First Servant]. Come, take the basket and the lustral
water;
Pace round the altar.

I SERVANT.   Done it. What's the next?

TRYGAIOS. Take the firebrand, dip it in the water!
Tremble, you lamb! Bring out the barley seed.
I'll hold the basin. Cleanse your hands—that's it—
Now scatter the seed to the audience—

[First Servant *makes a rude noise.*

What, done already?

I SERVANT.   Yes! For the men
Got bags full o' seed—

TRYGAIOS.   But what about the women?

I SERVANT. They'll get it tonight from the men, won't they?

TRYGAIOS. Now let us pray. . . . Who's here? Are there enough
Good men gathered together?

I SERVANT.   The Chorus is 'ere.

TRYGAIOS. You call them good?

I SERVANT.   We soused 'em in lustral water
And they never batted an eye . . . .

TRYGAIOS.   Come then, to prayers . . . .
O Peace most holy, O queenly goddess,
Mistress of dances, mistress of marriages,
Receive our sacrifice.

1 SERVANT. O most worthiest of all to be honoured,
    Receive our sacrifice.
    (And don't you do what them flighty flirts do,
    Ogling at doorways, 'alf an inch open,
    And if you 'as a mind to 'em—
    In they pops! And if you turns your back on 'em—
    Out they peeps! No, don't you do nothing
    Of *that* sort with *us*.)

TRYGAIOS.   No, by heaven!
    But show yourself, in your naked nobility,
    To your true lovers, loyally patient
    For thirteen years.
    Let cease the din and rumble of battle
    That we, in truth, may name you—'Peacemaker'.
    Stop the rumours, the 'exclusive information'
    Of liars in-the-know
    That we, in wartime, babbled to each other.
    But mix us Greeks in a sweet elixir
    Of love and friendship, tolerance and good temper.
    And furnish our market with every luxury—
    Cucumbers, garlic, pomegranates, apples,
    And little tunics for slaves.
    And let Boeotia send us her poultry,
    Geese and ducks, plovers and pigeons,
    And from Lake Copaïs, EELS by the basket!
    Oh, and let Melanthios come too late and
    Not an eel left, and let him moan (—it's
    Out of his own play)
    'I die, I die, bereft of my darling,
    Bedecked in jelly'—and let everyone laugh!
    O Mistress hear our prayers!

1 SERVANT. Now carve 'er up like a cook. 'Ere, take the knife.

TRYGAIOS. No! No!

1 SERVANT.   For why?

TRYGAIOS.   Peace doesn't care for victims.
    Nor blood on the altar. Take the beast indoors
    And do it there. Then bring the thighs out here!
    Hurray! The lamb is saved—for the chorus-master!
                    [*Exit* First Servant *with the sacrifice.*

CHORUS.   But you, since you're staying,
                   Get the firewood ready
                   And whatever else you need.

TRYGAIOS.   Don't I just look the part
                   Of a diviner laying
                   His sacred fire?

CHORUS.   To the life!
                   —As we expect from you!
                   Is there anything you forget
                   That a wise original
                   Exploring mind would do?
                   You do it all, and more!

TRYGAIOS [*laughing*]. The fire's caught, but it's blinding your
    diviner!
   I'll bring the table out. We won't need the boy to.

CHORUS.   —It's a joy to praise the man!
                   —There's nobody would not!
                   —Think of all he braved for us,
                   Our holy City saved for us,
                   —The envy of us all, his name
                         Shall never be forgotten!

                   Re-enter First Servant.

1 SERVANT. 's all done. 'Ere, sir, you take the thighs and cook
    'em.
   I'll go and get the entrails and the cakes.

TRYGAIOS. I'll attend to this . . . . You ought to have come before.

1 SERVANT. Well, here I am. Didn't think I'd been long—

TRYGAIOS. Roast these properly, please. Now, who's this bounder
   With the laurel crown on his head?

                   Enter Hierocles.

1 SERVANT.   —Looks pretty cocky!
   —Come off it, you!—Must be some prophet I reckon.

TRYGAIOS. No—it's Hierocles the oracle-expounder
   From Oreos.

1 SERVANT. And what's 'e coming in aid of?

TRYGAIOS.   To object to
   Our truce I should think—

1 SERVANT.   Go on! It's the savoury smell
  As attracts him.

TRYGAIOS.   Pretend not to notice him.

1 SERVANT.   Right!

HIEROCLES. What sacrifice is this? To whom?

TRYGAIOS.   Don't say a word.
  Just go on cooking—*and keep your hands off the meat*!

HIEROCLES. Will you not say to whom you sacrifice?
  This tail exhibits favourable omens . . . .

1 SERVANT [*aside*]. It's doing very nicely, oh darling Peace!

HIEROCLES. Lo, now, commence—and hand me the first cut!

TRYGAIOS. —Cook it properly first!

HIEROCLES.   —'Tis done enough.

TRYGAIOS. —You do too much, whoever you are. [*To* Servant.]
    Keep carving;
  Where's the table? Bring the libation, please . . . .

HIEROCLES. See that the tongue be separately excised . . . .

TRYGAIOS. We know what to do, thank you. But do *you* know—

HIEROCLES. Yes?

TRYGAIOS.   How to hold *your tongue*? O holy Peace
  We sacrifice to—

HIEROCLES.   You poor deluded fools!—

TRYGAIOS. Speak for yourself!

HIEROCLES [*well away*].   —In your folly ignorant
  Of the will of the gods, you, ill-considering men,
  To covenant with quarrelsome apes—
                          [First Servant *bursts with laughter.*

TRYGAIOS. Why are you laughing?

1 SERVANT.   I like his 'quarrelsome apes'!

HIEROCLES. You timorous zanies trusting the cubs of foxes
  That are crafty of soul and cunning in wit—

TRYGAIOS.   I wish
  Your lungs were as hot as this meat, you damned imposter!

HIEROCLES. If the holy nymphs and goddesses have not imposed
  Upon Bakis, Bakis not upon mortal men;
  Nor, I repeat, the nymphs imposed on Bakis—

TRYGAIOS. To hell with you, shut up, you and your Bakis!

HIEROCLES. —Not yet is the destined hour for the bonds of Peace
To be loosed. Nay, nay, ere that time come—

TRYGAIOS. —This bit of meat'll be sprinkled with salt!—

HIEROCLES. —Not yet is it behovely to the blessed
Gods to desist from the clash of arms, before
The wolf lies down with the lamb—

TRYGAIOS.   You stupid fool,
How can the wolf lie down with the lamb?

HIEROCLES.   Doth not
The beetle in terror break most nauseous wind?
Doth not the flustered finch bring forth blind young?
Even so not yet, not yet is the Hour of Peace
Come in its due time . . . .

TRYGAIOS. Then what is to happen? Never stop fighting?
Or just draw lots as to who shall suffer the more?—
When, with mutual treaties, we could rule Greece in common?

HIEROCLES. Shalt thou teach the crab to advance as straight as a die?
Never!

TRYGAIOS. Shall you dine in the Council Chamber again, my
friend?
Never!
No, nor go on getting away with all this claptrap!

HIEROCLES. Shalt thou make the prickles of the hedgehog smooth?
Never!

TRYGAIOS. Will you ever stop imposing yourself on the people?
—Never.

HIEROCLES. In accordance with what oracle do you sacrifice to the
gods?

TRYGAIOS. The best. Wasn't it Homer who wrote:
'Duly the thighs they burned and ate the tripe and the innards,
Then poured out the libations; and I was the guide and the leader';
[*With edge.*] 'None to the soothsayer gave the shining beautiful
goblet.'

HIEROCLES. No. I do *not* know that: the Sybil never said *that*.

TRYGAIOS. But deep-browed Homer spoke the truth when he said:
'Tribeless, lawless, and heartless is he that delighted in bloodshed,
Bloodshed of kith and kin, heartsickening, horrible, hateful.'

HIEROCLES. Take heed, lest a kite deceive your vigilance
And seize the sacrifice—

TRYGAIOS.   My goodness, yes!
Look out for that: that's a really terrible future—
For the entrails! Now pour the libation out
And give me a piece of the roast.

HIEROCLES.   I take it
I may help myself?

TRYGAIOS [*not taking notice*]. Libation, pour the libation . . .

HIEROCLES. Pour one for me, and hand me out a helping—

TRYGAIOS [*mocking*]. That is not yet behovely to the Blessed
    Immortals.
Nay, for before that hour—*we'll* pour the libations
But *you'll* buzz off . . . .

                              O Mistress Peace abide
With us for ever . . . .

HIEROCLES.   Fetch the tongue hither!

TRYGAIOS. Take yours away!

HIEROCLES.   Pour the libation . . . .

TRYGAIOS.   Take that! [*Spits at him.*

HIEROCLES. Will *nobody* give me a bite?

TRYGAIOS.   Not a scrap for you,
Till the wolf lies down with the lamb!

HIEROCLES.   By your knees, I—

TRYGAIOS. No luck, however you beg. You will never make smooth
The hedgehog's prickles! Here, you spectators,
Will you share in our feast?

HIEROCLES.   But what about *me*?

TRYGAIOS. Oh, go and eat your Sibyl!

HIEROCLES.   By all that's holy,
You two shan't eat alone—if you won't give me any,
I'll take some—it's all in common!

TRYGAIOS.   Beat this Bakis,
Beat him!

HIEROCLES. I call to witness—

TRYGAIOS.   —*I* call to witness
That you're a greedy crook. Here, use this stick.

1 SERVANT. No, *you* do that! I'll peel the skins off him
He's pinched from other sacrifices. Off with 'em—
You wolf in sheep's clothing. Look at him naked,
Black as a crow from Oreos! Shoo! Fly off home!

[*Exeunt* Trygaios *and* First Servant, *chasing* Hierocles *off.*

CHORUS.   I delight and I delight
                      To be delivered
                      From helmets and iron-rations!
                      For I abhor battles,
                      But I adore lazing
                      By the fire with my cronies—
                      And a snappy blaze
                      Of brittle logs uprooted
                      In the height of summer,
                      And chestnuts roasting
                      In the glowing embers,
                      And perhaps a slap and tickle
                      Or a tumble with Thratta
                      While the wife's in her bath.

   For there's nothing sweeter when the seed is sown,
   And god is gracious with a fostering shower,
   Than to run into a neighbour and remark:
'What shall we do, Comarchides, how shall we pass the time?
Speaking simply for myself *I* should be pleased to drink,
While the rain god does our work for us; I'll chivvy up the wife
To roast three measuresful of beans, and mix some barley in
And choose some figs— You! Syra! You fetch Manes from the
   field,
For it's not at all the time of day to strip the vine of leaves,
Or hoe the roots—already the soil is moist enough—
And someone bring me out a brace of finches and a thrush!
Then there ought to be some beestings, and four helpings of cold
   hare:
(Unless the cat has got 'em: what it was I couldn't say,
But there *was* a scrabbling in the night) but if there *are*, bring
   three—

And give my dear old da the fourth—and ask Aeschinades
For myrtle boughs with berries on—and as it's on the way,
Give Charinades a call, to drop in for a drop—
While all the time the kindly gods are busy with our crops!'

> When the cicala sings
> In its old sweet mode,
> I love to contemplate
> The Lemnian grape
> Already growing ripe,
> The earliest to swell.
> Then I see the fig full-bellied
> And, wherever it is choice,
> I pick and eat, with joy,
> And murmur 'Happy hours';
> And grating up some wild
> Thyme I make a cordial,
> Growing comfortably stout
> All the summer long.

This is better than a captain's visage, odious to the gods,
With his crests and scarlet tunic he asserts is Sardian-dyed,
It is fast, it will not run—it's funny, when he comes to *fight*,
How his terror turns it yellow; and *he's* fast, *he* runs all right,
With his triple crest all quivering—and we're left to carry on.

But when they're safe at home they do intolerable things,
Making out the roll-calls and monkeying with the names,
Take *this* one out; put *that* one in; to suit their private whims.
Off to the front tomorrow; some poor devil's got no rations,
He never dreamed that he was posted till he stopped to glance
At the military notice on the statue of Pandion,
Then he sees his name and rushes off, his face as green as grass.

They do that to us country folk—the townee's treated better—
Detestable to god and man, the only thing *they* know
Is how to throw their shields away, but if the gods are good
They are going to account to *me* for all the wrongs they've done,

> These lions among ladies,
> These foxes in the fight.

Re-enter Trygaios.

TRYGAIOS [*happily*]. What a party! Oh friends, what a wedding
   party!
Here, take this crest—wipe down the tables—
No other use for it— Serve up the meal cakes,
The thrushes—and lashings of hare and dumplings.

Enter Sickle-maker.

SICKLE-MAKER. Where's Trygaios?

I SERVANT.   Stewin' thrushes.

SICKLE-MAKER [*with joy*].   Trygaios!
My *dear* chap! *What* a good turn you've done me,
Making peace. For nobody bought my sickles
While the blasted war was on—but now I can sell 'em
At fifty drachmas a time.
                  And look at my friend here—
Sells water casks for the farms. Now, take as many
Sickles and casks as you like—all free—come on, *take* 'em,
And *this* too. [*Jingle of money.*] Out of our sales and our profits
We're *giving* you these—they're wedding presents!

Enter Crest-maker *and* Spear-burnisher.

CREST-MAKER [*utterly low*].   Trygaios . . . .
Trygaios, you've ruined me, *ruined* me, *ruined* me . . .

TRYGAIOS. What's up, you misery? Have you got a crestache?

CREST-MAKER. My life, my livelihood—you've utterly destroyed it,
   Me and my matey—he's a spear-burnisher.

TRYGAIOS. This couple of crests—what d'you want for them?

CREST-MAKER. What d'you offer?

TRYGAIOS.   I wouldn't like to say.
Mmmm . . . *yes* . . . you seem to have put a *lot* of work
In the binding, here.—Three measures of dried figs?
How about that? I can do with some more dusters.

CREST-MAKER [*gloomily*]. Go in and get the figs. . . . 'Sbetter than
   nothing . . . .

TRYGAIOS [*angrily*]. Tchah! Take 'em away! They're moulting!
   They're no good!
I won't give a fig for 'em!   [*Another moan off.*
                  Heavens, who's this now?

Enter Breastplate-seller.

BREASTPLATE-SELLER [*North Country*]. Eeee, what's the use? And
such a gradely breastplate,
Ten minas' worth o' work in it . . .

TRYGAIOS.   *You* won't lose;
Offer a fair price—it's absolutely perfect
—For a commode.

BREASTPLATE-SELLER. You insult me!

TRYGAIOS.   I can balance it—
Look, d'you see—on these three stones. Good, isn't it?

BREASTPLATE-SELLER [*morosely*]. I'm hanged if you use such a
valuable thing for—   [*He thinks better.*
D'you mean you'd *pay* ten minas, for a commode?

TRYGAIOS. Why not? d'you think I'd sell my arse for less?

BREASTPLATE-SELLER. Well, where's the brass?

TRYGAIOS [*with a mock shriek*]. No use! it pinches me!
Take it away. I won't buy it!
              [*Exeunt* Sickle-maker, Crest-maker, Breastplate-seller.

Enter Trumpet-maker.

TRUMPET-MAKER [*rather a sissy*]. Trygaios!
What can I use this bugle for? Sixty drachmas it cost me—

TRYGAIOS. Pour lead into the mouth—then, if you lay
A long stick on the top—you could play cottabos.

TRUMPET-MAKER [*angrily*]. Don't pull my leg—

TRYGAIOS.   Then here's another idea:
Pour lead in, as before, get little cords
And hang a balance on it—you could weigh
Figs for farm-labourers—

                                        [*A snort of rage.*
              —Hi! wait a minute . . . .

Enter Helmet-maker.

HELMET-MAKER [*in despair*]. O gods have mercy! I'm done for,
utterly done for!
These helmets were worth a hundred drachmas each—
What shall I do with them? *Who* will buy them now?

TRYGAIOS. Take 'em to Egypt—you could sell 'em there.
They are *perfect* measures, for their laxatives . . . .

TRUMPET-MAKER. Poor Helmet-maker, we're finished, both of us.

TRYGAIOS. But what's *he* got to grouse about—

HELMET-MAKER [*bitterly*].   Me? *Grouse?*
 [*In agony.*] What will anyone *do* with my helmets now?

TRYGAIOS. Fix on handles (you could stick the price up),
  And sell 'em as wine cups.

HELMET-MAKER [*with a sigh*]. Spear-burnisher, come away . . . .

TRYGAIOS. No, no—I'll buy his spears, I really will!

SPEAR-BURNISHER. How much?

TRYGAIOS.   Cut 'em in half, I'll take 'em,
  A drachma a hundred, they'll do fine for vine-poles!

SPEAR-BURNISHER [*a noise of fury*]. He's hopeless! We'd better
  go—
            [*Exeunt* Trumpet-maker, Helmet-maker, Spear-burnisher.

              Enter two Boys.

TRYGAIOS. Good-bye then and good riddance! Ah, and I see
  The little boys are coming out for a wee-wee.
  I suppose they'll practise what they're going to sing—
  Now you, my lad, what are *you* going to sing?
  Come here and tell me; give me the first line—

1 BOY.   I sing of the younger heroes
               Whose bloody deeds we—

TRYGAIOS. Cut the younger heroes, you little wretch!
  Don't you know it's *peace*, you ignorant dolt?

1 BOY [*trying again*]. Then slow the armies came to grips
               Across the fatal field,
           Till with a ringing clash of skin
               Each from the other reeled;
           Buckler on buckler, shield on shield,
               Uprose the battle din.

TRYGAIOS. Shield and buckler? *Stop reminding me!*

1 BOY [*uneasy*]. Then rose the shout of victory
               Then sank the dying groan—

TRYGAIOS. I'll give you groans, by heaven! I'll make you sorry!

1 BOY. What *shall* I sing then? Tell me what you like?

TRYGAIOS. 'On the good roast beef they feasted'
  —Something like that.

> [*Not quite sure of the words.*

> Then all the choicest food was served
> And each man as he would,
>   Partook of what he fancied—
> And a little did him good . . .

1 BOY.   Then they feasted and unharnessed
>   Their fiery foaming steeds,
> And they rested from the battle,
>   Being tired of doughty deeds—

TRYGAIOS. Good! Good!—They were tired of war, and so they
  feasted . . . .
  Go on, my dear, sing how they were tired of war and feasted.

1 BOY.   And when the feast was over,
>   Each calling for his casque—

TRYGAIOS. Gladly, I bet—casks of the good red wine—

1 BOY.   —Forth issuing from their turrets
>   Took up the warlike task!

TRYGAIOS. Confound you and your wars, you little brat.
  You sing of nothing but wars. Now, who's your father?

1 BOY [*as though everyone should know*]. My father?

TRYGAIOS.   Yes, *your* father!

1 BOY.   Lamachos!

TRYGAIOS. I might have known it: that fire-eating, war-monger-
  ing . . .
  Go to the spearmen—you go and sing to them. [*Exit* First Boy.
  Where's Cleonymos' boy?

2 BOY.   Here, sir.

TRYGAIOS.   You sing, boy—
  You wouldn't sing of wars—not with *your* father.

2 BOY [*sadly*].   Some foreign warrior,
>   Sorry I am to say,
>   Is flourishing the shield
>   I jettisoned today—

TRYGAIOS. Tell me, m' little cock, are you mocking your father?

2 BOY [*on, inexorably*.]. But *life* it was I saved,
　　　　　　My life, and—

TRYGAIOS. —Shamed your family. But let's go in.
　I'm sure you'll be word-perfect in *that* song,
　With a father like yours . . . 　　　　　　[*Exit* Second Boy.
　　　　　　　　　　Now all you guests!
　Fall *to*, eat *up*, gulp *down*, don't leave a morsel,
　But chumble and champ away with top and bottom,
　For what's the point of having sets of mashers
　Like yours, if you don't use them?

CHORUS. We're not ungrateful for the hint, Trygaios!

TRYGAIOS.　　Yesterday—you were starving.
　　　　　Today—just come and get it!
　　　　　Hare isn't on the menu
　　　　　Every day of the week and when you
　　　　　Think of it afterwards,
　　　　　I assure you you'll regret it
　　　　　If you don't-take-this-chance!

CHORUS. Keep holy silence, let the bride be summoned, let all
　people
　Dance and rejoice. And very soon, we shall be free to carry
　Our implements to the fields—when we have celebrated
　And poured the due libation—and got rid of Hyperbolos!
　　　　　Let us pray to all the gods
　　　　　To grant to the Greeks riches;
　　　　　Harvest and fig and vintage;
　　　　　Let our wives bear us children,
　　　　　And every good thing we lost
　　　　　Be restored to us, and the glittering
　　　　　Sword be forgotten.

TRYGAIOS.　　Come, darling, to the field,
　　　　　My bountiful, my beautiful,
　　　　　Lie with me there.
　　　　　Hymen Hymenaios O!

CHORUS.

Thrice blessed, truly owed
Your fair and just reward!
Hymen Hymenaios O!

1 SEMI CHORUS.

What shall we do with her?
What shall we do with her?

2 SEMI CHORUS.

Let all her yield be reaped!
Let all her yield be reaped!

1 SEMI CHORUS.

We who are in the van,
Bear up this joyful man!
Hymen Hymenaios O!

2 SEMI CHORUS.

O keep a happy house,
In work harmonious,
Your ripening fruits in view!
Hymen Hymenaios O!

1 SEMI CHORUS.

His fig is firm and full.

2 SEMI CHORUS.

Her sweets have yet to swell.

TRYGAIOS.

Say so, and take your fill
Of food and drink with us.

CHORUS.

Hymen Hymenaios O!
Hymen Hymenaios O!

TRYGAIOS.

Adieu, adieu, my friends;
But follow to the feast;
I invite you one and all!

GLOSSARY AND INDEX OF NAMES

Admetos: a mythical king, famous for his goodness.

aegis: carried by Athene (and Zeus), used to frighten or protect.

Aeschylus (525–456): the great Athenian tragedian; fought at Marathon.

Aether: the upper air.

Agamemnon: commander of the Greeks in the Trojan War; killed on return by his wife's lover.

Aigeus: legendary king of Athens, father of Theseus; the Aegean Sea named after him.

Aigina: island opposite Athens, captured and occupied by Athenians, including probably Aristophanes' family.

Alcibiades (c. 450–404): Athenian politician, ward of Pericles and pupil of Socrates.

Alcmaionidai: noble Athenian family; legendarily had violated a sanctuary.

Amphipolis: city on north Aegean coast; scene of battle, 420.

Apollo: god of healing, music and prophecy, archery, and the sun (Phoebus).

Arcadia,-ady: remote mountain area of the Peloponnese, subject to Sparta.

Archeptolemos: proposed peace terms for Sparta in 425, rejected by Cleon.

archon: one of nine annual principal state officials in Athens, chosen by lot; one archon gave his name to the year.

Ares: god of war.

Argos,-ives: Greek city-state inactively allied to Athens in 420.

Aristides (c. 520–c. 468): Athenian empire-building leader.

Artemis: virgin goddess of hunting; sister of Apollo.

Asclepios: healing god.

Aspasia: clever Milesian woman, mistress of Pericles and, after his death, of Lysicles.

Athamas: in one myth, about to be sacrificed when rescued.

Athene: goddess of Athens and intelligence; daughter of Zeus.

Attic: adjective (and noun for the Greek dialect) of

Attica: the area of which Athens was the chief city.

Bacchanals: festivals for, or worshippers of, the god Dionysus (Bacchus).

Bakis: the archetypal oracle-speaking prophet.

Bellerophon: mythical subject of a play by Euripides; rode the winged horse Pegasus; was thrown trying to ride to heaven.

Boeotia: next Greek district, north and west of Attica.

Brasidas: Spartan general, killed at Amphipolis, 422.

Brauron: Attic site of a cult of Artemis.

Byzantium: modern Istanbul; often under Athenian rule in 5th century; had iron coinage, exceptional at the time.

Camarina: Greek city in southern Sicily.

Caria: region in south-west of modern Turkey.

Carthage: rich city in modern Tunisia.

Cecrops: mythical first king of Athens.

centaurs: monsters, upper part human, lower part horses'.

Cerberus: legendary dog guarding Underworld.

Chairephon: a notable disciple of Socrates.

Chalkis, -idian: chief city of Euboea; revolted against Athens 446, but defeated and became tributary ally again.

Chaos: the initial void in Greek cosmology.

Charybdis: legendary whirlpool in the sea.

Chersonese: the Gallipoli peninsula.

Chios: Ionian island, loyal to Athens until 413.

Chorus-Master: wealthy citizen appointed to present a play at his expense.

cicala: insect; modelled in gold as a brooch, traditionally worn by noble Atticans in their hair.

Cleisthenes: late 5th-century Athenian mocked as effeminate.

Cleon: son of a tanner and leading Athenian politician after Pericles' death (429); attacked Aristophanes for his (lost) play *Babylonians* in 426; victorious general at Sphacteria, 425; killed at Amphipolis, 422.

Cleonymos: Athenian mocked for being a coward soldier, fat, and greedy.

Copaïs: lake in Boeotia famous for its eels.

Copros: Greek for 'shit'; an area of Athens.

Cordax: old woman's solo funny dance, traditional to Old Comedy.

corybantes: frenzied worshippers.

cottabos: game of aiming the last of the wine in one's cup at some small object.

Crates: Athenian comic poet (fl. 450).

Cratinos (c. 484–c. 419): Athenian comic poet with a successful career behind him; heavy drinker; made a come-back in 423, when his *Bottle* won a first prize.

Croesus: king of Lydia (c. 560–546), of proverbial wealth.

Cronos: leader of the Titans, father of Zeus.

crows: 'to the crows' = 'to hell'.

Cynthia: Artemis; Kynthos a hill on Delos.

Datis: gave his name to 'datisms', foreigners' mistakes in speaking Greek.

Delos: sacred island in the Aegean, legendary birthplace of Apollo and Artemis; ceremonially purified by Nikias in 426.

Delphi: place of the famous oracle of Apollo; Dionysus its god during three winter months.

Demeter: goddess of vegetation, especially corn.

Demosthenes: Athenian general in Peloponnesian War, with many successes up to 424; executed, 413.

Dionysus (Bacchus): god of wine, whose festivals in Attica were the Great Dionysia in Athens in the spring and the Rural Dionysia in the winter.

donkey's shadow: proverbial for a pointless bone of contention.

Ecbatana: capital of Media.

Electra: in Aeschylus' *Choephoroi*, went to her father Agamemnon's tomb and found there a lock of her long-lost brother Orestes' hair, which she recognized, as a sign that he was back.

Eleusis: town in Attica with secret rites ('mysteries') of Demeter.

Enyalios: a war god.

Ephesus: city on west coast of modern Turkey, with famous temple of Artemis.

Erechtheus: legendary king of Athens.

Euboea: long island off Boeotia and Attica; from 445 much of it allotted, after conquest by Athens, in settlements to Athenians.

Eupolis (c. 445–c. 410): successful Athenian comic playwright.

Euripides (c. 485–406): writer of many tragedies; avant-garde in Aristophanes' eyes; his mother supposedly a herb-seller.

Ganymede: legendary beautiful boy, cup-bearer to Zeus.

Glanis: an invented prophet; the name of a fish.

Gorgias (c. 483–376): sophist and teacher of rhetorical style in Athens.

Harmodios and Aristogeiton: 6th-century Athenians who plotted against the tyrant Hippias and were celebrated in a popular drinking song.

Hecate: goddess associated with ghosts and black magic.

Heliasts: jurymen in an Athenian court (Heliaia originally the court of appeal).

Heracles (Hercules): legendary hero, famous for strength (and greed).

Hermes: messenger god, associated with fertility and travelling; often represented by Hermai, or upright stones, each with a head on top and a phallus.

Hermippos: comic playwright in Athens, slightly older than Aristophanes.

Hippias: tyrant of Athens (527–510).

Hyperbolos: leading popular politician and orator in Athens after Cleon; in favour of the war against Sparta; advocated expedition to Sicily with fancies of ultimately conquering Carthage; ostracized in 417 and died in 411.

Ino: mythical subject of a play by Euripides.

Io: cry for help, especially (*Io Paian*) of Apollo.

Ion of Chios (c. 490–c. 421): well-known poet in Athens.

Ionia, -ic: the area, and Greek dialect, of west and south of modern Turkey.

Isthmian Games: biennial athletic festival in Corinth.

Karkinos: 5th-century Athenian tragic playwright.

Keramikos: potters' (or ceramic) quarter of Athens; funeral ground there.

Knights: Athenian cavalry.

Lamachos: Athenian general; killed in 414.

Lamia: a bogey monster.

Lasos (born c. 548): rival poet to Simonides in Athens.

Lenaia: Dionysiac festival held in Athens early in the year; foreigners would not attend.

Leto: a Titaness, mother of Apollo and Artemis.

Lycos: patron hero of Athenian jurymen (or dicasts).

Lydia: highly civilized region on west coast of modern Turkey.

Lysicles: an Athenian leader for a while after Pericles' death; the 'sheep-seller' of *Knights*, 132.

Magnes (born c. 500): Athenian comic playwright.

Maiotic Lake: the Sea of Azov.

Marathon: on Attic coast, site of most famous victory of the Greeks over the Persians (490).

Maricas: play by Eupolis (421) attacking Hyperbolos as Aristophanes had attacked Cleon in *Knights*.

Megacles: name used in Alcmaionidai family.

Megara: town on isthmus of Corinth, supported Sparta from about 445; in 432 Pericles embargoed its trade with Athenian Empire to try to starve it to submit—a prime cause of the Peloponnesian War; known for its garlic and simple humour.

Melanthios: 5th-century Athenian tragic playwright, mocked for gluttony.

Memnon: mythical son of Dawn, killed at Troy.

Miletus, -esian: city of Caria, tributary ally of Athens; its tribute doubled in 424.

Miltiades: Athenian general at Marathon, 490.

mina: = 100 drachmai.

Morsimos: 5th-century tragedian.

Naxos: large island tributary to Athens.

Nestor: aged Greek leader in Trojan War.

Nikias (c. 470–413): expert Athenian general.

Noman: who Odysseus said he was to the Cyclops Polyphemus.

obol: 6 to a drachma.

Odeon: hall in Athens used as a courthouse and for musical competitions.

Odysseus: Homeric Greek leader, famously clever; got into Troy in rags, and out of Polyphemus' cave by clinging on under a ram's belly.

Olympus: highest Greek mountain, thus home of the gods; also name of a famous flute-player.

owl: bird of Athene.

Paean: god of healing, equated with Apollo; hymn or call to him.

Pallas: Athene.

Panathenaia: Athenian festival held in midsummer with much sacrificing and feasting; the Great Panathenaia every fourth year.

Pancration: unarmed athletic contest of boxing and wrestling.

Parnassus: sacred mountain with Delphi below it.

Paros: large island tributary to Athens.

Peleus: resisted seduction, in one myth, by Acastus' wife; outcast for trying to seduce her, but safeguarded by a sword provided by the gods; later married Thetis and became father of Achilles.

Peplos: robe of Athene, carried in procession at the Panathenaia.

Pergasé: area of Athens.

Pericles (c. 495–429): greatest Athenian statesman and popular leader; subjugated Euboea; issued decree against Megara, 432; friend of Phidias.

Phales: personification of the phallus.

Pharsalos: city in Thessaly.

Thales: early 6th–century Milesian philosopher and astronomer.

Theognis: tragedian contemporary of Aristophanes.

Themistocles (c. 528–c. 462): Athenian statesman; created strong navy and fortified Piraeus; exiled and died in Persian Empire; once thought to have committed suicide.

Thespis: 6th-century Athenian playwright and actor.

Thetis: mythical wife of Peleus, mother of Achilles.

Thrace: large eastern Balkan region, north of Greece.

Thucydides: leader of Athenian upper class c. 445 (not the historian).

Titans: pre-Olympian divinities, children of Heaven and Earth.

Tlepolemos: mythical figure, caused death of Likymnios in what might have been a chariot accident.

Tritons: mythical mermen.

Trophonios: oracle-god in Boeotia; honey-cakes given to placate the snakes in his cave.

Typho: hundred-headed monster, son of Tartarus and Earth.

Zeus: father god of sky and order.